Graham Greene's
Catholic Imagination

AMERICAN ACADEMY OF RELIGION
ACADEMY SERIES

SERIES EDITOR
Kimberly Rae Connor, University of San Francisco

A Publication Series of
The American Academy of Religion
and
Oxford University Press

AMERICAN ACADEMY OF RELIGION

Graham Greene's Catholic Imagination

MARK BOSCO, S.J.

OXFORD
UNIVERSITY PRESS
2005

OXFORD
UNIVERSITY PRESS

Oxford   New York
Auckland   Bangkok   Buenos Aires   Cape Town   Chennai
Dar es Salaam   Delhi   Hong Kong   Istanbul   Karachi   Kolkata
Kuala Lumpur   Madrid   Melbourne   Mexico City   Mumbai   Nairobi
São Paulo   Shanghai   Taipei   Tokyo   Toronto

Published by Oxford University Press, Inc.
198 Madison Avenue, New York, New York 10016

www.oup.com

Oxford is a registered trademark of Oxford University Press

Library of Congress Cataloging-in-Publication Data
Bosco, Mark.
Graham Greene's Catholic imagination / Mark Bosco.
p.   cm.—(American Academy of Religion academy series)
Includes bibliographical references and index.
ISBN 0-19-517715-0
1. Greene, Graham, 1904—Criticism and interpretation.   2. Christianity and literature—
Great Britain—History—20th century.   3. Christian fiction, English—History and
criticism.   4. Greene, Graham, 1904—Religion.   5. Catholic Church—In
literature.   6. Catholics in literature.   I. Title.   II. Series.
PR6013.R44Z63158 2004
823'.912—dc22   2004006716

H 5482 5912.

9 8 7 6 5 4 3 2

Printed in the United States of America
on acid-free paper

Contents

Acknowledgments

There are many people who aided in bringing this book to completion. I want first to express my special gratitude to David Stagaman of Loyola University Chicago and Albert Gelpi of Stanford University for their thoughtful, challenging comments and always stimulating conversation throughout the writing of this book.

Likewise, my work has benefited from countless conversations on Graham Greene with many people, more than I can name here. However, I must mention Leonor Pokorny, John Chandler, Michael Garanzini, and Robert Burns. I am grateful for their friendship and encouragement and, most important, their thoughtful reading of drafts of the text.

To Kimberly Rae Connor of the University of San Francisco, her friendship and her help were essential in finding a home for the book. I want to thank the editors and support staff at Oxford University Press who have brought this book to publication in such a professional manner.

Finally, I want to acknowledge the steady support of my brothers in the Society of Jesus and my family—my sisters Lisa, Diana, Michele, my brother Christopher, my Aunt Carol, and, most of all, my mother and father. Their faith, hope, and love have instilled the development of my own Catholic imagination.

Portions of chapters 2 and 4 of this work originally appeared as an article entitled "From *The Power and the Glory* to *The Honorary Consul*: The Development of Graham Greene's Catholic Imagination" in the journal *Religion & Literature*. Reprint permission by the University of Notre Dame, *Religion & Literature*, Volume 36, Issue 2 (Summer 2004).

Graham Greene's
Catholic Imagination

I

Catholicism

Graham Greene's Pattern in the Carpet

There does exist a pattern in my carpet constituted by Catholicism, but one has to stand back in order to make it out.

—Graham Greene

In a book-length interview with Marie-Françoise Allain published late in Graham Greene's life, Greene described the imaginative role that Catholicism played in his long writing career by making the allusion cited above to his literary hero, Henry James.[1] It is a fitting metaphor for the manner in which Catholicism's *difference* is often inscribed in many of Greene's characters, plots, and themes. From his publication of poems in 1925 to his posthumously published dream diary in 1992, Greene's 67 years of writing included over 25 novels, 2 collections of short stories, 2 travel books, 7 plays, 2 biographies, 2 autobiographies, film scripts and film criticism, and countless literary and journalistic essays. If Catholicism is not the very fabric of many of these texts, it is always a thread that helps to bind his literary preoccupations into a recognizable pattern.

Much has been written about Greene's relationship to his Catholic faith and its privileged place within his texts, especially in the criticism prevalent during the heyday of the Catholic literary revival of the first half of the twentieth century. Greene's cycle of novels, beginning with *Brighton Rock* in 1938 and concluding with *The End of the Affair* in 1951, stands as the gold standard of what is often referred to as the "Catholic novel" in English literature.[2] The commentary surrounding these novels exemplifies a high level of interdisciplinary engagement between both religious and literary scholars. Part of the fascination of both readers and critics alike is the way in which Greene's religious imagination challenged the narrow or straightforward assessment of any orthodox Catholic metaphysical or hermeneutical claim embodied in his texts. Greene's unorthodox treatment of orthodox ideas raised ambiguities and made it difficult to definitively clarify his attitude. Because of this critical fixation with religious un/orthodoxy in so much criticism of Greene, he has been labeled at various times a Manichean, Jansenist, Pelagian, Quietist, and existentialist.[3] As much as Greene denied this in himself, the extreme situations of his characters and plots lend weight to such accusations of heresy being imposed upon him and upon his characters. In truth, Greene's paradoxical literary expression of Catholic faith is never offered as a comforting way out of the discomforting realities of modernity. Rather, Catholicism serves to raise the standards, heighten the awareness of the fallen sense of the world, and challenge characters to respond to extreme situations in full knowledge of what is at stake. Religion—and Catholicism in particular—inevitably becomes part of Greene's dark and seedy terrain, an imaginative ground from which Greene's creativity draws inspiration. Yet determining just how important that religious terrain is, and how "Catholic" it is, has been a source of contention throughout the development of Greene criticism.

This chapter thus attempts two separate but related investigations: first, a summary assessment and critique of the "Catholic" genre in twentieth-century literature and Greene's place in this literary heritage; and second, an appraisal of Greene's own relationship to Catholicism as it is expressed in interviews, essays, and biographical details. The first part of this investigation will help expand the historically conservative context that presently defines the Catholic novel. By reformulating the relationship of theology and literature in broader terms, a more nuanced understanding of Graham Greene's Catholic imagination arises, one that is historically situated in the tumult of the Catholic Church's own development after the Second Vatican Council. The second part of this investigation gives evidence to Greene's ongoing dialogue with and immersion in the theological development of Catholicism throughout his life, challenging any reduction of the imaginative role that religion plays in the creation of his texts, especially in static and fixed notions of Christian and, specifically, Catholic orthodoxy. Both of these investigations offer evidence for a central premise of the overall argument of this book: that Catholicism is more textured and complicated than the usual schematic framework often expounded both in studies of the Catholic novel and in Greene studies in particular. If such is the case, then it is possible to explore a Catholic imagination that engages Greene throughout his long writing career.

The "Religion in Literature" Debate

> After the death of Henry James a disaster overtook the English novel
> . . . for with [his] death the religious sense was lost to the English
> novel, and with the religious sense went the sense of importance of
> the human act. It was as if the world of fiction had lost a dimension:
> the characters of such distinguished writers as Mrs. Virginia Woolf
> and Mr. E. M. Forster wandered like cardboard symbols through a
> world that was paper thin.[4]

Any discussion of Graham Greene forces the critic to come to terms with the role that the religious imagination plays in his literary creation. In countless literary articles and interviews of the 1930s, 1940s, and 1950s, he bemoaned the loss of the "religious sense" in the English novel; for Greene, that sense became intimately tied to Catholicism, a faith tradition that could still evoke a metaphysical understanding of good and evil in the world and within an individual. His articles on writers of the period highlight this point. In his *Collected Essays* (1969), Greene writes that Conrad "had retained of Catholicism [an] ironic sense of an omniscience and of the final unimportance of life under the watching eyes . . . in scattered phrases you get the memories of a creed working like poetry through the agnostic prose" (140). On Somerset Maugham, he notes that "[Maugham] cannot believe in a God who punishes and he cannot therefore believe in the importance of a human action. . . . Rob human beings of their heavenly and their infernal importance, and you rob your characters of their individuality" (154). He notes that in Dickens, "evil appears only as an economic factor, nothing more. Christianity is a woman serving soup to the poor."[5] Only in James does Greene see an appreciation of the supernatural quality of evil.[6] It is thus helpful to delineate the genealogy of this condition within the English novel in order to understand how both reviewers and literary critics have often classified Greene as the *malgré lui* of "Catholic" novelist.

It was not until the early nineteenth century that British literary and philosophical writers began to reflect critically on the relationship between literature and religious belief. This dialogue within the English Protestant heritage found its literary expression in such writers as Samuel Taylor Coleridge, William Wordsworth, George Eliot, and Matthew Arnold, to name just a few. Their work describes the historical trajectory of literature in terms of a *Deus Abscon-ditus*, of religion evermore eclipsed by Enlightenment rationalism, science, and philosophical idealism. What is left of the "religious sense" in nineteenth-century literature is expressed in either the moral allegories of George Eliot and Charles Dickens or in the poetic-philosophical displacement of religious feeling in many of the English romantic poets. The impression that religion had lost its power within British culture gained force in the Victorian elegies that mourned the loss of meaning in bourgeois culture and the implicit loss of religious belief. Eliot's *The Waste Land*, published in 1922, became the leit-motif of the early twentieth century, expressing the disillusionment, confusion, and seeming chaos that afflicted the generation of artists still reeling from World War I. Some writers persisted in offering substitutions for the traditional role that religion played in literary creativity: H. G. Wells placed his faith in science and the machine; G. B. Shaw in an optimistic secular humanism; D. H. Lawrence in the primal instinct of a lost sexual vitality; W. H. Auden, C. Day-Lewis, and Stephen Spender in their flirtation with an English socialism that could counteract the negative effects of an impersonal modern state. Many intellectuals in the 1930s and 1940s turned to orthodox religious belief in the Anglican Church, most notably T. S. Eliot, C. S. Lewis, Dorothy Sayers, and, later, Auden. Surprisingly, after World War I organized religion had regained some cultural prestige, a fashionable alternative for many British intellectuals looking for a cultural edifice that could stand up against the chaos, violence, and meaninglessness around them. Thus in the early part of the twentieth century, Christianity, along with its rivals Marxism and psychoanalysis, found a place at the cultural table of intellectual debate.

The Protestant perspective of these English literary figures matched the philosophical and theological investigations of such influential Protestant thinkers as David Friedrich Strauss, Søren Kierkegaard, Paul Tillich, and Nor-throp Frye. These authors, like their literary relations, begin with an initial supposition: the world of Western civilization is in religious decline. Much of the impetus of their writing was to "shore up the fragments" of religious thought against "the ruin" of modernity in order to accomplish the difficult task of correlating the importance of religion to human existence. This valuable critical heritage is still a dominant model today for studying the relationship of literature and religion, effectively placing theology at the service of explicat-ing literature and assessing the concerns of literary criticism.[7] At the risk of simplification, this model follows the path of Paul Tillich's famous dictum on the critical correlation of cultural question to theological answer: "Religion is the substance of culture and culture is the form of religion."[8] If religion is to find a home in contemporary literature, the logic goes, it can no longer be understood in terms of orthodox systems of belief, religious markers, or theological nomenclature; rather, religion must be reframed in existential or psychological terms, so that literature has religious value because, at its heart, it expresses ultimate concern, mystery, or the infinite in human life. It assumes, in effect, that good literature, as a human artifact, has a latent, unconscious theological character that manifests itself in the uncertain, the tragic, or what Tillich called the "demonic" aspect of contemporary life. Though Tillich's ontotheological perspective is correlated to his conception of existentialism in the mid-twentieth century, his approach is felt in much of contemporary criticism that still marks the "religious" attribute in literary works in terms of disruptions, ruptures, or Derridean notions of difference and absence. The historical impact of endeavoring to read texts from such a "religious" perspective has meant that rarely if ever do the imaginative contours of Christian theology support or impinge upon literary interpretation. Theological questions, when acknowledged at all, are made to serve as a second-order philosophical language for literary studies. Indeed, theological interpretation of literary texts has been mostly displaced today by various strains of postmodern theory and secular ideology, making a "theological reading" of someone like Graham Greene a mere historical footnote in the history of Greene criticism.

The "Catholic" Novel as Literary Genre

Situated within any discussion of the religious dimension in literature is the rise of the "Catholic novel" in the early twentieth century. The Catholic novel in Europe originated in the neoromantic and decadent forms of French literature in the nineteenth and early twentieth centuries as a reaction against the dominant discourse of Enlightenment philosophy and the antireligious doctrines of the French Revolution.[9] Such writers as Joris-Karl Huysmans, León Bloy, Charles Péguy, Georges Bernanos, François Mauriac, and Paul Claudel made the Catholic novel into an accomplished literary form that opposed positivist thought and defended the spiritual reality of human life in terms of a distinctly Catholic ontology and epistemology. These authors drew their poetic and thematic material from their common Catholic experience and beliefs, framing and structuring their artistic vision through the lens of Catholic dogma, symbolism, and religious conversion.[10] Thus, the Church's sacramental life; its complex rituals, doctrines, and mystical tradition; and its emphasis on the primacy of theological aesthetics over rational modes of theological discourse served to address and critique the reigning ideology of bourgeois, materialist French society. Catholicism was both a reactionary critique of the state of religious decline in modernity and also a powerful theological, philosophical, and artistic alternative to this seeming decline.

In terms of theme and plot, the French Catholic novel contained many classic ingredients. David Lodge, in the introduction to François Mauriac's *The Viper's Tangle*, succinctly describes these key attributes in the following manner: "the idea of the sinner 'being at the heart of Christianity' (Péguy's phrase), the idea of 'mystical substitution,' the implied criticism of materialism, [and] the tireless pursuit of the erring soul by God, the 'Hound of Heaven' in Francis Thompson's famous metaphor."[11] Another basic ingredient that heightened the tension of the genre's narrative and plot is the conflict between the corrupt flesh and the transcendent spirit, usually devised as sexual tension between male and female protagonists, ascending to a spiritual suffering that finds its reference in Christ's crucifixion. What is remarkable about these French Catholic authors who typify this genre is the accessibility of their writing to those who do not share a Catholic sensibility.

Paralleling the Catholic revival of France was the very different experience of English Catholicism, a minority tradition in predominantly Protestant England. It was not until the 1840s that Catholicism gained some legitimate status in England. Following from this legal victory and aided by John Henry Newman—a convert from Anglicanism's own religious revival, the Oxford Movement—a small but effective Catholic revival flourished in England for over one hundred years. From the beginning it was dominated by English converts who shared a vision of the world as fallen, or in Newman's words, "implicated in some terrible aboriginal calamity." English Catholicism, and especially for those who converted to the faith in the early twentieth century, involved a decidedly intellectual constituency: writers, poets, artisans, theologians, and clergy who had found the Anglican dispensation either intellectually untenable or too compromised by political collusion with the state.[12] This era's diversity of Catholic converts and their works—the political and social articles of G. K. Chesterton, the poetry of Siegfried Sassoon and Edith Sitwell, and the exegetical texts of the priest-scholar Ronald Knox, to name just a few—allowed Catholicism a distinct voice in the intellectual life of England at the time.[13]

With the novels of Evelyn Waugh and Graham Greene, the Catholic genre found a popular preeminence in England in the 1930s and 1940s. Waugh's conversion was anchored in his belief that the essential truths of Catholicism had been dissipated by an English society uprooted from its Catholic birthright. His early satires humorously exposed modern society as a vacuous spectacle adrift from its roots. Beginning with the novel *Brideshead Revisited*, published in 1944, he attempted to use Catholicism not only to frame the issues and crises of modern society but also to offer Catholicism's vision and doctrine as

an antidote to the present crisis in Western, and specifically English, civilization. Waugh's later books, true to the author's own religious conversion to
Catholicism, portrayed characters searching for the certainty and the triumph
of a creedal faith that had been obscured or eclipsed by the mores and values
of modern European society. Waugh's political and social conservatism fit
nicely into Protestant categories of what an "English" expression of the Catholic
novelist might look like.

Graham Greene, also a convert, shares with Waugh much of the same
Catholic concerns and issues in his writing, but in many ways he comes closer
than Waugh to dramatizing the themes of the Catholic novel as embodied by
his French contemporaries. The classic ingredients elucidated by David Lodge
concerning François Mauriac's Catholic vision—the sinner at the heart of
Christianity, mystical substitution, a critique of materialism, and God as the
Hound of Heaven—can be found in many of Greene's most celebrated works.
These novels—Brighton Rock (1938), The Power and the Glory (1940), The Heart
of the Matter (1947), and The End of the Affair (1951)—illustrate Greene's own
absorption in the French Catholic literary revival, of which more will be said
in the following chapter. Greene takes Péguy's famous text "Le pécheur est au
coeur même de chrétienté" as the epigraph of The Heart of the Matter, but it
could be the epigraph and the theological lens for all of his novels from this
period: the spiritual life of the sinner has the privileged status of experiencing
"the appalling strangeness of the mercy of God."[14] Greene's novels of the
1930s, 1940s, and 1950s, like those of Waugh, Mauriac, and Bernanos, were
constantly discussed in terms of how well or how ambiguous was the correlation of character and plot to the Catholic theological categories of scholastic
thought. The dialectical nature of counter-Reformation Catholicism, attempting to stand against both Protestant religious discourse and the materialism
and secular ideologies of the modern age, found its literary expression in these
Catholic writers of the early part of the century.

Yet there has been a growing consensus by critics in the 1970s and 1980s
that the Catholic novel as genre, with its formulaic themes and theological
certitudes, has disappeared as Roman Catholicism shed its opposition to serious engagement with the modern world.[15] Gene Kellogg notes that the genre
"began when the isolation of the world's Roman Catholic communities started
to break down in the nineteenth century, and which tapered off—perhaps
ended—when Roman Catholics 'joined the modern world' after the Second
Vatican Council."[16] More derisively, Albert Sonnenfeld eulogizes the Catholic
novel's demise by maintaining that "Vatican II marked the legitimization and
consecration of a host of modernist longings that were both a reflection and a
cause of the 'decline and fall' of that possibly perverse and reactionary nostalgia

which made the Catholic Novel possible."[17] The effect of Vatican II, these scholars note, is that Catholic *difference*, which had such clear and defined contours
in opposition to Protestant hegemonies in politics, philosophy, and theology,
lost its ability to engage the creative imagination of Catholic writers. These
critics interpret the net effect of the Second Vatican Council as the Church's
assimilation into modernity, an intellectual appropriation of Catholicism to the
philosophical and theological concerns of Enlightenment discourse. The dialectical stance of the Church toward the outside world was so diminished or
buried under an ambivalent Christian humanism that the explicit markers of
a Catholic culture and orthodox creed were no longer visible.

If Greene was an astute student of the Catholic literary revival of France
and a major contributor to its success as a viable genre in England, labeling
him in such a constrictive manner proves difficult, for Greene's artistic concerns and his vision of reality transgressed the theological boundary, as well
as the historical era, of the Catholic novel. As much as Greene's texts evade
such a simple designation, there is a redundancy and uniformity in the criticism from this period, especially in terms of assessing Greene's position in
the literary canon. Many Catholic critics of the time championed Greene's work
for manifesting their faith in such a popular medium, even as they became
obsessed about whether the author and his characters were Pelegian, Manichean, or Gnostic heretics. Even those critics who concurred that Greene's
religious themes are paramount in interpreting his novels argued that his creativity as a writer came from a very limited and biased point of view. David
Pryce-Jones's 1963 study, which looks almost exclusively at the religious aspect
of Greene's texts, reproaches his use of Catholicism as merely a clever tactic
on the author's part to superimpose paradoxical situations into his melodra-
mas.[18] Still others of the period lamented that so much attention had been
given to the Catholic dimension in these novels. John Atkins complains in his
1957 comprehensive study that the constant attention paid to Catholicism and
theology obscures the more important literary themes and issues, noting that
"Greene's work is valuable as social commentary and much more as individual
(including personal) revelation . . . the theology is on the surface, planted there
rather weightily but it is a surface growth."[19] Thus, from the beginning Greene
criticism has been polarized by what one makes of the religious sense, a quality
that Greene claimed was of utmost importance to the modern novel. The argument continued even after Greene rejected the formal elements of the Catholic novel genre in his works following his famous Catholic cycle. Consequently, the critical community—those both sympathetic and unsympathetic
to a religious reading of the novel—by and large assigns to his most famous
works the rubric of the Catholic novel, whereas his later works are often clas-

sified in political and psychological terms because secular concerns seem to predominate in his themes and plots. Even in the most recent study of Greene's fiction, Cates Baldridge perpetuates this schematization: "His novels of the fifties and beyond are in an undeniable sense 'post-Catholic' and even 'post-Christian'—at least when contrasted with those of the forties."[20] This inherent dichotomy exists in much criticism of Greene: his "Catholic" versus his "post-Catholic" novels or the early "religious" versus the later "political" or "secular" ones.[21] Trying to place Greene in either camp exposes the problem of the pre-scriptive understanding of the Catholic novel, which reached its zenith before the Second Vatican Council. And yet an attempt to understand Greene's vision and artistic expression of a Catholic sensibility begs for a different model in which to engage the relationship of literature and theology, one that is not wedded to a conservative and scholastic Catholic context of the Catholic literary revival but a broader, historical context that can still be discerned as Catholic. Are there ways, then, in which the dialogue between theology and literature might continue so that a more fruitful approach to the developing religious imagination of Greene's work might be perceived?

Theology and Literature: An Imaginative Alternative

A reformulation of the interdisciplinary conversation between theology and literature has taken place, thanks in part to the postmodern concerns of both theology and literary criticism. The theological trajectory can be found in the thought of the theologian David Tracy, who attempts to reinvigorate the cor-relational and hermeneutical heritage by proposing a "reading" of texts deemed classic—those that have founded or formed a particular culture and/or contin-ually disclose an excess and permanence of meaning. A keen reader in the hermeneutics of Hans-Georg Gadamer and Paul Ricoeur and thus sensitive to the postmodern epistemological dilemma, Tracy holds that all classics, espe-cially religious ones, express both "a radical stability become permanence and radical instability become excess of meaning through ever-changing recep-tions."[22] Any conversation on the reception of such works requires one to ex-plore the text so that the theological "answers" of religion are critically assessed in light of modernity's "questions," at the same time that the cultural "ques-tions" of literature are situated in the light of critically held truth claims of a theological tradition. Furthermore, Tracy claims that the religious dimension in art, especially in literary texts, is not something externally brought to bear on the text but stands as the imaginative ground of the text, as a constructed or deconstructed "horizon" of every cultural artifact. The religious dimension of any text is not something foreign. In this way Tracy further clarifies Tillich's insight into the relationship between cultural question and religious answer by making the correlation mutually inclusive, more dialogical, more interdependent. Theology is not merely an unchanging apparatus that literary artists can use but also an imaginative milieu that is in constant development within a culture.

Tracy offers three theological paradigms that help interpret the contemporary situation: a paradigm of transcendent manifestation (a metaphysical insight into concrete reality as exemplified in such writers as Mircea Eliade and Karl Rahner), a paradigm of prophetic proclamation (a call to heed the strangeness and otherness of religious faith as exemplified in such writers as Karl Barth and H. Richard Niebuhr), and a paradigm of action/praxis (the political and liberation theologies of resistance and hope). These three Christian responses are imaginatively rendered in either analogical or dialectical language. Analogical language views reality in ordered relationships that express a similarity-in-difference, building on a prime analogate as reference and focus; dialectical language views reality as necessarily in need of radical theological negations, a deconstructive therapy of sorts that exposes fundamental illusions in knowledge and reality. Tracy holds that the dialogical nature of theological reflection is best when analogical and dialectical religious languages engage one another, producing a more constructive interpretation of the situation of contemporary life.[23]

Tracy's understanding of the analogical and dialectical imagination is most fruitful for the study of literature and theology. He traces the analogical imagination as a Catholic tendency in Christianity and the dialectical imagination as a Protestant one. The two are dialogically related, together offering fuller insight into the complex nature of religious belief and practice in the religious imagination of an artist. Building on Tracy's work, critics have tried to delineate the analogical and dialectical imagination in contemporary culture. Andrew Greeley, to take one example, has popularized Tracy's dense theological insight by offering numerous sociological studies that explicate the Catholic imagination at work through a comparison of statistical evidence about the political and cultural habits and tendencies of American denominations in the United States. Without absolutizing these tendencies, he offers insightful critiques about the "difference" expressed in Catholic artists whose works are in dialogue with a predominantly Protestant cultural heritage.[24]

Tracy's thesis has brought new attention to the critical work of the late William Lynch, who explored in numerous articles the philosophical and theological contours of the imagination from a distinctly Catholic perspective.[25] In books such as *Christ and Apollo* (1960) and *Images of Faith* (1973), Lynch attempts to illustrate how theological traditions make a claim on the imagination and its full development. At the same time, he critiqued the imaginative constructs of the literary arts of the twentieth century, pointing out exaggerations and distortions that truncated the religious character of the imagination. Lynch's methodology grants that religious doctrine and dogma—in this case the Christian understanding of the Incarnation, the Trinity, Salvation, and the Fall—help shape the imaginative way in which the work of a cultural artifact is understood and received. Like Tracy, Lynch holds that the imagination is an interpretive act of the whole person, not relegated to a separate intellectual act of signification. Both Lynch and Tracy, then, extend the traditional approach of theological analysis in literature by claiming that literary works can be understood in terms of a theological imagination at play in the text. They allow that religious doctrines, practice, and the dramatic sweep of religious narrative can coalesce into an ideological vision manifested imaginatively in poetic, literary, and dramatic texts.[26] They argue that theological considerations are not just applications to the text but also actually inform the text's literary expression.

If theology has reassessed its relationship with literature over the last quarter century, so too has literary criticism placed renewed emphasis on the role of religious and theological concerns in the creation of literary texts. Ironically, the critical assumptions of materialist, postmodernist conversation have begun to investigate the relationship between theological texts and literature. Rejecting the monologic preeminence of Enlightenment reason and the focus on the self as subject of knowledge, many postmodernist thinkers argue that these notions are artificial constructs with little foundation in reality. The Enlightenment and the modernist metanarrative of reason are nothing but the arbitrary connection between words in a text, and the self as subject is nothing but one's social location in a complex and shifting world. Reality is only a network of fluid, amorphous, affective, ambiguous relationships, fusing together notions of subject and object. There is thus a postmodern preoccupation with ambiguity, affectivity, indeterminacy, irrationality, and otherness. Because theology and religious practice have been marginalized by the metanarrative of Enlightenment ideology, some postmodern critics have found this very marginality a worthy study because it serves to indicate a continual irruption of otherness and strangeness into culture and society.[27]

Paul Giles, whose analysis of American Catholic writers and filmmakers builds on Michel Foucault's interpretation of language as ideological discourse, notes that religion is one among many discursive strategies available to the maker of cultural texts. Giles has fruitfully noted how the Catholic imaginations of artists offer different readings of culture. As a minority position in both England and America, Catholicism becomes an ideological engagement with Protestantism, mapping out alternative visions and fictions.[28] Religion, it seems, and especially the Catholic aesthetic and the historical heritage of Catholic theology, has its own textuality, its own status as a work of art, full of ruptures and tainted with fluctuating signifiers. As the critic Ellis Hanson aptly puts it: "Catholicism is itself an elaborate paradox. . . . The Church is at once modern and yet medieval, ascetic and yet sumptuous, spiritual and yet sensual, chaste and yet erotic, homophobic and yet homoerotic, suspicious of aestheticism and yet an elaborate work of art."[29] Thus, at the end of the twentieth century, there is a paradoxical inversion of the Protestant and Catholic positions: whereas historically the dialectical tendency of Protestant ideologies had acted to deconstruct a premodern, pre-Reformation Catholic decadence in culture and society, Catholic ideologies are now being engaged to critique what has devolved into a form of decadent secularism, formed out of the Protestant ideologies that dominate British and American society. Within contemporary circles, both public and academic, there is a critical revival of Catholic discourses—a revival of Thomistic-Aristotelian "virtue ethics" in philosophy, a developed theological aesthetics in theology, a recovery of the importance of liturgy in ritual studies, and a renewed look at Catholic spiritual traditions— that help to expose the assumptions of post-Enlightenment, post-Reformation modernity and offer a Catholic alternative discourse of engagement.

Of course, much of the postmodern option toward the play of ambiguity, irrationality, and rupture assumes the very dichotomy of Enlightenment thinking, between intellect and affect, rational certainty and subjective feeling. Religion and theology are consigned to being one among many artificial, historical constructs, and the truth claims of theology (its practice and doctrines) are upended by the nihilistic nature of much poststructuralist thought. And yet this postmodern "moment" does allow for a reconsideration of religious narrative, symbol, and ritual that helps chart an inherently logical system of thought and belief evidenced in works of literature. This renewed interest in the language of theology and religious doctrine in terms of religious paradox— and not merely as rationalistic contradiction or repressive ideology—places in high relief the role that an analogical imagination plays in holding such beliefs and systems together. Thus, David Tracy's notion of the analogical/dialectical imagination and the postmodern stresses on religion as "discourse" both widens and renegotiates the relationship between literature and theology, suggesting, implicating, and critiquing possible syntheses that refuse to separate the religious imagination from the literary, which refuse, in effect, to throw out the philosophical and aesthetic heritage of Christianity (and in this case, Catholicism) from the discourse of modern thought. The dialogue implies a perspective in which the tension between the analogical and dialectical languages of the religious imagination does not work to negate the other and, at the same time, critiques any secular ideology in which intersubjectivity is either exiled into the discipline of theology or reduced to some materialist construct in the discipline of literature.

In terms of the Catholic novel—a categorization of many of Graham Greene's works—the theoretical assumptions of writers such as Tracy and Lynch encourage critics to understand its historical terrain in a way that extends beyond the boundaries of a too narrowly defined genre. Rather than seeing the Catholic novel as merely a historical phenomenon in which Catholic themes remain a constant, structured, and "orthodox" religious reality in a text, they advocate a more fluid and open-ended designation beyond adherence to any religious catechism or explicitly "Catholic" plots. This more permeable assignation of the Catholic novel into terms that stress the imaginative contours of writing allows critical space in which to see the way in which religious rituals and theological doctrines inform the world of a text. It articulates predispositions in the Catholic imagination, such as the obsession with the effects of the doctrine of the Incarnation on human life, the philosophical and scholastic understanding of personhood and the place of community, the sacramental reality that stresses divine immanence in concrete reality, and the biases and prejudices of gender that pervade the Catholic tradition. Taken together, these tendencies exhibit a way of seeing and valuing reality that is often embodied in the characters, plots, and thematic material of authors who engage Catholicism as both a faith experience and a historical tradition. Catholic difference is maintained but in less antagonist terms.

Furthermore, this emphasis broadens the notion of the Catholic novel by situating its development in relationship to the historical developments in Catholic theology over the last half of the twentieth century. As the Second Vatican Council began to give privilege to and accentuate new paradigms in the Catholic Church's self-understanding and in its relationship to the modern world, so too there is a marked transformation of the religious imagination of writers engaged in that faith tradition. Graham Greene is just such a writer who profits from broadening the vantage point, for he illustrates the problems and the preoccupations that have formed both the consciousness and the religious imagination of the twentieth century.

The "Novelist Who Happens to Be a Catholic"

Graham Greene was born in 1904 into a prominent English family whose religious affiliation was nominal at best. He both lived and was educated at the

Berkhamsted School, where Greene's father was headmaster, and he finished his education at Balliol College at Oxford in 1925. Having fallen in love with Vivien Dayrell-Browning, a recent convert to Catholicism, Greene, only 22 years of age, converted in order to marry her. As he often admitted in countless interviews, his true loyalty was to Vivien first and only secondly to the Church. But what began as an intellectual conversion for personal reasons became, after his experience of the persecution of Catholics in Mexico, an emotional conversion too. Though Greene was to become estranged and separated from Vivien in 1948, he remained married to her throughout his life as he also remained in faith a Catholic, however tentative that affiliation became in later years.

Greene's first eight novels, the most successful of which were *The Man Within* (1929) and *Stamboul Train* (1932), explored the divided loyalties between the public and private realms of life, framed within the genre of the political, psychological thriller (what Greene early on called his "entertainments," only later to drop the distinction altogether). This balance of loyalty is a key theme throughout Greene's novels and finds historical reference in his experience of the double loyalties at public school. His anxiety over whether to be loyal to his father, the headmaster, or to his classmates caused him such stress that he underwent psychoanalysis when he was 16. It was also his experience with a class bully named Carter that helped form his awareness of evil and the consequences of betrayal in human interactions, all of which later shaped his works of fiction. In the article "The Lost Childhood" (1951) Greene remarks:

> When—perhaps I was fourteen at the time—I took Miss Marjorie
> Bowen's *The Viper of Milan* from the library shelf, the future for bet-
> ter or worse really struck. From that moment I began to write. . . .
> Why? On the surface *The Viper of Milan* is only the story of a war
> between Gian Galezaao Visconti, Duke of Milan, and Mastino della
> Scala, Duke of Verona, told with zest and cunning and an amazing
> pictorial sense. Why did it creep and color and explain the terrible
> living world of the stone stairs and the never quiet dormitory? . . . As
> for Visconti, with his beauty, his patience and his genius for evil, I
> had watched him pass by many a time in his black Sunday suit
> smelling of mothballs. His name was Carter. He exercised terror
> from a distance like a snowcloud over the young fields. Goodness
> has only once found a perfect incarnation in a human body and
> never will again, but evil can always find a home there. Human na-
> ture is not black and white but black and grey.[30]

Loyalty and betrayal was never a clear-cut thing for Greene. It could be subverted, and its opposite could become a virtue, for no side was always right. It was this sense of the psychologically divided mind and the clouded sympathies within the political and sexual realms that characterized the dark plots and anguished, alienated characters of his novels.

The experience of Greene the schoolboy provided Greene the convert with a reference point in understanding the black and gray of human life. Greene often quoted from A. E. Russell's poem "Germinal" in demonstrating the intersection of childhood betrayals and the religious imagination: "In the lost boyhood of Judas, Christ was betrayed."[31] This intersection between the psychological and the religious becomes creatively rendered in Greene's work beginning with *Brighton Rock* (1938), the book that launched Greene into the category of Catholic novelist. Greene turned to Catholic characters because he wanted "to examine more closely the effect of faith on action."[32] Greene believed that for writing to have any depth, it had to be based on a view of the human person as a supernatural being, brought to that moment when God confronts the person and grace encounters free will. In a 1978 interview, Greene noted, "The religious sense does emphasize the importance of the human act. It's not Catholicism, it's simply a faith in the possibility that we have eternal importance. A religious sense makes the individual more important and therefore it helps to put the character on the page."[33] His characters often have this heroic status, endowed with a religious sense of good and evil that preempts a bourgeois morality based merely on what is socially or legally right or wrong. It is this borderland of conflict—social, political, and spiritual— that becomes for Greene his primary interest. In "Letter to a West German Friend," Greene merges his sense of religious and political borders:

> Nearly forty years ago I stepped across such a frontier when I became a Catholic, but the frontier did not cease to exist for me because I had crossed it. Often I have returned and looked over it with nostalgia, like the little groups on either side of the Brandenburg Gate who on holidays stare across at each other trying to recognize a friend.[34]

Greene's novels portray characters that come to stand at the border of acceptance or rejection of personal salvation. As Georg Gaston notes, what connects all of Greene's novels to some degree is eschatology and the theme of possible redemption, whether explicit or muted in the text.[35] Thus, beginning with *Brighton Rock* and continuing through *Monsignor Quixote* (1982), Greene carries on something like a 40-year dialogue with God, subverting and transgressing the orthodox comforts of Catholic religious feeling so that extreme situations of faith, belief, doubt, and commitment may take center stage in his novels. If Greene admitted to creating Catholic themes in only "four or five books," the Greene reader senses the imprint of his religious consciousness throughout his entire oeuvre.

Yet Greene disliked being called a Catholic novelist and preferred instead "a novelist who happens to be a Catholic." He argued for this distinction by accepting John Henry Newman's position in *The Idea of a University*: "If literature is to be made a study of human nature, you cannot have a Christian literature. It is a contradiction in terms to attempt the sinless Literature of sinful man."[36] Greene elaborated his debt to Newman's perspective in his conversations with Allain:

> My books only reflect faith or lack of faith, with every possible human in between. Cardinal Newman, whose books influenced me a great deal after my conversion, denied the existence of a 'Catholic' literature. He recognized only the possibility of a religious dimension superior to the literary dimension, and he wrote that books ought to deal first with what he called in the vocabulary of the day, 'the tragic destiny of man in his fallen state.' I agree with him. It is the 'human factor' that interests me, not apologetics.[37]

And yet it was Greene's Catholicism that gave him a specific point of view throughout his literary career and brought a consistency to his art; without Catholicism he would not have developed the distinctive voice and style on which both his artistry and popularity flourished. From the beginning, Catholicism for Greene was never a system of laws and dogmas or a body of belief demanding assent or dissent but rather a system of concepts, a reservoir of attitudes and values, and a source of situations with which he could order and dramatize his intuitions about human experience.

Greene Criticism: Catholic and/or Post-Catholic?

With the success of *Brighton Rock*, Greene entered into his most productive years of writing, producing a series of novels that explored the boundaries and loyalties of religious faith as understood in the confines of the Catholic consciousness of his characters. As previously noted, critics of this period began calling him a Catholic novelist, a label that inadvertently worked to mark the restrictions of his talent. Fans of his earlier novels were amused by this supposed religious turn in a novelist who had heretofore shown mastery for melodrama and the psychological thriller. And yet the themes in Greene's early novels, beset with criminals and conspirators, alienated protagonists and their betrayal of loyalties, actually find expression in all his great novels of this middle period: the Catholic Pinkie in *Brighton Rock*, who conspires to marry Rose in the fallout of a gang murder; the whiskey priest in *The Power and the Glory*, who betrays his celibate vows by fathering a child; the convert Scobie in *The Heart of the Matter*, whose double loyalties to wife and mistress cause his suicide; and the adultery of Bendrix in *The End of the Affair*, who plays a game of loyalty and betrayal among his mistress, her husband, and her God. In each case, Greene's use of Catholicism extends the psychological and moral crisis of characters beyond their own deception and treachery and places it in confrontation with the objective reality of God. In the end, Greene illustrates that one's faith and belief in God is as treacherous a place as that of the world of politics and espionage.

Because of this intense confrontation with religious interiority and the clear parallels with Catholic French writers of the period, critics with a religious disposition often analyzed his texts in terms of dogmatic and apologetic concerns, often accusing Greene of mixed motives and Manichean tendencies. One of the most famous of these reviews concerned Greene's *The Heart of the Matter*, written by Evelyn Waugh, a close friend and fellow convert. In an otherwise praiseworthy appraisal, Waugh wonders if Greene has taken the doctrine of the *Felix Culpa* too far: "To me the idea of willing my own damnation for the love of God is either a very loose poetical expression or a mad blasphemy, for the God who accepted that sacrifice could be neither just nor loveable."[38] The space between the fallen nature of Greene's characters and the mysterious, inscrutable grace of God was feared to be too wide a theological gap for many of his religious compatriots, and Greene's disdain for traditional expressions of Catholic faith and piety in the institutional Church proved troubling to many in the pre–Vatican II environment of the Catholic Church.[39] These critics questioned implicitly the veracity of Greene's Catholicism because of the way in which he crossed the boundaries of Catholic orthodoxy. As Roger Sharrock notes, Greene the convert was continually compared at this time with François Mauriac, a friend and mentor of Greene, who "with the faith in his bones and a known, convincing regional background, was able to escape heresy. But did Greene's [faith] really exist or was it not the product of a personal trauma?"[40]

Other critics that have shown a secularist prejudice have claimed that Greene's Catholic novels show little originality and rely on religious dogmas as a device to heighten the melodramatic effects of his stories into a contrived seriousness. The religious struggles of his characters, it is argued, go against the grain of contemporary expressions of the psychological novel. If Catholic critics were hesitant to accept Greene's Catholic imagination during this most "Catholic" period of his career, secular critics took Greene to task for obscuring his humanism with religious tensions.[41] Indeed, since Greene's later novels eschewed the intensely religious dilemmas of his earlier Catholic characters, more contemporary criticism has been quick to divide his work into a Catholic and a post-Catholic period, with political and postcolonial concerns as the moral barometer of his later novels. Though there is some acknowledgement of the way in which religion continues to play a muted role in Greene's later works, the criticism articulates this diminution by perpetuating an understanding of religion—and specifically Catholicism—in the narrow terms of the Catholic novel genre, of affirming or denying some religious dogma as a central theme of the text. Greene's religious imagination apparently loses its claim to be recognizably Catholic outside the vested interests of creedal and eschatological crises that impinge on a character. The evolutionary development of Greene's religious imagination is discussed in terms of a rejection of Catholicism for a more idiosyncratic humanism.

Robert Pendleton, for instance, argues that Greene's Catholic novels were only a psychological and stylistic detour from his "Conradian masterplot," a perhaps unconscious attempt by Greene to create a genre that set him apart from the overt homage his thrillers owed to Conrad's narrative themes and protagonists. Building on Harold Bloom's well-known study, *The Anxiety of Influence* (1974), Pendleton suggests that Greene's Catholic novels operate as "deviations" and "displaced repetitions" of Conrad's interiorized thrillers. Greene's later novels, he argues, return to the larger influence of Conrad, where faith and belief are so marked by skepticism that they signify the loss of religious meaning for his characters.[42] And Cates Baldridge, in an otherwise nuanced discussion of the conception of God in Greene's novels, uses J. Hillis Miller's *The Disappearance of God: Five Nineteenth-Century Writers* (1963) to argue that Greene's obsession with divided loyalty illustrates the author's psychological and spiritual quest for "a consummation or a reconciliation or a reintegration that [he] can never quite—or at best only fleetingly—realize."[43] Baldridge concludes that Greene, like William Blake, created his own peculiar and powerful religious system that, seen over the span of his novels, divested itself of any orthodox form of Catholicism; rather, he argues that Greene's deity is imagined as one in the midst of cosmic entropy, emphasizing a God who is only worthy of the pity of failure, never a God who might triumph in the world, much less in the human person.

What is interesting about both Pendleton's and Baldridge's argument is how it returns to the Protestant English tradition that stresses in literature the absence of God, or at least God's virtual impotence and demise in the modern world. Also missing in much of the discussion that divides Greene's novels into Catholic and post-Catholic is any appreciation by such critics of the theological centrality of Catholic mediation, specifically in the human face of God in Christ and in the sacramental system of the Church. And nowhere does the literary criticism question the relevance to Greene's artistic imagination of developments in Roman Catholicism that resulted from the Second Vatican Council. Indeed, the evidence to do so is seen in the countless interviews and articles in which Greene continues to engage the social teachings of Catholicism and post-Vatican II theological texts, as well as in the subjects and themes of most of his late novels, *The Honorary Consul* (1974); *The Human Factor* (1978); *Doctor Fisher of Geneva, or the Bomb Party* (1980); and *Monsignor Quixote* (1982).

Charting a Late Twentieth-Century Catholic Imagination

Can there be found a larger, less rigid context in which to discuss the discursive and symbolic role that Catholicism plays in Greene's texts that honors the corresponding development in Catholic theology of the twentieth century? Catholic theology before Vatican II was primarily a hermetic, scholastic endeavor that stressed the individual's status before God in terms of moral precepts and ritual obligations. The revival of Thomistic thought in the early twentieth century began a conscious dialogue between the Church and the culture of modernity, arguing that the Church's philosophical and theological synthesis had an important role to play in both the social and political aspects of society. Jacques Maritain, for example, gave Thomistic philosophy a new cachet in the intellectual discussions about art and the role of the artist, holding that the artist's purpose was to create an "experience of life," not a mere reflection of it or some idealized form of it. For Maritain, that meant tackling the problem of evil and its ability to wreak havoc on the human condition. Maritain held up the Christian writer as an artist who had some idea of human potential, as well as the aspects that limit such potential.[44] Maritain's thought contributed much to articulating the conceptual foundations of the Catholic literary revival.

With the advent of the Second Vatican Council (1962–1965), there arose a dramatic shift in theological emphasis that affected the practice and attitudes toward Catholic belief in a number of important ways. First, the Council emphasized a theological "perspective from below," a methodology that stressed God's manifestation of grace on the horizontal plane of human relationship within and without the Church. The secular concerns of society, even the most profane, became possible pathways to the sacred. This emphasis is noted in renewed christological concerns that stressed the humanity of Christ as the hermeneutical starting point and in the emphasis of communal justice over personal acts of charity in the Church's social teaching.

Second, religious anthropology before Vatican II had stressed the individual's relationship with God in a vertical, one-to-one basis, so that individual salvation was seen as a private affair of piety and charity. The Council documents, most particularly *The Church in the Modern World*, reject the individualistic verticalization of the human being's relationship to God for a more social, horizontal perspective. As J. C. Whitehouse points out in his study of the human person in Catholic novelists, the Council began "a movement away from a picture of man as an individual in a unique relationship with his Creator through a new appreciation of existential freedom and ultimately to an image of the human being as a nexus of social relationships."[45]

Third, there was a reorientation of the sacramentality of Catholicism, so that sacraments are neither to be isolated in ritual actions stemming from an intermediating priest nor to be confined to the functionalism inherent in the theological concept of *ex opere operato*.[46] God's grace does not intervene solely in the priest's function but also in the diffusion of all the baptized members of the church community. All forms of human interaction with the world have the possibility of being sacramental, visible signs of God's invisible reality.

Fourth, there was a clear rejection of the body-and-soul dualism of human nature that was part of the legacy of Catholic thought. In an attempt at a more holistic understanding that took seriously the doctrine of the Incarnation, the body is not portrayed as at war with the soul; rather the body and the soul are consubstantial, sacred coconstituents of human life. The scandal of the Incarnation in Catholic thought is that the divine is found in the endeavors of the flesh, so that the spiritual life must be understood in part as the strivings of the flesh, just as the desires of the flesh must be understood as a possible path for the soul. This added theological emphasis on the human body grounded the Church's post–Vatican II social teachings on the dignity of the human person, the sacramental nature of human work, and the call for justice to meet the physical, as well as the spiritual, needs of people.

Fifth, there was a reorientation of the Church's self-understanding and its relationship to the outside world. The documents of the Council continually stressed the "pilgrim" nature of the Church as a "people of God," implying that it was at the same time holy and sinful, needing to be constantly renewed. As for the situation of the world, the documents recognized the need for a critical reading of the "signs of the times" in which the Church might more fully enter into the political and social struggles of peoples. In recasting the teaching *extra ecclesiam nulla salus*, the Church recognized that institutional Catholicism cannot claim to be exclusively the Church of Christ and is thus not the sole arbiter of salvation. Indeed, the Council explicitly states that non-Christian religions may also serve as instruments of salvation.[47]

It is true that after Greene's publication of *A Burnt-Out Case* in 1961, he extricated himself from the stylistic intensity of his character's Catholic interiority as the primary focus for formulating the crises in his novels. Whether a character's actions contributed to his personal salvation or damnation was no longer the paramount issue in his novels; rather, Greene's focus turned to human action deriving from political relationships that allegorized the human struggle in economic and moral terms. Most criticism has seen this as a "post-Catholic" maneuver on Greene's part, a turn away from the imaginative world of Catholicism. Yet Greene's artistic confrontation with his religious imagination parallels the developments in Catholic theology, doctrine, and liturgy since Vatican II. When Greene returns to explicitly religious themes in his late novels, he is not merely reworking the conflict of his previous "Catholic" cycle but is also engaged in a dialogue with the political concerns, as well as the religious crises, of belief that have become part of the experience of Catholicism since the end of the Council.

I am not suggesting that Greene was writing these novels only with Catholic social teachings and doctrinal controversies in mind. Indeed, his concern for the "human factor" is not necessarily embodied in Catholicism. Greene is not a theologian or a philosopher but a novelist. What I am suggesting is that there is an organic growth in his religious imagination that is reflected in his literary artistry as he lived in tension with his Catholic faith in the last half of the twentieth century. The restrictive ingredients of the historical genre of the Catholic novel obfuscate a consideration of the way in which his Catholic imagination continued to frame his work. Greene's ironic stance toward the use of theological categories in these later novels does not remove the issues of faith and belief from them but rather transposes them into political and social concerns in which justice, salvation, and even the mystery of divine grace might be manifested. Where Catholicism was more monolithic in his earlier novels, it now becomes part of a dialogue with the contemporary situations of his texts. In reading Greene's texts, we see how his religious imagination has developed, shifting emphases in the intervening years that saw the greatest change in the Catholic church in centuries.

The Religious Landscape of Greeneland

Graham Greene's conversion to Catholicism did not occur in a vacuum, and the simple rejoinder that Greene converted to marry Vivien belies the complex manner in which Catholicism engaged Greene's interpretation of life throughout his long literary career. The preoccupations of his religious imagination is illustrative of the dilemmas that have formed the consciousness of much of the twentieth century, and his vision is always in dialogue with the cultural and political world in which he found himself. It is important then to begin by delineating some of these characteristics of "Greeneland," the term used to describe the existential and religious geography of Greene's novels.

All the most important things in a writer's life, Greene often declared in interviews, happen during the first sixteen years. It seems true of Greene, for his creativity was shaped by the literary heritage of the Victorian and Edwardian age, a staple of his early reading. He greatly admired the novels of Henry James and Joseph Conrad, the adventure stories of Rider Haggard, the detective stories of G. K. Chesterton, and the many works of Robert Louis Stevenson, a family relation on his mother's side. In his *Collected Essays*, Greene shows his appreciation of each of these writers on the formative years of his imagination. His love of the political thriller and adventure owes much to Conrad, and his focus on the interior tensions in the consciousness of his characters owes much to James. Coupled with this, Greene's early years were marked by his discomfort at school: the divided loyalty between his father and his schoolmates, the loss of privacy, the acts of betrayal, the antiauthoritarian strain of adolescence—all contributing to his sense of the precariousness of his life and the injustices in the world. Greene's religious imagination is so deeply grounded in these early experiences that they thematically show up in all of his most deeply felt work.

Though Greene disparaged his youthful conversion to Catholicism as merely pragmatic, it was nevertheless an important act that had profound consequences on his friendships and his literary works. He read widely in theology and Catholic history under the influence of the Dominican scholar Bede Jarrett, a close friend of both Greene and his wife early in their marriage. In the 1930s through the 1950s Greene counted among his friends the English Jesuit theologians Martin D'Arcy and C. C. Martindale, and he often corresponded with them concerning his novels and plays. He was a close friend of Tom Burns, the publisher of *The Tablet*, still the leading intellectual Catholic journal of England, and served on its board of trustees until his death. By the late 1930s Greene's literary reviews in both *The Tablet* and *The Spectator* became more focused on the religious implications in novels and writers, taking to heart Eliot's maxim that literary criticism should be undertaken "from a definite ethical and theological standpoint."[48] When Greene left England to live in France in 1966, his reading and correspondence with Catholic theologians continued unabated, most notably with the liberal theologian Hans Küng, a theological advisor and framer of many documents of Vatican II. Furthermore, Greene's close friendship with the Spanish priest Leopoldo Duran and his friendship and support of many priests from Central America in the last decades of his life brought to full circle his engagement with Catholic culture and religious-political causes.[49]

His conversion and immersion in the intellectual and artistic discourses of his faith had the effect of positioning him in a religious intellectual history, both enabling him to critique the comfortable liberalism of his English Protestant roots while at the same time offering support for his creative turn to the religious interiority of his characters. In effect, Greene found in Catholicism a doctrinal and imaginative discourse that was compatible with his earliest experiences and gave him some objectivity in crafting the contours of his own creative obsessions. Catholicism thus gave him a consistent point of view as essayist, journalist, and novelist in the ever-changing pluralism of twentieth-century literary fashion.

As did many British intellectuals who converted during this time, Greene found solace and support in his reading of John Henry Newman. In the epigraph to his travel book on Mexico, *The Lawless Roads* (1939), Greene quotes from Newman's *Apologia Pro Vita Sua*, a text that documents the theologian's own gradual conversion to Catholicism:

> The defeat of good, the success of evil, physical pain, mental anguish, the prevalence and intensity of sin, the pervading idolatries, the corruptions, the dreary hopeless irreligion . . . inflicts upon the mind the sense of the profound mystery which is absolutely beyond the human situation . . . *if* there be a God, *since* there is a God, the human race is implicated in some terrible aboriginal calamity.[50]

Newman's outlook is found throughout Greene's narrative world, for like Newman he accepts the ontological and metaphysical existence of evil as a fact of life, as the "way of the world." If Greene denied creating a literary world in which evil existed in supernatural terms on a par with God's goodness, he did at least affirm that within the human person evil is real.

This "aboriginal calamity" is the world of Greeneland, a landscape filled with lonely, pathetic, and sometimes malevolent characters. Incidents of pursuit, acts of violence, and voluntary and involuntary betrayal populate a world set against a background of misery and squalor. Greene's characters live as exiles on the extreme edges of society, conscious of their failures and their betrayals of one another and, as is often the case, of their faith in God. Throughout his texts the eschatological certainties of both Christianity and Marxist ideology are always thwarted by the inevitability of human failure. Greeneland is thus an uncomfortable place for bourgeois religious piety—Catholic and Protestant—as well as Marxist ideology, precisely because of the optimistic assumptions about human nature and the eschatological utopias that pervade both these positions. Indeed, Greene implies that the hopeless causes that engage his characters are worthy of allegiance, specifically because they are unlikely to be manipulated and thwarted by success. Failure, as Terry Eagleton claims, is the one legitimate form of victory in Greene's novels, suggesting that the doctrine of the Incarnation finds its textual embodiment not so much in human creativity but in human failure—the tragic, radically fallen nature of humanity.[51] Though Eagleton overstates the case, it is true that the primary religious insight sustained throughout Greene's religious landscape is the Christian doctrine of the *felix cupla*, the happy effect of human sin as the cause of God's grace manifested in the Incarnation to an individual and a community. The Incarnation is revealed to characters when they discover that their sins or their suffering bring them into an analogical relationship with a suffering God in Christ. Even in Greene's least religious novels, his protagonists experience such a manifestation or Joycean "epiphany." His reluctant and often degraded heroes are ennobled by the way in which they come to understand and face their own failure and/or worthlessness before God or before those to whom they have committed themselves. There is thus always a dialectical strain in Greene's religious imagination, a critical response to what Greene considered the major flaw of his Protestant heritage: the denial of this aboriginal calamity that compromises all of the noblest of human aspirations.[52]

Greene's religious imagination is also fixated on the tension between belief and unbelief, mirroring throughout his novels the epistemological and existential dilemmas of his century. In this way he is a product of the Enlightenment and liberal establishment, choosing doubt as the premier virtue of humanity, claiming that "doubt like the conscience is inherent in human nature . . . perhaps they are the same thing."[53] Orthodoxy, or "right belief," is always open to doubt because there is never only one perspective in which to understand truth, and it is inevitably open to mystery. Of course, Greene subversively puts this ostensibly secular virtue at the service of a Catholic sensibility. He often highlights the virtue of doubt in the concluding remarks of many of his novels, wherein a priest comments on the possibility of redemption for the hero/antihero. This remark is usually at the expense of the complacency of

Catholic certitudes given by the institutional Church, so that doubt negotiates a wider space for divine presence and mercy. Thus, in the final pages of *The Heart of the Matter* (1948), the widow Louise worries that Scobie's suicide sends him to hell, to which Father Rank, the parish priest answers, "The Church knows all the rules. But it doesn't know what goes on in a single human heart" (272). And in as late a novel as *Monsignor Quixote* (1982), the priest-hero has a disturbing dream in which he watches Christ get off the cross before his persecutors, making the whole world know with certainty that he is the Son of God. As the priest awakens, he feels "the chill of despair felt by a man who realized suddenly that he has taken up a profession which is of use to no one . . . who must live without doubt or faith, where everyone is certain that the same belief is true" (70). Doubt is thus a two-edged sword for Greene's characters: it can allow for the ineffable and mysterious workings of faith to be recognized and honored, or it can lead to a rationalistic and ultimately skeptical stance toward the "human factor."

Greene claimed in a late interview that he understood faith and belief as two different realms: "What I distinguish is between faith and belief. One may have less belief as one grows older but one's faith can say, 'Yes, but you are wrong.' Belief is rational, faith is irrational and one can still continue to have an irrational faith when one's belief weakens."[54] Greene locates faith in trust and hope in God's love and mercy, whereas belief is found in human rationalization and institutionalization of God through theology and the Church. Doubt, whether in religious or political systems, is at the heart of the human enterprise because it checks any overt triumph of ideological excess. It suggests Greene's affinity to the dialectical power of Kierkegaard's "leap of faith," where trembling self-doubt, placed in extreme situations and on the precipice of despair, is honored above any religious pharisaism or political party line, even if it means relinquishing the power or comfort that comes from such institutionalized structures.

Thus, arguing that Greene has a discernible Catholic imagination cannot mean that Catholic *difference* is always in reference to the Protestant intellectual and religious heritage from which he came, that his conversion to Catholicism and his imaginative use of it was a *rejection* of his English cultural heritage. Rather, Greene's religious imagination finds in Catholicism a perspective, a place to stand, and in doing so, a place to reflect on and critique the world, including the world of Catholicism. David Tracy's theological nomenclature can help to map out the landscape of Greeneland. As a convert imbued with a modern, Protestant ethos, Greene's well-developed dialectical imagination is constantly challenging the more analogical tendencies of his professed faith. If the analogical imagination produces a religious discourse that is prone to an easy accommodation of differences in its desire for synthesis, order, and harmony, the dialectical imagination becomes a prophetic discourse that focuses on human uncertainty, negates formulaic claims on the nature of faith and God, and emphasizes the self-destructive forces at work in the human heart. Greene's texts constantly criticize the self-satisfied religious pietism he found in either Catholicism or liberal Protestantism, and he excoriates the institutional side of Catholicism for its certainty, its triumphalism, and its tendency to compromise with the political powers and principalities of this world. Greene embodied what the theologian Paul Tillich called the "protestant principle," the "protest against the tragic-demonic self-elevation of religion that liberates religion from itself for the other functions of the human spirit."[55] Indeed, in his book-length interview with Allain, Greene claimed, "I fear that I'm a Protestant in the bosom of the Church."[56] Greene's texts constantly enact this tension between the dialectical and analogical language of religious faith, which leads many critics to argue that his conversion never carried the full engagement of his heart or head. As one who disagrees with this assessment, I find that the transgressive play upon Catholicism in Greene's literary landscape—in terms of Catholic orthodoxy and the Church's claim to certitude—never denies the significance of his Catholic vision and its influence on his creativity; rather, this critique and transgression is purifying and deconstructive, a task of the dialectical tendencies in his own complex religious imagination.

Furthermore, the Catholic Church performed its own purification and renewal through the proceedings of the Second Vatican Council and in the years following. The focus and thrust of Catholicism took on new paradigms to articulate its role in the world, showing an evolution or, in Newman's phrase, a "development" away from the church's dialectical stand against the Reformation and the concomitant antagonism to Enlightenment thought in Western civilization to a more analogical stand toward the political and religious communities outside Catholicism. Greene inhabits this borderland too—a space in which his Catholic imagination evolves as his experience and study of Catholicism evolves throughout his life. The following chapters offer a consideration of the development of Greene's Catholic imagination by situating him in the two historical and theological milieus that dominate twentieth-century Catholicism: the Catholic revival in the first half of the century, in which his Catholic cycle of novels stand as a premier achievement, and the Vatican II and post–Vatican II concerns that found new expression in his later novels. Because there is such a wealth of religiously oriented criticism from Greene's Catholic cycle and a dearth of it in his late work, I am deliberately giving a short and focused analysis from this earlier period. To this end, chapter 2 analyzes Greene's own appropriation of the Catholic revival of the first half of the twentieth century, discussing two of his works from this period, *The Power and the Glory* and *The End of the Affair*. Chapter 3 discusses the theological contexts and developments of Vatican II, specifically in terms of how it transforms many of the classic features of the Catholic novel. Chapters 4 and 5 offer close readings of Greene's late novels that imaginatively render Catholicism and religious thinking in the context of post–Vatican II concerns. Finally, chapter 6 offers some concluding remarks on Greene as an exemplar of the Catholic imagination at work in a post–Vatican II, postmodern world.

2

The Greene/ing of the Catholic Novel

Greene's Appropriation of Oxford and the French Catholic Literary Revival

I've suddenly realized that I *do* believe the Catholic faith. Rationally I've believed for some time, but only this evening imaginatively.
—Graham Greene, letter to Vivien (undated, 1925)

One can believe in every point of the Catholic faith, and yet at times like this hate the initiator of it all, of life I mean.
—Graham Greene, letter to Vivien
(December 1925)[1]

Most people are only a very little alive; and to awaken the spiritual is a very great responsibility; it is only when they are so awakened that they are capable of real Good, but that at the same time they become first capable of Evil.
—T. S. Eliot, *After Strange Gods* (1930)

A French Catholic enters the church by the main door; he is interwoven with its official history; he has taken part in all the debates which have torn it throughout the centuries. . . . The work of an English Catholic novelist at first gives me the sensation of being in a foreign land. To be sure, I find there my spiritual country, and it is into the heart of a familiar mystery that Graham Greene introduces me. But everything takes place as though I were penetrating into an old estate through a concealed door unknown to me, as though I were advancing behind the hero of a novel through tangled branches

and suddenly recognized the great avenue of the park where I played when I
was a child.

—François Mauriac, "Men I Hold Great" (1951)

Graham Greene notes throughout his writings that his religious sense first
came to life in his childhood experience. The primary symbols of his faith are
all found in his early confrontations with the horror of and fascination with
the mysterious regions beyond the border of the safe and secure confines of
home. For Greene, this confrontation occurred in both an existential and textual manner. The anxiety and dislocation between his home and the "green
baize door" that separated him from the world of his school propelled Greene's
earliest sense of faith. He records this sense of a double life between these two
regions where he lived in *The Lawless Roads* (1939):

> I escaped surreptitiously for an hour at a time: unknown to frontier
> guards, one stood on the wrong side of the border looking back. . . .
> It was an hour of release—and also an hour of prayer. One became
> aware of God with an intensity—time hung suspended—music lay
> on the air. . . . And so faith came to one—shapelessly, without
> dogma, a presence above a croquet lawn, something associated with
> violence, cruelty, evil across the way. One began to believe in heaven
> because one believed in hell, but for a long while it was hell only
> one could picture with a certain intimacy.[2]

This religious sensitivity was further reenforced by his childhood reading of
adventure stories, thrillers, and romances, fostering within him a textual world
where evil could melodramatically come to life. For Greene, childhood was not
invoked in order to lament the loss of some pristine innocence that one tries
to recover; rather, childhood is already fallen: "Hell lay around them in their
infancy" is his subversive reformulation of Wordsworth's romantic notion of
childhood innocence. Childhood serves as Greene's touchstone to a primordial
honesty that he found lacking in adult life; there is a poetic clarity in childhood
experience that speaks to the veracity of the mixed motivations that a person
confronts. Thus, Greene's religious imagination is fused early on in childhood
memories, texts, and fixations about evil, loyalty, and betrayal. These obsessions
were to follow him wherever he went, including his more formal engagement
with his Catholic faith.

Greene converted to Catholicism in 1926; he published his first novel in
1929, and his first novel with Catholic characters, *Brighton Rock*, in 1938. In
that period of time he read and absorbed Catholic theology well beyond simple
catechism, especially in his understanding of the theologian John Henry New-

man. Greene once commented that it took him over a decade of being a Catholic to feel fully comfortable to write about Catholic characters and to see how the symbols and doctrines of his faith might find expression in his literary imagination.[3] He began his writing career when religion, and especially Catholicism, was having a surprising renewal in philosophy and literature, and Greene was a deft student of many of its leading figures. This chapter situates Greene during this Catholic revival, which artistically embodied a "kind" of Catholicism, one that is most apparent in the French Catholic authors of the early part of the twentieth century. Greene had great success in mining this rich tradition and incorporating its themes into his own religious imagination. It is from this period that he would write some of his best and certainly his most famous novels, two of which, *The Power and the Glory* and *The End of the Affair*, will be discussed at length.

Greene's Oxford Movement

The first volume of Norman Sherry's biography of Greene does much to contextualize Greene's early experience of Catholicism, instigated by his infatuation with Vivien Dayrell-Browning, a recent convert. Though Greene and his biographers are quick to point out that his conversion was an act to win Vivien in marriage, it is also true that Greene intelligently embraced this faith, taking both instruction and his theological reading very seriously. Vivien's religious conviction and quiet stability served to channel Greene's imagination, and it is in their correspondence that the religious overtones of his imagination first find expression. Sherry documents the abundant letters Greene wrote to Vivien during their courtship and the early happy years of their marriage. In the months before their wedding, Greene often wrote to her in hagiographic terms. With great enthusiasm he exclaims, "I can believe that miracles will be done at your grave. Only you should be the patron saint of lovers & depose that nonentity St Valentine," and a month later, "You are the most wonderful event in my life & would be in any one's. October 15 [their wedding date] will be a greater day than Cana, because all the water in the world will be turned into wine."[4] Greene's hyperbole and religious objectification of Vivien in these letters expressed early his attitude toward women as seen in his novels and plays. He has often been criticized for creating female characters that exemplify what might be called a Madonna/whore complex in which, with few exceptions, women are drawn as repositories of goodness or as egotistical temptresses for Greene's male protagonists. In his first novel, *The Man Within* (1929), the character Andrews, a smuggler on the run, takes refuge and falls in love with

Elizabeth, whose feminine spiritual force causes him to confront his divided loyalties between her and his gang.[5] Andrews is at first frightened by her goodness and he flees from her, only to give in to the temptation of another seductive young woman instead. Disgusted with himself for such a betrayal and in a state of panic, he runs back to Elizabeth, who takes him in as he declares his love for her. In the end, Elizabeth dies while protecting Andrews from his pursuers, and he in turn surrenders himself to the law. As an act of atonement for her death, he declares to the authorities that he is her murderer. This reification of women into categories of either sanctity or temptation fills many of Greene's novels, an artistic rendering that fully resonated in the Victorian world of romance. Yet it could be noted that it is even more pronounced a tendency in a Catholic sensibility that ritually venerated Mary, the Virgin Mother of God, and Mary Magdalene, the reformed prostitute. Greene's highly romantic vision of women mirrors the nineteenth-century Catholic reflection on women, seen not as equals of men but as Madonnas, agents of some finalizing grace and ultimate redemption. Greene's female characters find a home in the mythic descriptions of women and in the spiritualizing of the feminine that still lingers in some Catholic discourse.

Vivien, a resident of Oxford, introduced Greene to a Catholic circle of friends and scholars that had a profound effect on him. One such friend was the Dominican historian Bede Jarrett, the founder of the Oxford Dominican House, Blackfriars. Jarrett received Vivien into the Church and acted as godfather to the couple's first child, Lucy Caroline. Jarrett's books, *Mediaeval Socialism* (1913) and *Social Theories of the Middle Ages 1200–1500* (1926), were both influential in framing Greene's political vision. In them Jarrett gives evidence of forms of socialism that were supported by various strains of medieval life. He documents the role of theologians, monastic leaders, church and state lawyers, social reformers, and feudal lords in articulating a society that argued that land and wealth should be held in stewardship as opposed to ownership. It is interesting that he devotes a chapter to medieval conceptions of communism, its place among the mendicant religious orders, and the sanction of "poverty" as the essential element of religion, much to the chagrin of the hierarchy and state authority of the time. Jarrett concludes by examining the rise of the privatization of property, its delusory effect on the guild society of the medieval age, and the theological documents by church theologians of that time in defense of communitarian use of property.[6] There are great affinities in Jarrett's texts to Greene's developing political vision, where the ideals of social and economic equality found in Marxist and communist ideologies are framed by Greene within religious paradigms. Greene's insistent treatment of the ambiguous relationship between Catholicism and Marxism/socialism appears in many of his novels, and the religious foundations for such a dialogue between the two stems in part from Greene's close reading of Jarrett's texts.

Another Oxford don that had tremendous influence on Greene's Catholicism was the nineteenth-century convert John Henry Newman. Greene has pointed to Newman as the premiere Catholic thinker who gave shape to his faith, giving him justification, as we have seen, to distinguish himself as a "novelist who happens to be a Catholic."[7] Newman's theology served Greene well in two important respects: as a fellow English convert, Newman's own personal struggle to enter the church is centered within the political and philosophical conflicts raised by an English Protestant heritage fully engaged with Enlightenment thought; and Newman's stress on a developmental vision of Christianity took stock of the evolutionary process of religious belief. Both of these points in Newman's thought bear further comment, for they reverberate throughout both Greene's novels, as well as through the countless interviews that have questioned his understanding of faith and his struggle for belief.

Ian Ker, the eminent Newman scholar, notes that "Newman's intellectual conversion did for the most part precede a more experiential and imaginative discovery of Catholicism."[8] Newman's phenomenology of conversion is thus first articulated as a discovery of the intellectual soundness between modern Catholicism and the early church fathers. The *Apologia Pro Vita Sua* serves in part as a methodical justification for leaving the Anglican Church for the "truth" of Roman Catholicism. Though his *Apologia* attempts to challenge the reigning Protestant concerns over the concept of religious truth, there is still embedded in Newman's text Cartesian discourses on the dilemma about the certainty of oneself and of God. His reflections raise a specter of personal doubt that echoes Enlightenment concerns about truth and certitude. In Newman's conception of God, there is a strong hint of Descartes' *cogito*, where divine reality is subjected to one's own mental ideas. This subjective turn to the interiority of the individual, paralleled by other contemporary Protestant thinkers such as Kierkegaard, is evident in Newman's somewhat circular justification for his conversion:

> I am a Catholic by virtue of my belief in a God; and if I am asked why I believe in a God, I answer that it is because I believe in myself, for I feel it impossible to believe in my own existence (and of that fact I am quite sure) without believing also in the existence of Him, who lives as a Personal, All-seeing, All-judging Being in my conscience.[9]

Knowledge of oneself and knowledge of God is pressed into a tautology in which God seems to exist as an objective, spiritual reality in the conscience of a subject. The bifurcation between knowledge and experience, subject and object, in Enlightenment thought is quite opposed to the Catholic scholastic tradition, with its mixture of Aristotelian realism and Thomistic metaphysics. Educated in a distinctly non-Thomistic theological methodology, Newman brings to his discourse on conversion a decidedly Protestant inflection to his notion of certitude and belief.

Thus, in discussing the foundations of his belief, Newman's logic of religious certitude is built on the ground of probability or, more precisely, on "accumulated probabilities," in which "absolute certitude . . . was the result of an assemblage of concurring and converging probabilities."[10] He notes that this reasoned discernment led to his conversion, and "if any Catholic says in consequence that I have been converted in a wrong way, I cannot help that now."[11] It is the sense of reasoned probability, and its concomitant need for certitude, that most reflects the Protestant consciousness of Newman's awareness. He realizes that it might sit uneasily with the minds of Catholics precisely because of its Pascalian reserve for probability and theological wagering. If Newman echoes the Jansenist Pascal, so does Greene, for he has spoken of his conversion in similar terms, at first as an intellectual probability and only later as an emotional conversion discovered in his journey to Mexico during the religious persecutions. Greene wavered between belief and disbelief most of his life, and he often spoke of it in conditional statements, as in a late interview: "If there is a God, the Catholics probably come nearest to getting Him right."[12] Having one's religious faith not always in harmony with the doctrinal belief statements of one's faith was a constant starting point for Greene. The dilemma appears in many of his novels, most notably in A Burnt-Out Case (1961), where Greene claims in the introduction to "give dramatic expression to various types of belief, half-belief, and non-belief, removed from world-politics and household preoccupations."[13]

Newman's Apologia works seriously to undermine what has consistently been the Cartesian domain of Protestant theological epistemology, but in his most personal revelations one sees the Cartesian dread of the severed "I" appear, the individual mind isolated and alone in the world, needing certitude. It surfaces most strikingly in the following reflection:

Starting then with the being of a God . . . I look out of myself into the world of men, and there I see a sight which fills me with unspeakable distress. The world seems simply to give the lie to that great truth, of which my whole being is so full; and the effect upon me is, in consequence, as a matter of necessity, as confusing as if it denied that I am in existence myself. If I looked into a mirror, and did not see my face, I should have the sort of feeling which actually comes upon me, when I look into this living busy world, and see no reflexion of its creator.[14]

This very personal confession illustrates the complexity of doubt and uncertainty in Newman's early stage of conversion, a period that led him into a "winter of desolation" (1841–1845) before his entrance into the Church. The dread of the isolated mind, adrift in a world suffering some "aboriginal calamity" that Newman so eloquently describes, is a religious sensibility threaded throughout Greene's understanding of the human predicament. Newman's musing on "the greatness and littleness of man, his far-reaching aims, his short duration, the curtain hung over his futurity, the disappointments of life, the defeat of good, the success of evil, physical pain, mental anguish, the prevalence and intensity of sin which is beyond human solution" became the epigraph for Greene's travel book, *The Lawless Roads*, but it could stand as a description of the theological terrain for much of Greene's work. The Cartesian dread that Newman assumes—of self, of existence, of the void—finds a theological expression in Greene's literary work.

Greene's *via negativa* toward religious faith—a belief in evil that opened up space for belief in goodness—is not as sui generis as some critics contend, for even a cursory reading of Newman's writing leads to the same conclusion. In the last chapter of his *Grammar of Assent*, Newman's apologetic essay for Christianity, he claims that all religion "is founded in one way or other on the sense of sin," and one's search for faith must be "conducted under a deep sense of responsibility." Christianity alone becomes "that gift of staunching and healing the one deep wound of human nature."[15] In his published sermons Newman emphasizes the experience of suffering in Christian life as a sign of God's love. Though he notes that suffering has no sanctifying influence in itself and can even imprison persons and make them selfish, he also argues that it "arrests us: . . . it puts, as it were, a finger upon us to ascertain for us our own individuality" and carries us on "to the contemplation of Christ." In the strong words of a preacher, he warns: "Be sure of this: that if He has any love for you, if He sees aught of good in your soul, *He* will afflict you, if you will not afflict yourselves. He will not let you escape." Newman concludes another sermon with the same agonistic, hounding rhetoric, highlighting the dialectical tones in his theology: "If there were no enemy, there could be no conflict; were there no trouble, there could be no faith; were there no trial, there could be no love; were there no fear, there could be no hope. Hope, faith, and love are weapons, and weapons imply foes and encounters."[16]

Such dialectical "encounters" are the common fare of Greene's novels: the whiskey priest versus the lieutenant in *The Power and the Glory*; the believing Sarah versus the unbelieving Bendrix in *The End of the Affair*; Pinkie and Rose's Catholic world of good and evil versus Ida's utilitarian world of right and wrong in *Brighton Rock*; Major Scobie's tortured conscience in conflict with his own sense of responsibility and pity in *The Heart of the Matter*. These novels are character studies of persons who, though they resist heroic elevation or self-satisfying identification, come to an extreme situation that awakens their conscience and, in the process, humanizes them. Greene's Catholicism was nurtured by Newman's stress on the subject's interior struggle with religious experience in a world of disbelief, and his characters are exemplars of those placed in extreme encounters with faith, hope, and love. In Newman's thought, Greene found a theological voice that matched his own profound sense of corruption, in both human society and the dread of the divided self.

The other aspect of Newman's thinking that influenced Greene's religious imagination was his theory of development in religious doctrine, arguably his most original theological contribution. Newman contends that the study of dogma shows "how the great idea takes hold of a thousand minds by its living force . . . so that the doctrine may rather be said to use the minds of Christians, than be used by them." He argues in a classic passage that religious doctrines are brought out rather than obscured by development:

> It is indeed sometimes said that the stream is clearest near the
> spring. Whatever use may fairly be made of this image, it does not
> apply to the history of a philosophy or belief, which on the contrary
> is more equable, and purer, and stronger, when its bed has become
> deep, and broad, and full. . . . In time [the doctrine] enters upon
> strange territory; points of controversy alter their bearing; parties
> rise and fall around it; dangers and hopes appear in new relations;
> and old principles reappear under new forms. It changes with them
> in order to remain the same. In a higher world it is otherwise, but
> here below to live is to change, and to be perfect is to have changed
> often.[17]

Newman's sense of doctrinal development echoes in this instance a Hegelian notion of dialectical philosophy, which sees thought in terms of a progressive resolution, a philosophical perspective far removed from the static understanding of revelation and dogma in Catholic scholasticism.[18] It nonetheless gave him a perspective in which to discuss the differences between authentic developments and historical corruptions in the history of Christianity. Contrary to the classical scholastic treatment of dogma as a fixed truth, Newman argued that Christianity's doctrinal expression, and implicitly Catholicism's ecclesiological structure, is historically situated and, therefore, is always an act of interpretation of Revelation. Newman's work brought to the fore the hermeneutical element of belief at a time when Catholic philosophy and theology were decidedly classicist in worldview. Newman interpreted his own conversion in this way, not as a dialectical break with his Protestant heritage but in continuity with his intellectual and spiritual growth. His quest for some better articulation of faith's relationship with knowledge allowed him to admit to Protestant criticism of Roman Catholic deficiencies: "There may indeed be holiness in the religious aspect of the Church, and soundness in her theological, but still there is in her the ambition, craft, and cruelty of a political power."[19] Though this sentence was written before his entrance into the Catholic Church, it nonetheless exposes the situation of the convert whose cultural heritage is bound up in the Protestant dispensation.

Greene found sustenance in Newman's thought, for it offered theological insight into his own difficulty with the intricate formulations of doctrine. Greene would forever view doctrine as an attempt to rationalize away the mysterious and supernatural quality of Catholic faith. In all his novels he attaches little importance to orthodox pronouncements and pejoratively sets up the rationalized articulation of dogma as a foil to the spiritual insight of his characters. Furthermore, Greene embodies Newman's perspective by creating narratives that excoriate the empty pieties and political collusions of a historically situated Catholicism. The reader is constantly struck by Greene's criticism of a Church whose members find an easy accommodation with wealth and power and do not mirror the plight of the poor and the suffering. If Greene's understanding of Newman was at times selective, it nevertheless became the first formative lens in which his inchoate faith finds resonance in Catholicism: the struggle between belief and unbelief, the pervasiveness of evil in the world, the experience of suffering, and the developing awareness of the primacy of one's conscience. These become the primary tensions of his religious imagination.

Crossing the Channel

> God is very often the good temptation to which many human beings
> in the long run yield.
>
> —François Mauriac, La Pharisienne (1946)

If Greene found a theological lens from Newman's understanding of faith, he discovered from the French Catholic literary revival a lens for the theological drama of his Catholic cycle of novels. This literary revival emerged in the 1870s and 1880s as a reaction to the political anticlericalism and the intellectual positivism prevalent in French society. Artists and intellectuals converted or reconverted to Catholicism, finding in it a mystical, romantic defense against the "reign of Science" that inundated nineteenth-century philosophy and theology.[20] By using Catholic tropes and themes as the material for their literature, these artists created a specific literary vision of Catholicism, one that engaged the historical crisis in French culture by paradoxically accepting the charge by critics of the compromised spiritual condition of the Catholic Church. The revivalists were prophetic in denouncing both the rationalism of the state and the bourgeois Christianity that made a too easy concourse with capitalist society. To meet their philosophical adversaries on their own ground, they formulated Catholic ways of thinking and imagining that took on a negative, dialectical methodology, oftentimes rivaling their non-Christian contemporaries in cynicism and pessimism. Catholicism was never served up with triumphant, epistemological certainty or morally uplifting drama; rather, it was inscribed in the midst of fallen humanity, a place of constant struggle where grace oftentimes shines forth. Catholic ways of seeing and valuing were engaged not so much to fix the tragedy of the world but to transform the way in which one lives in that world. Greene was quite familiar with many of these French writers; his *Collected Essays* contain substantial articles on Léon Bloy, Charles Péguy, Georges Bernanos, and François Mauriac. His grasp of the dialectical function of Catholicism in these writers found easy resonance with his own conversion and affiliation with the institutional church.

Léon Bloy was perhaps the most striking writer of the Catholic revival. His autobiographical novel, *Le Désespéré* (1886), and his more famous work, *La Femme Pauvre* (1897), convey the wretchedness and despair of unseemly heroes and heroines who are assaulted by the injustices of life. Bloy thought it his prophetic mission to announce the looming catastrophe that would follow the modern defection from Christianity. Kurt Reinhardt argues that Bloy "was the first among European Christian novelists to point out the dangers of a provincial pharisaical denominationalism, and he was one of those few who defined religious faith in terms of risk and resolute daring in personal existential action."[21] Bloy's ultramontanist Catholicism did not deter him from upbraiding the veiled apostasy of the contemporary Church, declaring that "the bourgeois, even when he is a good Catholic, believes only in this world, in the expedient and the useful. He is incapable of living by faith in another world and refuses to base his life on the mystery of Golgotha."[22] His work praises poverty as the only legitimate imitation of Christ, and it sees in the mystery of human pain and suffering the enshrinement of God's divine pain as experienced in the folly of the cross. In his affirmation of the Absolute at the expense of the world, Bloy's work is at times violent, passionate, and vengeful in its dialectical vision. Greene admired the "indestructible honesty and self-knowledge" of Bloy's convictions, referring to him as a "religious man but without humility, a social reformer without disinterestedness, he hated the world as a saint might have done." Yet he was highly critical of his literary talent: "One reads [Bloy] not for his characters, who are painted only deformity-deep, not for his story, but for the occasional flashes of his poetic sense."[23] Greene used one such poetic flash from Bloy as his epigraph for The End of the Affair: "Man has places in his heart which do not yet exist, and into them enters suffering in order that they may have existence." And Bloy's words echo through the whiskey priest's dying thought: "He knew now that at the end there was only one thing that counted— to be a saint."[24]

Charles Péguy, more than Bloy, was influential in developing two important themes interlaced throughout this period of Greene's work: the sinner as the heart of Christianity and the idea of "voluntary damnation" as a reflection of Christ's divine substitution on the cross. Greene's homage to Péguy is found in the last pages of Brighton Rock, when Rose goes to a priest for confession. She regrets not committing suicide so as to join Pinkie in his death and damnation. The priest tells her the following story to give her comfort:

> There was a man, a Frenchman, you wouldn't know about him, my
> child, who had the same idea as you. He was a good man, a holy
> man, and he lived in sin all through his life, because he couldn't
> bear the idea that any soul could suffer damnation. . . . This man de-
> cided that if any soul was going to be damned, he would be damned
> too. He never took the sacraments, he never married his wife in
> church. I don't know my child, but some people think he was a
> saint.[25]

Greene also refers to "Péguy challenging God in the cause of the damned" in The Lawless Roads; and in his article, "Man Made Angry," he compares Bloy to Péguy, focusing on the latter's readiness to suffer damnation for all those who suffer in Hell.[26] Greene's epigraph for The Heart of the Matter is Péguy's sanctified sinner at the heart of Christianity, lending authorial ambiguity to the reader's reaction to Scobie's suicide.

Grahame Jones, in his comparison of Greene and Péguy, argues that Greene was so taken by the implications of Péguy's idea of voluntary damnation that "Greene makes Péguy into a Promethean figure, challenging the might of God, willing to damn himself to protest against the damnation of others."[27] This preoccupation with Peguy's religious theme is in every novel of

Greene's Catholic cycle. It is suggested in Rose's wish to join Pinkie in suicide in *Brighton Rock* and embodied in *The Power and the Glory* when the whiskey priest mournfully prays for his illegitimate daughter: "O God, give me any kind of death—without contrition, in a state of sin—only save this child."[28] And voluntary damnation becomes more than just a prayer in *The Heart of the Matter* and *The End of the Affair:* in the former Scobie actually carries out the challenge issued by Péguy, deliberately damning himself for the sake of others; in the latter, Sarah struggles with the irony that winning her wager with God— to have Bendrix brought back to life if she gives up the affair—makes her life, separated from her lover, feel like a living hell. The hinge of dramatic action for both of these novels depends on this doctrine of substituting oneself for the sake of the other, a participation in Christ's mystical substitution on the cross, whereby Christ willingly takes the place of sinful humanity. Greene explores the theological idea in the extreme, transgressively pushing it to its ultimate dramatic potential. However selective Greene's reading of Péguy, one sees the Frenchman and his specific grasp of Catholicism embraced in Greene's most theological novels.

Georges Bernanos, like Bloy and Péguy before him, denounced the distortion of Christianity into respectable and genteel mediocrity, protesting in his works the collusion of the French Church hierarchy with the rich and powerful. Hans Urs von Balthasar's study of the author notes the depth of his anger at the condition of the Church: "Bernanos truly followed the Reformer to the very border of revolt. It is doubtful whether he suffered less than Luther interiorly at the scandals offered by the church."[29] His *Sous le Soleil de Satan* (1926) and *Journal d'un Curé de Campagne* (1936), written while Greene was solidifying his own literary vision, illustrate what Bernanos thought Christian life was like "under Satan's sun." His protagonists are often saint-heroes whose virtues lie not in superheroic, conventional saintliness but in their human frailty. Ann Begley remarks that "Bernanos' saints do not surpass humanity; they assume it."[30] Many of these saint-heroes are priests who serve as theological scapegoats. The priest of the *Journal d'un Curé* cries impulsively, "I'll answer for your soul with mine," and in *Sous le Soleil* the character Mouchette is redeemed by the priest's own life. Bernanos' concept of "mystical substitution" echoes Peguy's notion of "voluntary damnation" and Greene's appropriation of it, though in Bernanos emphasis is not so much on the dialectical protest of the injustice of the suffering as it is on the desire to participate mystically in Christ's agony on the cross.

In his article on Bernanos (1968), Greene says that "he belongs in the company of Léon Bloy rather than of François Mauriac . . . to the world of angry men, to a tradition of religious writing that stretches back to Dante, 'who loved well because he hated.' " Though Greene found Bernanos' literary style uneven, he writes appreciatively of both *Sous le Soleil* and *Journal d'un Curé* as texts in which "there is no catharsis . . . his stories are open wounds which refuse, like the stigmata, to heal."[31] Yet it was Bernanos' bold portrayal of evil personified that Greene most admired, a depiction of a somber but malicious adversary at work in the world that cannot be reduced to mere psychology or human ignorance. Of Satan's appearance as a character in *Sous le Soleil*, Greene writes that "this is surely one of the great scenes in literature, the scenes which suddenly enlarge the whole scope of fiction and like new discoveries in science alter the future and correct the past. Never again will it be possible to write off the infantile devils of *Doctor Faustus* with their fire-crackers and conjuring tricks."[32] Greene's attention to the reality of evil at work in the world and his use of theological scapegoats in his Catholic cycle shows great thematic kinship to Bernanos' works.

Of all the French Catholic authors of this period, it is François Mauriac whom critics have found most influential on Greene's artistic development. Phillip Stratford's scholarly study, *Faith and Fiction: Creative Process in Greene and Mauriac* (1964), makes the strongest case for the affinity between the two artists and, by implication, an affinity for the French influence on Greene's religious imagination. Stratford notes that at the beginning of his literary career, Greene began reading Mauriac's work. He read in English translation Mauriac's *Therese* in 1930, *Vipers Tangle* in 1933, *God and Mammon* in 1936, and *The Life of Jesus* in 1937.[33] Greene's great respect for Mauriac extended into a lifelong friendship. He was personally responsible for getting Mauriac's complete works translated into English when still a director of the publishing house Eyre and Spottiswoode. Mauriac was always grateful to Greene for extending his readership into the English-speaking world, an important factor, Mauriac thought, in his winning the Nobel Prize for Literature in 1952. During the literary criticism of the 1940s and 1950s, Greene and Mauriac were often compared, and both authors discussed in interviews and articles how their works converged or diverged in respect to the other.

Stratford highlights their biographical and textual similarities while acknowledging the creative ways in which they differ in matters of both style and temperament. He notes that both Mauriac and Greene have written about their "lost childhood" as the source of their vocations as artists, as well as the crucial moment when their religious obsessions solidified in lifelong themes for their writing; both went through a religious crisis or conversion early in their adult life that sparked their most creative and intense period of work; both achieved their best effects by creating a distinct atmosphere in their settings and in their attention to plot; and both understood the creative act of writing as grounded on a respect for the individuality, mystery, and spiritual dimension of their characters.[34] Stratford notes that for Mauriac it was Catholicism that gave him the religious sense that ultimately found its creative outlet in literature, whereas for Greene it was not religion but literature that gave support to his innate religious sensibility.

By his own account, Mauriac claims that his faith was rooted in his Catholic Jansenism, emphasizing a moral code and discipline that constantly stressed the reality of sin, guilt, and the potential dangers of worldly pleasures. Mauriac speaks of his early Catholic formation as a vaccine: "Many others have been born in it and have swiftly escaped from it because the inoculation of Faith did not 'take' on them. But I belong to that race of people who, born in Catholicism, realize in earliest manhood that they will never be able to escape from it."[35] Living up to this religious discipline was never easy for Mauriac; his passionate nature often repelled him from the demands of Catholic practice. Blaise Pascal, the seventeenth-century defender of Jansenism, became the greatest influence on his theological and literary imagination. Under the inspiration of Pascal's life and conversion, Mauriac's religious themes correlate well with much of Pascal's thought.[36] Theodore Fraser's study of Mauriac asserts Pascal's effect on the novelist:

> [Mauriac's] fiction resonates with many of Pascal's major themes:
> the 'grandeur and misery' of the human condition; the intuitive way
> of thinking and knowing about God rooted not in the intellect but in
> the heart; the notion of the hidden God and His mysterious chan-
> neling of grace; the need to wager everything on the probability of
> His existence; and the inability of human love to satisfy the cravings
> of the human heart.[37]

Like Pascal, Mauriac saw an inherent tension between human nature and supernatural grace, a theological position that held sway in much of Catholic discourse before the revival of Thomism in the early twentieth century. Neoscholastic theology maintained that God's grace was extrinsic to human existence, "poured into" receptive souls as if a supernatural material reality. To fulfill their spiritual destiny, human beings had to overcome their physical nature, to transcend the limitations of the flesh.[38] Mauriac's novels thus fixate on the struggle to overcome the temptations of the lower, natural order because they stand in the way of grace. For Mauriac this meant creating characters who, in their weakened state, are attracted to sin and evil, usually embodied in overt sexual passions, obsessive domination of one over another, or the craving for pleasure and wealth.

In the novel *Le Baiser au Lépreux* (1922), Mauriac tells the dark tale of a beautiful young woman who is forced by her family to marry a sickly man to better the financial state of the two families. Very much in love with his wife but knowing that she detests him, the husband sacrifices his life for hers by aggravating his sickness and hastening his death. His wife, aware of his great sacrifice, is so transformed that she renounces a young lover that she has courted on the side and decides to live chaste and alone the rest of her life. The story treats desire, disgust, and renunciation as the progressive fulfillment of her spiritual destiny; at the same time, it condemns the Catholic bourgeois families who colluded in forcing this event. The same holds true for *Thérèse* (1927), though here Mauriac valorizes the title character's attempt at murder because her extreme situation sets her apart from the conniving mediocrity of her family and husband. Thérèse's arranged marriage to a boorish husband compels her to contemplate an act of evil. Discovered to be slowly poisoning her husband with arsenic, she is locked up by the families in order to save face and, after much suffering, is told to give up her daughter, leave for Paris, and never to return to Bordeaux. Though she stands as a criminal and outcast, Mauriac's sympathy is with Thérèse, making the novel's final judgment and condemnation rest on her family. Thérèse is thus one of Mauriac's tragic studies of a woman who risks all to get out of her encaged life, becoming in the end a sort of saint. Mauriac subverts orthodox notions of saintliness in order to offer a kind of Catholic vision that fulfills Péguy's axiom of the sinner at the heart of Christianity.

Greene held Mauriac in high esteem and found in him support for his own understanding of the art of fiction. Mauriac, Greene claims, is important to the English reader because "he belongs to the company of the great traditional novelists: he is a writer for whom the visible world has not ceased to exist, whose characters have the solidity and importance of men with souls to save or lose, and a writer who claims the traditional and essential right of a novelist to comment, to express his views." As to his craft, his characters "exist with extraordinary physical completeness," such that we can "wipe out the whole progression of events and we would be left still with the characters in a way I can compare with no other novelist." Plot is used "not to change characters . . . but to reveal characters—reveal them gradually with an incomparable subtlety. His moral and religious insight is the reverse of the obvious: you will seldom find the easy false assumption, the stock figure in M. Mauriac." Greene ends the article with Pascal: "This modern novelist, who allows himself the freedom to comment, comments, whether through his characters or in his own 'I', again in the very accents of Pascal. . . . If Pascal had been a novelist, we feel, this is the method and the tone he would have used."[39]

Mauriac and Greene were hailed as "Catholic" novelists, and the dubious distinction had the effect of creating a critical correspondence on each other's work. As a convert in Protestant England, Greene saw much of the difference between Mauriac and himself in terms of their location: "Roman Catholicism takes on extraordinarily different forms in different countries."[40] Catholicism's broken tradition in England produced a polemical and self-conscious Church when it was reestablished in 1851. Characterized by such literary figures as Hilaire Belloc, G. K. Chesterton, and Evelyn Waugh, English Catholicism proclaimed the Church Triumphant, a kind of Catholicism that Greene's novels shunned. French Catholicism, by contrast, did little proclaiming; it embodied more comfortably the Church Suffering, passively enduring the infliction of modernity. Greene was drawn to this vision in no small way by his study of Mauriac and by his travels to Mexico. Greene spoke to the point in a series of lectures in Belgium, published as *Essais Catholiques* (1953), suggesting that the French novelist comes from "an uninterrupted tradition of Christian state of mind, thought, and style. . . . When a door opens in a novel by Mauriac, even before one leaves the shadows to enter the well-lit room where the characters are assembled, one is aware of forces of Good and Evil. . . . This awareness is, in general, banished from the English novel." Greene claims that in ever pragmatic and doubtful England, "the Apostle Thomas should be the patron saint of people in my country, for we must see the marks of the nails and put our hands in the wounds before we can understand."[41] In a lecture entitled "A Message to French Catholics," Greene recalls two personal events when he saw such "marks of the nails" and came to understand the suffering Church:

> I had the opportunity a few months ago at 5:30 in the morning, to
> listen to the Mass in a small Franciscan church in the South of Italy
> and to see, when a sleeve slipped, the horrible wounds on his
> hands, feet, and side, which Father Pio had had for a quarter of a
> century. In the semi-darkness of this early morning, I remembered
> another event I witnessed. It was in 1938 in Holy Week and at the
> very end of the Mexican persecutions. . . . No priest had the right to
> enter a church, all the masses were secretly said in private houses;
> but on Good Friday, the Indians went down from their mountains
> and spread into the crowded churches. It was ten years since they
> had listened to the Mass, they did not know how to speak Spanish
> and Latin. But they did their best to reconstruct the ceremony of the
> mass using their secret idioms, which are different in each village.[42]

His fascination with the Franciscan stigmatic Padre Pio and the oppressed Indians of Chiapas, Mexico, would be touchstones of Greene's faith throughout

his life. In interviews and essays he recollected that in times of personal religious doubt, he would call to mind these two events from his life.

Mauriac also saw differences with Greene's religious imagination, which
arose from nationality. Having claimed that one enters English Catholicism
through a "hidden door in the wall," Mauriac goes on to suggest that Greene
"broke like a burglar, into the kingdom of the unknown, into the kingdom of
nature and Grace. No prejudice troubles his vision. No previous experience
conditions his own explorations . . . it could be said that he has no model of
saintliness in mind, only corrupt nature and all-powerful Grace."[43] Mauriac's
preface to the French edition of *The Power and the Glory* presses the point
further:

> What I found most authentic in Greene's novels is Grace . . . [it is
> the] Truth that man does not know. With his English education and
> Protestant tradition he sees this truth in a light altogether different
> from the one we, French Catholics, are familiar with, coming as we
> do from a Jansenist tradition. He enables us to rediscover Christian
> faith; his solutions to the problems posed by Grace and salvation are
> free from the rigid categories of our theologians and casuists. The
> liberty he grants to God over mankind is at once terrifying and reas-
> suring because, at the final count, God is love and if nothing is pos-
> sible to man, everything is possible to Eternal Love.[44]

Mauriac appreciated the *lack* of Jansenism in Greene's work, an interesting
statement given the propensity of many critics of the period to label Greene in
this way. Greene's theological "given" is the fallen state of humanity, the starting place for Jansenism too. But like the novels of his French Catholic contemporaries, Greene's stories do not end in such pessimism. Rather, they portray
characters that sense their fate as inextricably linked to a fallen world, only to
have this *other* fate break into the world's fatality to create a new fate—a destiny.
In scholastic terminology, divine grace surmounts nature and transforms it, a
theological vision very amenable to the French Catholicism of the literary revival. One could even argue that the thematic relationship to Jansenism in the
novels is more stylistic than theological, a way of heightening the tension and
dramatizing the struggle between fallen nature and divine grace; thus, the
novels mirror the agonistic conflicts of Manichaeism and the wide chasms of
Jansenism without succumbing to the dualistic doctrines of either.[45] In terms
of nature and grace, there is never any suggestion in Mauriac or Greene that
nothing good could come from human nature. Indeed, having set up the conflicts of their novels, both authors are at pains to eschew an easy division

between the divine and human, good and evil. Grace is not condescending, as if handed down to the unfortunate, but operates from the level of misfortune. It is the manifestation of grace in the midst of fallen nature that most provoked their imaginations.

Greene and Mauriac share many other attitudes as well. Phillip Stratford argues that Greene learnt from Mauriac how to transform his melodramatic style into tragic realism.[46] The great feat of Mauriac and the French authors was to "Christianize" the tragic imagination, so that one is brought to religious faith, commitment, or insight by a path that seems foreign to what one would consider the normal route. As William Lynch observes in *Christ and Apollo* (1960), Christian tragedy "produces an extraordinary impact of beauty and exaltation in the spectator, yet paradoxically the spectator is brought to the experience of deep beauty and exaltation, but not by way of beauty and exaltation."[47] Such is the case for the dramatic realization of tragedy by Greene and his French counterparts: their characters do not flee the world or see faith as an escape; they come to discover grace in the realm of their finite and often destructive lives. Greene absorbed from this fecund literary movement the basic elements of a Catholic theological aesthetic and transposed them into his own literary expression. He shares with these authors the theological preference for the prodigal and social outcast to express the principle that Christ came to save "that which was lost." Their religious sensibility stresses the insufficiency of the bourgeois status quo, acute attentiveness to the terror that conditions much of modern life, and a haunting preoccupation with the reality of death. If Mauriac was more concerned with the traditional French fiction of "betrayal of the spirit by the flesh," Greene's awareness of betrayal was embodied more in the actions and deeds of the adventure novel. If sexual passion becomes the impetus of religious awakening for Mauriac's characters, Greene's heroes are usually roused more by moral choice and physical action. But unlike his French counterparts, it is not the angst of bourgeois European life that Greene emphasizes in his Catholic novels; rather, it is the horror, the ugliness, and the violence of life in oppressed and dehumanized situations. Once again, Newman's "original calamity" is the stark focus of Greene's setting and the springboard for his plots. Whether the gang wars of Brighton, the poverty of Mexico, the corruption of Sierra Leone, or the blitz of London, the external horrors of life are startlingly evoked. These novels continue the theological perspective of the Catholic literary revival, but always in terms that affirm Greene's taste for melodrama and action.

Two of Greene's novels, *The Power and the Glory* and *The End of the Affair*, can serve as textual bookends for a discussion of Greene's Catholic literary imagination from this period of his writing, for they embody those thematic elements that historically would help to define the Catholic novel as a unique genre of the early twentieth century. I propose to look briefly at the following theological tendencies expressed in these works: the theological aesthetic that structures the novels, the ways in which God's presence/absence is portrayed, and the relationship of secularist ideology to religious faith. Each will help to illustrate the development of Greene's religious imagination when we turn to his later, post–Vatican II religious works.

The Power and the Glory of a Catholic Aesthetic

Greene's most famous novel reenacts an archetypal story of pursuit and betrayal, specifically drawn in Catholic terms by making the chase motif operate on two levels: the first is the whiskey priest's attempt to flee from the pursuing forces of a Mexican state in which Catholicism is treasonable and punishable by death; the second is the discovery that the priest is even more intensely pursued by the power of God's grace. The whiskey priest has lived as a fugitive among his flock for the past 10 years, descending into a morally ambiguous world. He is forced to confront his life without the bourgeois values that he has personified through most of his priesthood: "It had been a happy childhood, except that he had been afraid of too many things, and hated poverty like a crime; he had believed that when he was a priest he would be rich and proud—that was called having a vocation."[48] He knows himself to be a bad priest who, in a state of drunkenness, has conceived a daughter and betrayed the vows of his priesthood. He feels a poignant disorientation from the church because this "five minutes of love" with the woman, Maria, "seemed to him now so unimportant [because] he loved the fruit of it" (128). In his covert ministry, he is tormented by the fact that he puts others in political jeopardy when they hide him from the authorities, as well as moral jeopardy by tempting them to betray him for monetary reward. His faith is tested anew at each place he hides. After arriving at a relatively safe location, he makes the fatal choice to return to the province to hear the confession of an American gangster, ensuring his own arrest and execution. The novel ends with the ideological conflict between the priest and the pursuing atheist lieutenant, drawing out the novel's central oppositions and ironies: loyalty and betrayal, hope and despair, success and failure, the desire for peace and the necessity for subversive activity. The morning of his execution, the priest feels he has been a terrible disappointment to God, yet the structure and the texture of the story leave the reader with no doubt of his sanctity. Greene masterfully conveys a strikingly contemporary hagiography that has a popular and immediate appeal beyond its religious signification.

The novel contains all the obvious ingredients of the classic Catholic novel ubiquitously found in the French authors discussed above. The whiskey priest is Péguy's "sinner at the heart of Christianity," who realizes that Christ is intimately linked with every sinner: "It was for this world that Christ died; the more evil you saw and heard about you, the greater glory lay around the death. . . . It was too easy to die for what was good . . . it needed a God to die for the half-hearted and the corrupt" (97). The priest participates in a "mystical substitution," a theological form of scapegoat in which he takes upon his shoulders the sins not only of the world but also of the Church (its corrupt leaders and its superstitions), rightly pointed out to the priest by the lieutenant in their final conversation before his execution. Added to this is the more explicit desire of the priest to damn himself for the sake of his daughter's life. There is also the extended criticism of the materialist ideology of the lieutenant, as when the priest's faith entails the dignity of the individual over the state: "That was the difference . . . between his [the priest's] faith and theirs, the political leaders of the people who cared only for things like the state, the republic: this child was more important than a whole continent" (82). And the lieutenant contemplates the future in Marxist fashion: "It was for these [children] he was fighting. . . . He was quite prepared to make a massacre for their sakes—first the Church and then the foreigner and then the politician" (58). Finally, God as the Hound of Heaven, pursuing the priest through the labyrinth of his fallen nature, stands as the central religious lens of the novel, exposing God's presence in the least expected of places.[49]

Yet there are more formidable manifestations of Greene's religious imagination at work in the novel that decidedly locate his theological vision in the Catholic world before the Second Vatican Council. The most striking is the way in which the understanding of Christ serves to illustrate a profoundly Catholic theological aesthetic. Roman Catholicism, more so than other Christian denominations, has deeply embedded in its tradition the understanding that an aesthetic apprehension of reality can open up a person to religious faith and conversion. It is an aesthetic drama because an individual is grasped by the form of Christ and is thus shaped by that form. The theologian Hans Urs von Balthasar has traced this theological aesthetic throughout Christian history and notes its prevalence in the last century in the French Catholic literary revival.[50] It is important to understand the mechanics of such a "Catholic" aesthetic in order to see just how deeply Greene's religious imagination creatively embodies it.

Von Balthasar begins his discussion of a theological aesthetic by noting that the metaphysical notion of beauty as a "transcendental" finds literary expression in Christian Revelation, whereby the Incarnation of Jesus Christ is the event in which God's story and the human story intersect. In this one life, divinity and humanity dramatically come together. Christ becomes, in effect, the ultimate "Form" of God's objective Beauty, not only radiating the transcendental beauty of Absolute Being, but also expressing it in a definitive way, even when hidden in the mystery and painfulness of the cross. The aesthetic form of Christ thus stands as the measure of all being, granting a significance to all creation beyond its singular significance. The human person is attracted to the Christ-form by fascination, wonder, and desire, a theological process of eros, of being drawn to beauty and lured to the Christ-form, an ascent of human desire to God.

This aesthetic is at its most theological in a consideration of the cross of Christ, for death on a cross is by all accounts a terrifying and ugly event and yet paradoxically manifests beauty. Though the cross has the appearance of an unbearable form, beauty "embraces the most abysmal ugliness of sin and hell by virtue of the condescension of divine love, which has brought even sin and hell into that divine art for which there is no human analogue."[51] On the surface the cross—when viewed without receptivity to what it reveals—appears only as the brokenness of beauty; yet it is precisely in brokenness that the cross is the witness of a kenotic, self-emptying transparency, drawing the beholder up into a hidden beauty, the self-sacrificing communication of the Absolute.

The logic of this theological insight into God's love can be stated in the following terms: Jesus' mission is to proclaim the love of God, yet experience of finite life gives the appearance that there is no God of love but only an empty universe filled with suffering; how, then, does God reconcile love with the experience of suffering? He sacrifices himself as a manifestation of presence, compassion, and companionship. By surrendering his life, Christ enables the human person to *see again* a horizon of absolute love. "The Gospel of the Cross," von Balthasar argues, "is not the crowning of a human drama with divine victory: rather the drama of human dissolution as a whole becomes the expression of eternal love."[52] The believer's participation in this Christ-form is a continual unfolding of moments when beauty, hidden in the ugliness and terror of life, shines forth. Ultimate participation is granted to the believer through the freely chosen self-sacrifice made out of love for such beauty. Von Balthasar documents this theological aesthetic—of being drawn into the Christ-form as one's own—dramatically rendered in ancient and modern philosophy, theology, literature, and drama, and most profoundly exemplified in the early twentieth century by the French Catholic authors. It is here that

Greene's own relationship to this literary tradition can be found as a Catholic influence on his religious imagination.[53]

Greene's specific genius places this aesthetic at work in the wasteland geography of the persecuted Church in Mexico. The whiskey priest undergoes a change of vision through his sinfulness and suffering. What he first thinks ugly—the poor, the prison hostages, the mestizo companion who betrays him—is seen to be a manifestation of God's presence. The priest initially understands all these encounters as further signs of the absence of God in the world, and yet they function to reconstruct for him the criteria by which that presence is measured. True to the theological tenet of the *felix culpa*, the "happy fault" of Adam's sin, the priest's spiritual enlightenment comes not because he disavows or escapes his sinfulness but precisely because of it. In being brought low he sees beauty shining forth, or as the priest reflects, he feels "the shock of human love" when observing his illegitimate daughter. Key to this perspective is the priest's analogical understanding of the similarity in the dissimilarity of everyone he meets. As he attempts to flee the mestizo, the priest ruminates that "at the center of his own faith there always stood the convincing mystery—that we were made in God's image. God was the parent, but He was also the policeman, the criminal, the priest, the maniac, and the judge" (101). While in prison he is moved with affection for his fellow prisoners, noting that "he was just one criminal among a herd of criminals. . . . He had a sense of companionship which he had never experienced in the old days when pious people came kissing his black cotton glove" (128). And when a woman complains to him about the ugliness around her, the priest voices the heart of a theological aesthetic:

> Such a lot of beauty. Saints talk about the beauty of suffering. Well,
> we are not saints, you and I. Suffering to us is just ugly. Stench and
> crowding and pain. That is beautiful in that corner—to them. It
> needs a lot of learning to see things with a saint's eye: a saint gets a
> subtle taste for beauty. . . . When [they] saw the lines at the corners
> of the eyes, the shape of the mouth, how the hair grew, it was im-
> possible to hate. Hate was just a failure of imagination. (130–131)

The novel climaxes with the whiskey priest participating fully in the Christ-form by returning to the wounded criminal, an act of compassion and a commitment to that which he now sees as truly beautiful. His execution is a final participation in the cross, and the text implies the full stature of the religious aesthetic in the final pages of the novel. In this way Greene actualized a distinctly Catholic tradition of a theological aesthetic, of putting on the form of Christ as the standard of one's true self before God.

Yet critics continually charge Greene with an unorthodox theological vision because he textually conceives of God in terms that either confuse the Father with the Son or force the term "God" to mean only the Creator at the expense of the Incarnation of Christ. Jae Suck Choi notes that Greene often turns God into the scapegoat, a title usually reserved for Jesus. Cates Baldridge claims that Greene's Catholic characters rarely think of Christ at all, so that the center of divine weakness is not portrayed at Calvary as much as in the very vulnerability of the Godhead itself. And Daphna Erdinast-Vulcan argues that Greene so dissolves the distinction between the Father and the Son that the Christian archetype of self-sacrifice is embodied not in the Son as much as it is in the Father.[54] It is true that *The Power and the Glory*, like all of Greene's Catholic cycle, expresses a God known primarily in suffering, a concept more in keeping with the understanding of Christ, the Son of God. Yet these critics seem to miss the theological aesthetic just articulated, where the whiskey priest *becomes* the Christ, the objectification of the Christ-form, participating in that form by being emptied of his bourgeois Christian piety and sacrificing himself for his criminal brother. True to Greene's own thematic obsessions and borrowed heavily from his appreciation of the French Catholic novelists, the form of the Catholic priest expands into a lived identification with Christ. He enacts and repeats the role of a victim-God, undergoing the painful drama of the cross, where, like Christ, he will doubt himself, doubt the trustworthiness of God, second-guess what he is about to do, experience painful regret, and be betrayed by nearly everyone in whom he has invested. As William Lynch observes, "There are no shortcuts to beauty or to insight. We must go through the finite, the limited, the definite, omitting none of it lest we omit some of the potencies of being-in-the-flesh."[55] The whiskey priest, in effect, becomes an *alter Christus*, another witness to the presence, the compassion, and the companionship of God in a world of suffering. The God that the priest comes to know at the end of his life is a God who knows suffering, who sees suffering as the only way to be freely—and thus not coercively—at one with creation.

There is not only the symbolic weight of the *alter Christus* placed on the character of the whiskey priest. If he stands as a representative of what sainthood might look like in Greene's religious imagination, he also serves as the primary mediator of the presence of God through his sacramental service. Greene's whiskey priest is ontological in nature: he is different and set apart not in moral virtue but in virtue of his ritual functions. When the young Coral Fellows asks the priest why he does not simply renounce his faith, he answers, "It's impossible. There's no way. I'm a priest. It's out of my power" (40). Even Padre José, who has married his housekeeper and tries to live comfortably, suffers the pangs of conscience in betraying who and what he is before God.

Acutely aware of the disjunction between his priestly duty and his own moral failure, the whiskey priest notes that "after a time the mystery became too great, a damned man putting God into the mouths of men: an odd sort of servant, that, for the devil" (60). When he tries to offer prayers for a dead infant, he can find nothing meaningful to say, yet realizes that "the Host was different . . . that was a fact—something you could touch" (151). And in his final conversation with the lieutenant, he retorts that "it doesn't matter so much my being a coward—and all the rest. I can put God into a man's mouth just the same—and I can give him God's pardon. It wouldn't make any difference to that if every priest in the Church was like me" (195). This sense of a functional *ex opere operato* expresses the ontological difference of both the priesthood and its mediating function that pervades Greene's Catholic imagination.

On the surface of the text, the sacramental action of the priest is the sole vehicle in which to make God's grace present to the world, a religious notion that fits quite comfortably in the Catholic sensibility of the early twentieth century. This understanding of priesthood emphasizes a vertical relationship to God in which all participate through the actions of the priest. Greene's imagination focuses on the stable mediation of the sacraments (specifically of confession and the Eucharist) as a means to save one's soul. At first glance, a pietistic and private understanding of Salvation is affirmed in the text. Twice the whiskey priest voices such thoughts: "The Church taught that it was every man's first duty to save his own soul" (65), and later, "I have to get to shelter—a man's first duty is to himself—even the Church taught that, in a way" (155). And yet these serve as ironic statements, for part of the priest's growth comes in rejecting the catechetical teachings of his Church because they act to truncate his faith and his ability to care for those in need of his consolation qua priest. The text thus stresses the dialectical, deconstructive language of the priest's religious insights in the midst of his experience of the analogical, sacramental language of his Catholic faith. The tension is always there between the primacy of faith over a suspect institutionalization of that faith, as well as the mediating vision of the priest's sacramental role over a political state whose aim is to suppress that role.

Paradoxically, this overly narrow and reduced sense of God's mediation found only in the priesthood is affirmed in the text at the same time that it is ultimately subverted by the analogical stress of the divine image, the *Imago Dei*, in every person, whatever his or her peculiarities or corruptions. Greene theologically locates the Incarnation not only into the realm of cultic, priestly function of the sacramental presence but also in the horizontal presence of God in the mundane persons that surround the whiskey priest. If the biblical tradition asserts humanity in God's image, Greene extends the analogy to its extreme. There are no exceptions or irredeemables among human beings because God, through Christ on the cross, redeems the God-image in everyone. Elliot Malamet articulates in poststructuralist terms how this effects the theological ramifications of the novel:

> Greene substitutes one sign-system for another, replacing the conventional Christian indicators with a whole other methodology of signification. The loss of [the priest's] chalice or the breviary does not displace the priest's hermeneutic frame of reference. He interprets humanity itself as a series of traces of God, seeing the divine in not only parent figures and priests, but in criminals, policemen, lunatics, and lovers. . . . Hence, Greene's penchant for recognizing the flexibility inherent in signification; the signs of God are everywhere, seeing as they need not be contained within the traditional borders of orthodox Christian symbols. Human beings reflect and circulate God's image on earth and thus forestall any possibility of the deletion of presence from the world.[56]

I believe Malamet overstates the case in one respect: if Greene's replacement of "the Christian indicators" affirms a wholly different sense of signification from *conventional* orthodoxy, it is done in order to affirm a deeper understanding of what is conventionally understood and expressed by Catholicism. The whiskey priest, deprived of the liturgy, reduced by his loss of breviary, altar stone, chalice, and congregation, must recover the traces of God's grace in the very presence of those persecuted. As the political state attempts to eliminate any trace of that presence, so the priest is pushed to find that trace in places hitherto undetected. As Malamet suggests, Greene neatly converts "the loss of the signs of the Church into an opportunity to restore the ubiquity of the divine. The delay in capturing the priest gradually allows for his own acknowledgement and reidentification with the priesthood as an irreplaceable conductor of God."[57] The text thus produces two movements of grace: the cultic function of priesthood works in tandem with the doctrine of the *Imago Dei* to reconstruct how God's presence is both mediated and measured in a fallen world.[58]

A final aspect of Greene's theological imagination in the novel is expressed in the ideological conflict between a persecuted Catholicism and a ruthless, secular socialism. Greene's sympathy for a dialogue between these two discourses partially comes from his reading of Bede Jarrett, the Dominican scholar at Oxford who was an important friend in the early years after his conversion to Catholicism. This conflict structures the entire novel. The lieutenant, described throughout the text as priestlike in his cause and in his sense of secular vocation to help the poor, desires to obliterate the church even if it means shooting hostages to ensure the capture of the priest. Greene goes to great length in the text to show how similar the two are in their ideals and goals, if not in their temperament. Indeed, the lieutenant is at times portrayed sympathetically, for he is endowed with a moral character and sense of purpose traditionally associated with the priesthood. But as Maria Couto has pointed out, *The Power and the Glory* structures the confrontation between social justice and faith in antagonistic terms: "Religion and politics, the Church and the state, are in opposite camps. The priest is a member of the establishment to be wiped out so that social justice can prevail; the lieutenant, member of another establishment, leads the crusade."[59]

The lieutenant considers blood to be the price for being socially progressive, declaring to the priest that the God of his Catholic Church supports the toleration of the abject poverty of the poor. The whiskey priest responds to the lieutenant with an argument that still causes many critics to cringe: "We've always said the poor are blessed and the rich are going to find it hard to get into heaven. Why should we make it hard for the poor man too? . . . Why should we give the poor power? It's better to let him die in dirt and wake in heaven—so long as we don't push his face in the dirt" (199). Yet this quietism is tempered by a latent political theology in which the political is articulated on the personal level. The whiskey priest counters the temptation to abstraction inherent in secular progressive politics of the time by attempting to convince his young daughter of her personal worth over any political notion of the human person: "I love you. I am your father and I love you. Try to understand that you are so important. . . . You must take care of yourself because you are— so necessary. The president up in the capital goes guarded by men with guns— but my child you have all the angels of heaven" (82). In the end the timely arrival of the priest's replacement in the book's final pages suggests that it is the whiskey priest's vision that may eventually win the ideological battle, one person at a time.

It must be said that Catholicism for Greene is central to the political landscape of the text not because it offers a superior ideological platform from which to live or govern society but rather because it offers a vision that criticizes any ideology that reduces humanity to a materialist construct.[60] Greene is at pains to show in the text the similarities between the priest and the lieutenant—their desires for a just society, their single-minded quests, and their respect for one another. The priest calls the lieutenant a "good man" to his face, and the lieutenant can grudgingly admit to the defrocked Padre José that his prisoner is "not a bad man." Yet it is clear that the lieutenant has won a pyrrhic victory in eliminating the last priest in the state: "The spring of action seemed to be broken. He looked back on the weeks of hunting as a happy time which was over now for ever. He felt without a purpose, as if life had drained out of the world" (207). As if to underscore this emotion, the lieutenant falls asleep and dreams fitfully, but all he can remember of the dream is "laughter, laughter all the time, and a long passage in which he could find no door" (207). His "spring of action," his quest for social justice, ends in a laughter of ridicule with no exit in sight.

That same evening the priest dreams of a strange eschatological banquet at which he eats six large plates of food at a café table placed before the high altar during Mass. He pays no attention to the Host, the "God over the altar," until his glass begins to fill with wine and he sees Coral Fellows, the child who once secretly hid him in his flight from the lieutenant. Though the whiskey priest is at first oblivious to the Mass in progress around him, Coral Fellows taps out a code in Morse that soon is joined by the priest at the altar and an invisible congregation along the aisles. The young Coral who risked her life giving him food and shelter—she who had an instinctive bond with the hunted priest—awakens the priest to the relationship between Coral's saving action to the event that is before him at the altar. The religious code of Catholicism is not felt in the dream until all together tap out in Morse code the word "News" for the whiskey priest, suggesting that this banquet manifests the Good News of the "God over the altar" only when connected to the good actions for the sake of others. The code and the truth that is encoded reveal that a just society must be grounded not in any political abstraction or privatized religious ritual but in a service to others that enacts the Christ-form of selfless love.

The novel ends with another nameless priest knocking at the door of the boy who, at the beginning of the novel, was bored by the clichéd piety of his mother's faith. The boy sees differently now, sees the deception of the lieutenant's vision of a better world, a vision fostered in an angry revolution that loses sight of the importance of the individual. In the end, Catholicism is not valorized as some exceptional organization that will always triumph but as a code that emphasizes the human in the wake of a modern wasteland of political ideology. Greene thus subverts an accommodating Catholic orthodoxy not to deny it but to emphasize the humanism in its theological vision. In *The Power and the Glory*, he continues the Catholic aesthetic so richly developed in his French Catholic literary contemporaries. In this novel, Greene's religious imagination conforms more than any other of his texts to the kind of Catholicism celebrated as a unique literary genre of the pre–Vatican II Church.

The End of an Incarnational Affair

Ian Gregor comments that in "*The Power and the Glory*, Greene makes reference to the 'appalling strangeness of the mercy of God'; in *The End of the Affair* it becomes his *subject*."[61] A true enough statement this is, for Greene's Catholic imagination had been fully engaged in this "appalling strangeness" since writing *Brighton Rock* in 1938; and with *The End of the Affair* in 1951, Greene attempted to embody this strangeness in the adulterous affair between two people who stand ostensibly outside of Catholicism. Though some critics consider this the most Catholic of his novels because Sarah Miles spiritually ascends to a kind of sainthood, the novel is paradoxically devoid of any explicit Catholic consciousness in the characters. Greene gives Pinkie and Rose, the whiskey priest, and Scobie a theologically informed frame of reference in a shared Catholicism as they work out their intense inner struggles with God's strange presence; Sarah and Bendrix are given no such place to stand as they grope to claim the truth of their experience. Greene's genius is to place the story in the first-person narrative of an unbeliever so that the religious point of view is filtered through a highly unsympathetic consciousness. In this way it is very much a novel of God's strangeness at work in a thoroughly modern, agnostic world.

Set in London during World War II and immediately afterward, the story is told by the novelist Maurice Bendrix, who had begun a passionate love affair with Sarah, the wife of a senior civil servant living across from him at Clapham Common. Four years into the affair they are together in his apartment during an air raid. Bendrix goes downstairs and is buried under the front door in a bomb explosion. Sarah believes him to have been killed and when he recovers consciousness and goes back upstairs to their bedroom, he finds her on her knees. Unbeknown to him, she is vowing to "anything that existed" that if Bendrix is restored to life, she will give him up as her lover and return to her husband, Henry. This she does, and Bendrix assumes that she has ended the affair to be with another man. Eighteen months later and still in a jealous rage, he hires a private detective after meeting a distraught Henry in the commons. The detective reports on her movements and procures her private journal from her house. Reading the journal, Bendrix finds out about Sarah's vow and is relieved to know that she is still in love with him. Her journal tells of her visits to Richard Smythe, a rationalist preacher whom she hopes will convince her of the futility of her vow but whose words only make her believe even more strongly. At first hating and resentful of the God she now believes in, she later comes to a deeply felt peace. In a late journal entry she begs God to take her peace and give it instead to her ex-lover. Bendrix is convinced that he can compete against a God he does not believe in and tries to confront her. Sarah avoids him, runs away in the rain, and dies from pneumonia a week later. Bendrix and Henry find out that Sarah was under religious instruction with a Father Crompton, yet Bendrix bitterly advises Henry not to give her a Christian burial. At her cremation, he discovers from Sarah's mother that she was secretly baptized a Catholic at age two. After this revelation, coincidences keep piling up that imply Sarah's intervention: Sarah's mother arrives just as Bendrix unthinkingly prays to Sarah to stop a seduction in progress; the detective Parkis tells of his son's cure of stomach pains after the boy dreamt that Sarah came and touched him; and the preacher, Smythe, is cured of the strawberry mark on his cheek, kissed by Sarah at their last meeting. In the end, Bendrix moves in with Henry at his invitation, still hateful and jealous of Sarah's lover/ God in whom he too has reluctantly come to believe.

In his autobiographical *Ways of Escape*, Greene comments that the inspiration of the novel came from reading Baron von Hügel's study of St. Catherine of Genoa, the fifteenth-century mystic known for her service to victims of the plague. This work led him to quote from another provocative article by von Hügel: "The purification and slow constitution of the Individual into a Person, by means of the Thing-element, the apparently blind Determinism of Natural Law and Natural Happenings . . . nothing can be more certain than that we must admit and place this undeniable, increasingly obtrusive, element and power *somewhere* in our lives: if we will not own it as a means, it will grip us as our end."[62] Aware that he was interpreting this passage contrary to von Hügel's intent, he nonetheless fused in his mind the erotic, bodily (and thus, incarnational) mysticism of St. Catherine as a naturalistic way to portray the inevitability of belief for Sarah. Sarah's sexual encounter with Bendrix becomes the occasion for her religious encounter with God. Forced to confront Sarah's convictions in her diary, Bendrix is reluctantly and defiantly led to the same place.

Once again Greene's text contains the classic elements of the Catholic revival: the adulterous Sarah at the heart of Christianity; her willingness to give up everything for Bendrix's life; the upended rationalist ideologies of both Smythe and Bendrix; and the amorous God who hounds Sarah and, at the end of the novel, hounds the unwilling Bendrix. It has the usual obsessions found in Greene's novels, a story of parallel pursuits, journeys, and betrayals. And yet critics observe that the novel is closer in technical form and in psychology to Greene's French contemporaries, especially François Mauriac. There is less action and melodrama and instead a discourse on the reflections and observations of the interior motivations of the main characters. Through the use of first-person narrative, the emotionally distraught and thus unreliable narrator, the constant time shifts and flashbacks, the use of letters and a diary, and the spiritual debate between art and life, Greene echoes more resonantly here with Mauriac's literary style than in any other novel.[63]

Critics have also quarreled about whose story it is, Bendrix's or Sarah's. Greene has so richly represented the spiritual awakening of both characters that it is difficult to categorize whose journey is the major focus.[64] It attests to Greene's success that the dual tension exists throughout the novel: it is at once a story about sainthood but is told by an unsympathetic narrator, himself a primary subject of the story and its harshest critic. In his role as narrator-novelist, he imposes meanings on his relationships; as critic, he questions the veracity of these very same meanings. The novel presents two competing versions of the end of the affair by shifting from Bendrix's reconstruction of past events and the counterversion found in Sarah's diary. If the point of view is initially weighted in favor of Bendrix, the diary gives us a strong counterpoint. The reader, like Bendrix, finally succumbs to the aura around Sarah's diary. The authentic interpretation of events increasingly becomes Sarah's perspective, first through her personal reflections on her struggles to come to terms with her vow to leave Bendrix, and second, understood most emphatically at the end of her diary, when she addresses God as her spiritual lover.[65] Sarah's transformed inner life has an effect on Bendrix's interpretive claims, and he stands transformed in the end (his compassion for Henry is a primary example), though still full of the same hate and jealousy transferred from Sarah to God.

The Catholic matrix of Greene's religious imagination once again extends beyond the formal elements of the genre as articulated above. The theological aesthetic expressed by von Balthasar so evidently embodied in *The Power and the Glory*—of seeing the beauty of Christ in the most hidden and sordid of places and being transformed by it—is found throughout *The End of the Affair*, but even more subversively. Because Sarah has neither belief nor any rudimentary religious instruction, she is only convinced of her belief in God through the miraculous restoration of her lover. It is a vow made in an extreme moment, dialectical in its intensity to commit her to an "all or nothing" decision, which over time becomes an undeniable conviction of her belief. Only later does she develop any sense of faith, fostered precisely in the analogical realization of her sexual longing for Bendrix as a spiritual form of suffering. Like the whiskey priest who is stripped of every obvious, orthodox sign of God's presence, Sarah begins her journey without the benefit of material signs of God except for the body of her lover. The loss and abandonment that both the whiskey priest and Sarah face lead them to put their faith in signs of divine presence in the least likely of places: for the priest it is revealed in the *Imago Dei*, the divine image analogously rendered in the poor, the ugly, and the persecuted; for Sarah, it is in an affair, the sexual fulfillment and loss that she knows with Bendrix analogously rendered into an erotic mysticism of love for the suffering body on the crucifix. And finally, both become a vehicle of sacramental encounter with God: the whiskey priest mediates God's grace in his priesthood, and Sarah does so in her baptism.

The novel's theological aesthetic pushes most explicitly the spiritual *via negativa* of John of the Cross, a mysticism consisting essentially in a passionate exchange of love with God through a process of purification, trials and temptations, and deliberate detachment from external things.[66] The "dark night of the soul" entails the experience of utter abandonment by God, the person's spiritual identification with the absence of God felt by Christ at the crucifixion. Bendrix's reflections on the reconstruction of the events of his story note that his feelings for Sarah encompass an affinity with a kind of spiritual darkness. He compares his affair with Sarah as a secular dark night of the soul, a time when he knew a kind of mysterious peace in the midst of aridity and pain:

> The words of human love have been used by the saints to describe
> their vision of God, and so, I suppose, we might use the terms of
> prayer, meditation, contemplation to explain the intensity of the love
> we feel for a woman. We too surrender memory, intellect, intelli-
> gence, and we too experience deprivation, the *noche oscura*, and some-
> times as a reward a kind of peace. . . . Sometimes I don't recognize
> my own thoughts. What do I know of phrases like 'the dark night'
> or of prayer, who have only one prayer? I have inherited them, that
> is all, like a husband who is left by death in the useless possession
> of a woman's clothes, scents, pots of cream. . . . And yet there *was*
> this peace.[67]

And in Sarah's journal, written before the fateful bombing raid, she invokes the metaphor of the desert, with all its theological reverberations: "I know he is afraid of that desert which would be around him if our love were to end. . . . If one could believe in God, would he fill the desert?" She ends the entry by noting that Bendrix's jealousy and unhappiness "would drive me into such complete isolation that I would be alone with nothing and nobody—like a hermit, but they were never alone, or so they say" (91–92). The metaphor is continued in her diary after she leaves Bendrix, fully aware that she is now entering her own desert of despair.

The most provocative aspect of the novel thus turns on the human body as the fundamental sign of God's presence, whether they are bodies in pain, bodies disfigured, or bodies in erotic intimacy. Greene proposes to place the doctrine of the Incarnation at the center of his realistic novel, thereby pushing the ramifications of the doctrine to extreme moments of sexual ecstasy and of intense suffering because of the loss of the beloved's body. If God has become human flesh, the logic goes, then every finite body is a possible conduit of God's grace. It is the strongest claim of Catholic sacramentality in any of Greene's oeuvre, making "the appalling strangeness" of God's presence stand out in the profound realism of both Bendrix's critical, rationalist narration of events and Sarah's sometimes hysterical meditations in her diary.[68] Sarah's hysteria swings from savage hatred of a God she only slightly believes in to momentary glimpses into a spiritual peace. The novel's all-embracing metaphor of overt and obsessive sexual passion is reminiscent of Mauriac's heroine Thérèse, a character who has the same kind of extreme emotional states in the midst of a suffocating situation.

Bendrix always recalls the physicality of their lovemaking in vivid, concrete, visceral terms: "the brown indeterminate-colored hair like a pool of liquor on the parquet, the sweat on her forehead, the heavy breathing as though she had run a race and now like a young athlete lay in the exhaustion of victory" (49). His sexual affair with Sarah is so intense that he begins to discourse on it with religious, mystical vocabulary: "Eternity is said not to be an extension of time but an absence of time, and sometimes it seemed to me that her abandonment touched that strange mathematical point of endlessness, a point with no width, occupying no space" (51). Sexual love becomes the still point in time, a kind of death experience that is extraordinary and ineffable, a moment of "absolute trust and absolute pleasure, the moment when it was impossible to quarrel because it was impossible to think" (71). Sex with Sarah is so ecstatic that Bendrix is forced to consider it in terms of prayer, meditation, and contemplation as the nearest comparable experiences (47).

Sarah is one of the few women characters in Greene's vast repertoire who is described as beautiful. Indeed, she is very comfortable in her beauty, aware of the power of her body as the source of her charisma. Distraught about her vow to break up with Bendrix she wonders, "Why shouldn't I escape from this desert if only for half an hour? I haven't promised anything about strangers, only about Maurice. I can't be alone for the rest of my life with Henry, nobody admiring me, nobody excited by me" (98). Yet it is Sarah's meditations in which God is identified with the finite world of bodies that is central to the theological vision Greene constructs. God first becomes real for her as another suffering, naked body having every human attribute. The centrality of the body as divine signifier comes to its apex in her long diary entry of 2 October 1945, written after pausing in a Catholic church to get out of the rain:

[The church] was full of plaster statues and bad art, realistic art. I
hated the statues, the crucifix, all the emphasis on the human body.
I was trying to escape from the human body and all it needed. I
thought I could believe in some kind of a God that bore no relation
to ourselves, something vague, amorphous, cosmic, to which I had
promised something and which had given me something in return
. . . like a powerful vapour moving among the chairs and walls. . . .

[I saw] the hideous plaster statues with the complacent faces, and I
remembered that they believed in the resurrection of the body, the
body I wanted destroyed forever. I had done so much injury to this
body. . . . [I thought] of my own body, of Maurice's. I thought of certain lines life had put on his face as personal as a line of his writing:
I thought of a new scar on his shoulder that wouldn't have been
there if once he hadn't tried to protect another man's body from a
falling wall. . . . And so I thought, do I want that body to be vapour
(mine yes, but his?), and I knew I wanted that scar to exist through
all eternity. But could my vapour love that scar? Then I began to
want my body that I hated, but only because it could love that scar.
We can love with our minds, but can we long only with our
minds? . . .

And of course on the altar there was a body too—such a familiar
body, more familiar than Maurice's, that it had never struck me before as a body with all the parts of a body, even the parts the loin-
cloth concealed. . . . So today I looked at that material body on that
material cross, and I wondered, how could the world have nailed a
vapour there? A vapour of course felt no pain and no pleasure. . . . I
looked up at that over-familiar body, stretched in imaginary pain, the
head drooping like a man asleep. I thought, sometimes I've hated
Maurice, but would I have hated him if I hadn't loved him too? Oh
God, if I could really hate you, what would that mean? . . . I walked
out of the church in a flaming rage, and in defiance of Henry and
all the reasonable and the detached I did what I had seen people do
in Spanish churches: I dipped my finger in the so-called holy water
and made a kind of cross on my forehead. (109–112)

Sarah's reflections move from wanting to flee the body to looking at Christ's
body, to a consideration of Maurice's body, and then to a final insight into the
importance of the human body to God. An impersonal, vaporous, disembodied

spirit seems less believable to Sarah in this world of flesh. Sarah submits to a person—the person on the cross—even if this person is never addressed directly, only observed. The theological aesthetic is most pronounced here, for in discovering what is at stake in believing in this incarnated God, she becomes a more willing participant in that Christ-form, of identifying herself with the suffering Christ. The diary entry ends with her defiant baptismal gesture, crossing herself with holy water as she leaves the church. It is the transformative moment, the spiritual key to unlocking a mystical, even erotic identification with God.

Sarah's diary continues to swing from a willing surrender to God's pursuit of her to an intense desire for escape with Bendrix. That the experience of God and of Bendrix have become conflated in her mind is illustrated in the way she addresses God as "You," a term always used in addressing Bendrix: "I remembered the time when I had stuck my nails into my palms, and I didn't know it but You moved in the pain. I said, 'Let him be alive,' not believing in You, and my disbelief made no difference to You. You took it into Your love and accepted it like an offering . . . I wasn't afraid of the desert any longer because You were there" (113). Yet a month later she writes, "I'm not at peace any more. I just want him like I used to in the old days. . . . I'm tired and I don't want any more pain. I want Maurice. I want ordinary corrupt human love." In Augustinian fashion she ends the entry: "Dear God you know I want to want Your pain, but I don't want it now. Take it away for a while and give it me another time" (89). In her final letter to Bendrix, informing him that she will not go away with him, she writes, "I've caught belief like a disease. I've fallen into belief like I fell in love. I've never loved before as I love you, and I've never believed in anything before as I believe now. I'm sure. I've never been sure before about anything" (147). Even religious belief, Greene suggests, subversively carries with it bodily signification, a virus inscribed in Sarah's ailing body. But Greene poses another bodily image of religious belief that subverts Sarah's metaphor: her mother tells Bendrix after the cremation ceremony that Sarah was actually a Catholic. She confides that she had her daughter secretly baptized at the age of two, claiming, "I always had a wish that it would take. Like a vaccination" (164).[69] Sarah's body becomes the primary site for the totalizing love of an incarnate God. Belief is both a disease that consumes her in a mystical annihilation and abandonment of self and a vaccine that has silently inoculated her from taking any simple and easy route in her struggle with her vow to God.

The revelation of Sarah's secret baptism is an important factor in illustrating Greene's Catholic imagination. Greene once again wants to emphasize the mystery of sacramental grace in ontological terms, a visible marker of God's mediation in the life of a human being. Sarah's baptism stresses the vertical relationship with the divine, a work of God by the church that marks indelibly the soul of the baptized. In introductory remarks to the novel, Greene defends the baptism from hostile critics: "If we are to believe in some power infinitely above us in capacity and knowledge, magic does inevitably form part of our belief—or rather magic is the term we use for the mysterious and the inexplicable—like the stigmata of Padre Pio which I watched from a few feet away as he said Mass one early morning."[70] Magic, mystery, the inexplicable: all the domain of the Catholic religious tradition that Greene embraced, a tradition that understood itself and its theological vision in opposition to the rationalist, modernist world of scientific explanation.

The news of the baptism betrays Greene's enchantment with Catholic scholastic discourse on *ex opere operato* notions of grace so prevalent in this period of Catholic culture. But it does so in order to magnify the struggle in the text for any clarity about where truth lies—whether in mere coincidences or in a personal destiny. Bendrix has tried to write a novel of his own based on his claim to interpret what is happening to him and Sarah. The fact of the baptism places his claims in doubt, becoming Bendrix's final "crack" in his perception of events. He is forced to wonder if he too is becoming hysterical. The narrative of his thoughts is strikingly similar to Sarah's own changing attitudes in her diary: "I'm a man of hate. But I don't feel much hatred; I had called other people hysterical, but my own words were overcharged. I could detect their insincerity. What I chiefly felt was less hate than fear" (190). From the moment that the baptism is revealed, Bendrix reluctantly finds himself addressing a God he hates, afraid that he will "leap" as Sarah has leapt into religious belief. The form of Sarah's leap is theologically framed more in terms of kenosis than in existential choice: "I might have taken a lifetime spending a little love at a time, eking it out here and there. . . . You were there, teaching us to squander, like You taught the rich man, so that one day we might have nothing left but this love of You" (89). If Sarah is portrayed as "spent" but renewed in God's love through the accumulation of miraculous occurrences that populate the last pages of the novel, the text implies that Bendrix is actually not far behind her. Yet Sarah's baptismal "inoculation" keeps her from any simple and easy accommodation with her vow and growing religious belief; Bendrix is given no such assistance. Feeling spent and tired, he prays: "O God, You've done enough, You've robbed me of enough, I'm too tired and old to learn to love, leave me alone for ever" (192). The novel ends with Bendrix in medias res, struggling with his belief in God. His hatred and fear is similar to Sarah's moments of hatred and fear, an early expression of love in a spiritual desert. God is still hounding Bendrix, the reluctant believer.

What might be said of the relationship between secularist ideologies and religious faith in the novel? The political context is more muted than in earlier novels, but it is significant that the setting is London under siege, a tremendous moment of fear, destruction, and political turmoil. Beyond that background, Greene's religious imagination focuses on the competing visions of a religious and specifically Catholic belief system versus the modern, secular visions of atheism. There are three successive struggles in the novel: the first depicts Bendrix's misery and restlessness because of Sarah's betrayal; the second presents Sarah's spiritual struggle with faith and her troubled mind between seemingly contradictory loves; and the third portrays Bendrix's battle between his own complacent rationalism and an ever-encroaching religious belief after Sarah's death. Bendrix complains to God: "I don't want Your peace and I don't want Your love. I wanted something very simple and easy: I wanted Sarah for a lifetime and You took her away" (191). Sarah's withdrawal into faith and her struggle to maintain her vow destroy the possibility that Bendrix will achieve a simple and easy human affair. As the novelist-narrator of the story, he continually reminds the reader that "if this book of mine fails to take a straight course, it is because I am lost in a strange region: I have no map" (51). Having begun an affair in order to get material for a future novel about a civil servant, he finds himself writing on a subject very new to him, a territory in which he struggles to articulate the extremes of emotion felt outside the simple and the ordinary.

Part of the articulation of the *extra*ordinary comes in Sarah's debate with Smythe, the utopian atheist who stands as an ineffectual descendent of the lieutenant in *The Power and the Glory*. As in that novel, rationalist and utopian ideologies still portray the antithesis of the extraordinary world of faith. There is no doubt in the text that Christian faith serves as the preeminent criticism of the reigning modernist, antireligious discourses. Smythe even senses the futility of his philosophical positions when he realizes he has fallen in love with Sarah. Her concrete actions toward him upset the logic of his missionary zeal, and at the end of the novel he displays a kind of devotion to a sanctified Sarah, carrying a relic of her hair obtained after her death. In the characterization of Smythe there is little that has evolved in Greene's agonistic confrontation with secular atheism.

With Bendrix, on the other hand, there is quite a development. He is a more comfortable atheist than Smythe, unencumbered with any thoughts of religious faith because he thinks it irrelevant to modern life. At best God is a mathematical entity: "I find it hard to conceive of any God who is not as simple as a perfect equation, as clear as air" (11). Bendrix emphasizes that his way of love is "ordinary human love," understood as an uncomplicated consequence of biology: "Hatred seems to operate the same glands as love: it even produces the same actions" (27). He notes that Sarah's love for him is different, more difficult to reduce to such formulations, lacking the jealousy that is always surfacing in his longing. "I refused to believe that love could have any other form than mine," he reflects. "I measured love by the extent of my jealousy, and by that standard of course she could not love me at all" (54). Emotions are all part of an equation for Bendrix, something quantifiable and open to precise formulation. Love, hatred, and jealousy are mathematical fractions of biological drives, forever trying to cancel each other out. His relationship to Sarah continually takes him into a world where the equation founders. It is a new territory in which there is no escape into past reductions of human feeling and relationship.

If Bendrix fails at controlling the events that led to the demise of the affair, he at least wants to control its meaning. And yet even this is denied him as he ponders the relationship of his own literary craft to God's creative act. The first paragraph of the novel attests to Bendrix's fear of an omniscient author, arranging the scenes and imposing a plot:

> A story has no beginning or end: arbitrarily one chooses that moment of experience from which to look back or from which to look ahead . . . [for] did I *choose* that black wet January night on the Common, in 1946, the sight of Henry Miles slanting across the wide river of rain, or did these images choose me? It is convenient, it is correct according to the rules of my craft to begin just there, but if I had believed then in a God, I could also have believed in a hand, plucking at my elbow, a suggestion, 'Speak to him: he hasn't seen you yet.' (7)

Bendrix's agnostic and detached vision of his craft is immediately placed in doubt as he remembers the events of his affair. He thinks of his profession as one able to convey the truth of life, and his inability to control the ending of his story makes him question the very ability to make any totalizing claims on reality. And yet he notes that just as an author succeeds in bringing to life only certain of his characters, so too might God succeed only with the saints:

> Always I find when I begin to write there is one character who obstinately will not come alive. There is nothing psychologically false about him, but he sticks, he has to be pushed around, words have to be found for him, all the technical skill I have acquired through the laborious years has to be employed in making him appear alive to my readers. Sometimes I get a sour satisfaction when a reviewer

praises him as the best-drawn character in the story: if he has not
been drawn he has certainly been dragged . . . he never does the un-
expected thing, he never surprises me, he never takes charge. Every
other character helps, he only hinders. And yet one cannot do without him. I can imagine a God feeling in just that way about some of
us. The saints, one would suppose, in a sense create themselves.
They come alive. They are capable of the surprising act or word.
They stand outside the plot, unconditioned by it. But we have to be
pushed around. We have the obstinacy of non-existence. We are inextricably bound to the plot, and wearily God forces us, here and
there, according to his intention, characters without poetry, without
free will, whose only importance is that somewhere, at some time,
we help to furnish the scene in which a living character moves and
speaks, providing perhaps the saints with the opportunities for *their*
free will. (185–186)[71]

Being a saint, in Bendrix's estimation, makes one free and thus more alive
because saints have a different perspective and relationship to a society con-
ditioned to drag one into a complacent and agnostic irrelevancy. Greene is
subtly distinguishing in this text the Catholic *difference* in understanding contemporary secular and materialist culture: faith in God grants a poetry to one's
life. The reader realizes that Bendrix is comparing himself to Sarah, she who
"takes charge," who has that poetry in her to become more fully human. The
tendency in Catholic theological aesthetics to discourse on both the role and
the reality of beauty is threaded throughout the entire text. Sarah is drawn in
an ascent to the beautiful form of Christ on the cross, still hidden from Bendrix's spiritual perception. She leaps out of the bourgeois state of affairs reflected in both her easy-going agnosticism and an explicitly institutionalized
Catholic observance. In the process she is made into a thing of poetic beauty,
taking on that form that becomes for Bendrix another sign of God's presence,
however difficult a sign it might be for him.[72]

The End of the Affair is in many ways Greene's most persistently theological
novel. Closer in literary style to the French, and continuing the Catholic aesthetic so evident in that literary revival, Greene attempts to convey the com-
plexities of the appalling strangeness of God's grace. The political ramifications
are muted, but in his use of such transgressive categories as adultery and in
the bold dialogue of pronounced hatred of the Other because of its claim on
human desires, Greene relentlessly orients the theme to a wider audience outside a Catholic consciousness. It stands as the final work of his four-book
Catholic cycle, the apotheosis and limit of the genre for Greene's imagination.

Except perhaps for *A Burnt-Out Case* (1961), Greene never again attains in his novels the stylistic intensity of his character's Catholic interiority so pronounced in the genre. The novels of the next decade—*The Quiet American* (1955), *Our Man in Havana* (1958), *The Comedians* (1966), and *Travels with My Aunt* (1969)—still echo Catholic notions of salvation or damnation but no longer in explicitly religious terms. In these works Greene experimented with the political novel and comedy as a way to get at the moral and economic situations of modernity. His characters still find themselves in some "original calamity," but lacking is the strong undertone of the Catholic literary revival's thematic tensions that set his earlier novels apart. Most of literary criticism has seen this experimentation as a "post-Catholic" maneuver on Greene's part, a turn away from the imaginative world of Catholicism. Yet Greene's artistic confrontation with his religious imagination matured as Catholicism underwent the crucial years of the Second Vatican Council. The theological and ecclesial developments of the Council and their effect on Greene are the subjects of the next chapter.

3

Vatican II Con/texts and Greene's Catholic Imagination

The joy and hope, the grief and anguish of the people of our time, especially of those who are poor or afflicted, are the joy and hope, the grief and anguish of the followers of Christ as well. Nothing that is genuinely human fails to find an echo in their hearts. For theirs is a community of people united in Christ and guided by the Holy Spirit in their pilgrimage towards the Father's kingdom, bearers of a message of salvation for all humanity.

—*Gaudium et Spes* (1965)

All forms of "horizontally" mediated actions of salvation draw their actual saving significance from the "horizontal" appearance in this world of the man Jesus, the Son of God in person. Because all grace is a saving act of Christ—the "horizontalized," personal grace of God in this world—we can no longer conceive of any grace which does not come upon us from the horizontal level of our lives.

—Edward Schillebeeckx, *God and Man* (1969)

I must admit to being a fan of Hans Küng. Perhaps because I am an agnostic Catholic.

—Graham Greene, letter to Mary Pritchett (1979)[1]

I was delighted to get your essay with its generous and individual dédicace. The admiration is all on my side and the gratitude for help-

ing me to keep one foot in the Catholic Church. It's a delight to add this essay
to the five books [of yours] I have on my shelves.

—Graham Greene, letter to Hans Küng (1989)[2]

More Than a "Catholic Novelist"

Graham Greene was 47 years old when *The End of the Affair* was published in
1951. Inspired by his love affair with Catherine Walston, Greene had personally
felt the intense conflicts embodied in the book's religious themes. Paradoxically, the adulterous affair with Walston intensified Greene's identification with
Catholicism so much that he claimed in a love letter to her that "I'm not even
a Catholic properly away from you," and a year later, "the only way to love God
more than you is with you."[3] Though the obsessive and intense quality of such
theological tension in that novel is muted in Greene's next series of novels, it
found expression in his dramas written and successfully performed in the
1950s and 60s. Three of his plays, *The Living Room* (1953), *The Potting Shed*
(1958), and *Carving a Statue* (1964), consciously reworked the theological
themes that obsessed him during the 1930s and 1940s: mystical substitution,
doubt and the nature of belief, and God's pursuit of erring souls. His faith
perspective also appeared in many of his journalistic articles that touched on
the situation of Catholics in troubled spots around the world.[4] But his novels—
The Quiet American (1955), *Our Man in Havana* (1958), *A Burnt-Out Case*
(1961), *The Comedians* (1966), and *Travels with My Aunt* (1969)—lacked the
religious intensity of his earlier ones. Part of the reason is that Greene's own
Catholic fervor lessened during these decades, due in no small part to the
psychological trauma of ending his relationship with Walston. The tortured
love affair seemed to exhaust Greene's creative attachment to the Catholic
literary revival that helped make his reputation. In response to this, he exiled
himself from England and, consequently, the Catholic circle of friends who
supported him there.[5] By 1965, Greene had permanently settled in Paris and
Antibes, France, and had in interviews begun publicly distancing himself not
only from theological discussion of his novels but also from admitting a theological influence on his work.

As Greene traveled more frequently, the wider global concerns outside of
postwar Europe took center stage in his novels. The Catholic matrix of Greene's
imagination is still unmistakably present even as political struggles and moral
commitments to political situations displace the extreme religious dilemma of
his characters. This is illustrated in *The Quiet American*, a novel that explores
the complex relationship between French colonialists, communist insurgents,

and the growing American presence in Vietnam. Alden Pyle, the naive, "quiet" American, serves as Greene's subject in which to investigate the shift between European colonial rule and the new world order of U.S. economic and diplomatic interests. The imaginative world of Catholicism is minimal in the text, serving only as a political subtext in the plot when Vietnamese Catholics are under siege by insurgents. In this novel (and in the correspondence from his four extended journeys to Indochina) Greene still suggests that enclaves of Vietnamese Catholics stand apart from the ideological battle among the French, the communists, and the Americans in Vietnam. Catholic *difference* is still at play—a religious community that suffers as it is manipulated by opposing forces. And in the character of Fowler, the English journalist whose first-person narrative offers a nominal Catholic consciousness, Greene recreates his personal marital dilemma.[6] Fowler, like his creator, suffers from a broken marriage to a Catholic woman in England who, in this case, refuses him a divorce. In the novel Fowler betrays Pyle to the communist insurgents, thinking the betrayal will save innocent lives, as well as win back his Vietnamese lover, whom Pyle promised to marry. In the last words of the novel, Fowler longs for an absent God to whom he could confess his betrayal: "Everything had gone right with me since [Pyle] died, but how I wished there existed someone to whom I could say that I was sorry."[7] Though the novel voices the metaphysical distance between God and Greene's main characters, confessional tropes of Catholic remorse and guilt still reveal the religious sensibility underlying the text.

Greene's return to the political novel during this period is complemented by his attempt to temper his tragic imagination with comedy.[8] That humor is put to good effect in such works as *Our Man in Havana* and *Travels with My Aunt*, but in both books Greene's use of Catholicism becomes more a satirized, stereotypical cultural signifier than a religious lens through which to focus on reality. In *The Comedians*, his only novel written with the expressed political motive of bringing to light the oppression of a dictator, Haiti's Papa Doc, Greene uses comedy to expose the inadequacy of human agency to effect real change in the political order of that nation. Most of the novel's characters are outsiders to Haiti and would indeed be a comical ensemble if not for the horror inflicted on Haitians by the abuse of political power and the collusion of U.S. support of such a regime. Peter Mudford's political reading of the novel presciently notes the new cultural context in which Greene wrote: "In *The Comedians* ideological conflict has been reduced to the uncontrolled violence of the Tontons Macoute. . . . In a state where arbitrary violence and fear are the only instruments of government policy, betrayal ceases to have much meaning. . . . What is betrayed is not a faith but an underlying human dignity."[9] There is a sense in which Greene's position between the ideology of socialism and the metaphysical belief central to his Catholic cycle is made absurd by the unremitting dehumanization witnessed in Haiti during Duvalier's regime. The subhuman conditions of third world peoples, observed and analyzed by Greene in Haiti and other troubled places, would also become a central concern of Latin American theologians after the Second Vatican Council.

In the midst of such political and tragicomical landscapes during these decades of writing, Greene returned to the central question of faith and belief only in *A Burnt-Out Case* (1961). Set in a Catholic leprosarium in the Congo and owing much to Conrad's *The Heart of Darkness*, the novel tells the story of Querry, a world-famous Catholic architect who has lost all belief in God. He is the metaphorical leper, deadened to desire and love, as well as to psychological pain. In the growing relationship with his servant, a leper named *Deo Gratias*, and in his interactions with both the committed atheist Doctor Collins and the priests who staff the leprosarium, Querry is slowly cured of his despair and isolation. Yet the protagonist's new orientation toward faith in God is left ambiguous, for the novel ends with his murder at the hand of Rycker, a jealous husband who wrongly suspects Querry of impregnating his wife. Like many of Greene's previous texts, it is left up to those who survive to pronounce possible conclusions about belief. In the final dialogue that closes the novel, the atheist doctor maintains that Querry had learned merely a kind of fidelity in serving others, whereas the Father Superior, quoting Pascal, notes "a man who starts looking for God has already found him. The same may be true of love—when we look for it, perhaps we've already found it."[10]

The novel's investigation into the failure of religious belief to sustain the Catholic protagonist, Querry, was so pronounced that Evelyn Waugh personally wrote to Greene that he saw the book as a "recantation of faith." Greene responded to Waugh: "I wanted to give expression to various states or moods of belief and unbelief. The doctor . . . represents a settled and easy atheism; the Father Superior a settled and easy belief; Father Thomas an unsettled form of belief and Querry an unsettled form of disbelief."[11] In later remarks about the inspiration for writing the book, Greene clarified his position:

> Evelyn Waugh and I inhabited different wastelands. I find nothing
> unsympathetic in atheism, even in Marxist atheism. *My* wasteland is
> inhabited by the pious "suburbans" of whom I had too carelessly
> written—I had not meant the piety of simple people, who accept
> God without question, but the piety of the educated, the established,
> who seem to own their Roman Catholic image of God, who have

ceased to look for Him because they consider they have found
Him.[12]

Waugh was not alone in his attempt at diagnosing Greene's spiritual health,
for many of the reviews and critical essays read the novel as an indication of
Greene's burnt-out faith. The religious consciousness—or lack thereof—of
many of the characters in the novel has some resonance with Greene's earlier
Catholic cycle, and yet the novel stands apart from them because it explores
more narrowly and more suspiciously both a positive and a negative impact
that religious belief can have on a person's life. In creatively imagining a
broad continuum between Catholic belief and atheism in the modern world,
Greene reflects the discourse not only of French existentialist literature and
philosophy of the time but also of Catholic theologians at midcentury attempting to analyze different degrees of religious faith and kinds of atheism.[13] In
this way, the novel captures a development in Greene's religious imagination
that builds on and extends what I have been calling the classic ingredients of
the Catholic literary revival, for Greene now scrutinizes how faith in God (and
here, Greene presumes a Catholic notion of faith) takes on different levels of
religious commitment in his characters. The protagonist is "burnt" by his too
easily accommodated belief system and the institution that supports it. Querry
represents Greene's attempt to expose the difficult quest for authentic religious faith.

Greene's detachment from the theological constructions of the literary
revival and his effort at distancing himself from any branding as a Catholic
novelist coincided with the Church's convocation of the Second Vatican Council, an event closely followed by Greene and most Catholics during its four
yearly sessions. If Greene's religious imagination was indeed burnt-out, the
Catholic Church's desire to renew itself had just begun and Greene was to be
swept up in its wake. Vatican II began articulating Catholicism in paradig-
matically new ways, and the theologians of the Council that Greene continued
to read in the last decades of his life ultimately served to foster in him a renewed investigation in his literary texts into the centrality of Catholic ways of
thinking and feeling. Greene's embodiment of the theological issues of the
Council in his own religious imagination—the struggle for belief, for a justice
that is the fruit of faith, and for sacramental and liturgical renewal—illustrates
the developmental and piecemeal reception of the Council by Roman Catholics
in the 1970s and 1980s. Greene was keenly aware of many of the Catholic
thinkers influential at the Council, and their theological perspective engaged
his Catholic faith and the intellectual uncertainties surrounding his belief, reframing his sense of Catholic *difference* in his literary imagination.

From Criticism of the Modern to Critical Dialogue

European and American Roman Catholicism in the years immediately after World War II underwent an unprecedented resurgence in popularity because it seemed a refuge of order, discipline, and metaphysical meaning to a generation devastated by war, the Holocaust, and the atomic bomb. During the 1950s, the visible signs of a strong institutional Church were exemplified in the large number of men and women entering seminaries and convents. Postwar Catholicism, as the theologian Joseph Komonchak describes, had retained its idealized and nostalgic sense of its medieval culture, a time when "the Church possessed a monopoly of cultural definition, when social institutions embodied and confirmed its world-view and ethos."[14] It was the era of Pope Pius XII's formulation of the infallible doctrine of Mary's Assumption into Heaven, an event that occasioned Greene's most apologetic article about Marian devotion in the Catholic Church.[15] During this time, the issues in Catholic theological centers were still constructed in neoscholastic terms, but with a major shift of emphasis toward finding ways to engage the new world order. In the midst of the uncertainties of the cold war and the rebuilding of Europe, there was much optimism from within Catholicism, as well as in European and American political hegemonies, for pragmatic solutions to the problems in the world.

With Pope John XXIII's announcement in 1959 of an ecumenical council, there was great enthusiasm for a Church-wide *aggiornamento*, an adaptation of the church to the "signs of the times."[16] It was felt not only by Catholics but also by a wide range of intellectuals, both religious and secular. The Council became a point of interest especially to the political Left of Europe. The desire to engage in a dialogue between Marxist thought and Catholicism is illustrated in many books and journals of the 1960s, such as John C. Bennett's *Christianity and Communism Today* (1960), Adrian Cunningham's *The Slant Manifesto: Catholics and the Left* (1966), Roger Garaudy's *From Anathema to Dialogue: A Marxist Challenge to the Christian Churches* (1966), and Terry Eagleton's *The New Left Church* (1966). A few comments on the texts by Garaurdy and Eagleton will serve to illustrate the optimistic tenor of the dialogue provoked by the Council.

Roger Garaudy, the French Marxist philosopher and humanist, asks this question: Can there be a Christian-Marxist confrontation that is not merely an exchange of views but also a genuine intellectual cooperation? As an atheist, he urges this cooperation in order to deal with the proliferation of nuclear weapons between the superpowers. Quoting the Jesuit paleontologist Teilhard de Chardin, Garaudy agrees that if the human race is to survive it will not be by simple biological evolution "but because of a human choice which will have demanded, as Chardin said so well, 'the common front of all those who believe that the universe is moving forward, and that it is our task to make it move forward.' "[17] Garaudy proposes that there can be a synthesis between Christian and Marxist thought in terms of a fundamental humanism that works for the betterment of society, something shared universally by Christians and atheists alike.

On the Christian side, Eagleton, then a Catholic leftist literary critic, writes to persuade Christians that "being in the Church involves commitment to imaginative culture and the political left." He argues that Christianity "gives socialism a wholeness of concern, a simultaneity of emphasis, at a time when socialism needs to be healed in precisely this way—to regain a sense of its human depth while realizing itself as a practical force."[18] Eagleton even reinterprets the Catholic liturgy as a sacrament in which a Marxian notion of human alienation is healed by the selfless communication of God in Christ. In both Garaudy and Eagleton there was a desire, however naive it may seem in hindsight, for a cooperative relationship between Christianity and Marxism that would transform the Church, as well as the State. Greene had already been receptive to such dialogue since his Oxford days, especially through his friendship with the Dominican priest Bede Jarrett, whose scholarly studies of medieval forms of communism Greene had read and admired. Even though he was critical of Marxism as an ideology, Greene firmly believed that Marx's economic proposals were a more just economic system than those presented by American-style capitalism.[19] Greene's novels had often uncovered the similarities and differences between Marxist socialism and Catholicism. In these early comparisons, Marxist ideologies ultimately lose out to the religious impulses of Catholicism precisely because Marxist notions of human progress cannot ensure dignity for each human life. But as Greene continued to write into late life, that thematic opposition was tempered. His desire for some compatibility between the two became more pronounced as he searched out ways to think through his own loyalties and to come to terms with what he called "the human factor."

Thus the Second Vatican Council began a long-overdue effort by the Catholic Church to have a dialogue with the culture created in the West by the Enlightenment and the economic and political revolutions of the past two centuries. The Swiss-born theologian Hans Küng and his American contemporary David Tracy have jointly claimed that although conservative factions ultimately compromised the Council's aim at renewal, there was nevertheless the beginning of a paradigm shift in Catholicism. Starting with Thomas Kuhn's definition of paradigm as "an entire constellation of belief, values, techniques, shared by members of a given community," Küng notes that contemporary Catholic theology has felt the critical effects of changing paradigms, "a transitional period of uncertainty, in which faith in the established model began to waver, patterns of thought were seen through, bonds loosened, traditional schools dwindled, and a host of competing approaches made their appearance."[20] In the tension between faith and reason that demarcated the ideological differences of Christianity in the pre–Vatican II era, Küng argues that Catholicism's neoscholastic paradigm (the theological foundation of the Catholic literary revival of the first half of the twentieth century) was replaced by a "postmodern" paradigm that integrated some of the fundamental positions of the Reformation, the Enlightenment, and modernity.[21] In Küng's schematic, the neoscholastic Catholic paradigm stressed a hierarchical ordering in which faith stands higher than reason, grace higher than nature. Faith and reason, grace and nature, are not in opposition to each other; rather, reason and nature find their fulfillment and meaning in being directed toward their higher analogue.

In contrast are two other viable Christian paradigms. The first is the dialectical theology found in neoorthodox Protestantism (via Karl Barth), which sees the tension between faith and reason as a crisis: faith stands in opposition to reason, grace in opposition to nature. The other competing paradigm is liberal Protestantism and enlightenment philosophy, where the tension is resolved when natural science and philosophy fulfill the aims of religious belief, so that reason replaces faith, nature replaces grace. During the Second Vatican Council era, Küng suggests, the neoscholastic Catholic paradigm positively engaged the insights of Protestant dialectical theology by insisting that faith in God's revelation in scripture is the primary act of grace. The Council positively engaged the insights of the enlightenment and liberal Protestant tradition by accepting historical and hermeneutical methods to articulate that faith.[22] The effect was to place Catholicism at the center of a constellation of philosophical, political, and social movements of the mid-twentieth century in a manner that eschewed its previous triumphal, premodern, and often fortress mentality. It was a decisive shift in the way in which the Church understood itself and its mission in the world.

This shift is seen most markedly in the language of the Council. The emphasis on a continual, humanistic, inner renewal of the Church centered on the following key themes: the acceptance of historical consciousness in the articulation of the church's history and doctrine; the importance of an active role for the laity; the spirit of détente between the Church and the modern world; the modification of the Church's identity beyond clerical, institutional, and hierarchical terms to the more inclusive term "people of God"; the renewal in liturgical and devotional practices; the effort at interreligious dialogue; the clear affirmation of religious freedom to worship according to one's conscience; and the stress on human rights as fundamental to religious faith.[23] The rhetoric of reproach so prevalent in previous council documents was replaced with the rhetoric of affirmation and invitation. "Dialogue" became the buzzword of the Council, and as the Church historian John W. O'Malley suggests, "dialogue is horizontal not vertical, and it implies, if it is to be taken seriously, a shift in ecclesiology more basic than any single passage or image."[24] *Aggiornamento* and "dialogue" were the leitmotivs of a new ecclesiological paradigm for Catholicism, whereby "the Council, with all sorts of qualifications, was able to say that religion had to change to meet 'the needs of the times.' "[25]

The great sea change underlying all these issues was the acceptance of the "development of doctrine," where for the first time a Catholic council placed doctrinal and dogmatic theology under the scrutiny of historical exegesis and hermeneutical criticism. The Catholic belief that religious formulations of faith were immune to change was rejected.[26] The shadow of John Cardinal Newman, the nineteenth-century theologian so instrumental to Greene's own intellectual development as a Catholic convert, looms large over the Council. Newman had written that Christian revelation "is not a revealed system, but consists of a number of detached and incomplete truths belonging to a vast system unrevealed, of doctrines and injunctions mysteriously connected together" so that Revelation is "a doctrine lying within language."[27] Newman's perspective and critical methodology is precisely vindicated at the Council in the Church's insistence on a return to the historical sources of Catholic tradition, the development of doctrine, and an interpretive reading of "the signs of the times."

The condemnations of previous Church councils are gone, ending the Church's counter-Reformation protest against Protestantism and modernity. Yet because the Council never unambiguously inaugurated this paradigm shift, the documents reflect the tensions that survive in Catholic theological discourse and practice today. One senses the tension in the compromised quality of many of the Council documents, whereby formulations of the competing paradigms of neoscholasticism and historical-critical thought stand side by side in the text.[28] These competing formulations of the Council are still debated within Catholicism, for the historical developments and controversies around the issue of papal infallibility, artificial contraception, and the rules on celibate male clergy were to become crisis issues for a church in the midst of such renewal. With such compromise and ambivalence, the overall effect of the Council was to invite a critical and, for Catholics, an uncomfortable ambiguity into the very expression of being a post–Vatican II Roman Catholic. Indeed,

Greene expressed his own ambivalence with the Church's adaptation to modernity in a 1988 interview: "I haven't liked all that Vatican II did, but it was a breath of air, anyway."[29] In reformulating the nature of Catholicism in analogical language, metaphorical images, and homiletic inclusiveness, the Council tried to negotiate a careful but difficult balance between traditional Catholic identity and philosophical openness to modernity.

Both Vertical *and* Horizontal Catholicism

> Christianity and humanism are not opposites. Christians can be humanists and humanists can be Christians. . . . Christianity cannot properly be understood except as radical humanism.
> —Hans Küng, *On Being a Christian*

Vatican II was not a wholesale endorsement of modernity; rather, it attempted a dialogue that could articulate how Catholicism's philosophical and theological heritage might in fact help to shape both the believer and the unbeliever in modern times. If Catholicism had in the past stressed a vertical relationship between God and the human person, the new impetus of the Council was to imagine Catholicism in horizontal relationships that saw religious faith as affecting the social, political, intellectual, and scientific discourses of the period. Engaging atheism and secular humanism became a central concern of the Council, seen most fully in the *Pastoral Constitution on the Church in the Modern World*, commonly known as *Gaudium et Spes*.[30] The document affirms the goodness of the world and the fundamental dignity of human beings "made in the image and likeness of God." It offers a nuanced discussion on the quality and kinds of modern atheism, even admitting that it is "believers themselves [who] frequently bear some responsibility for this situation. For, in general, atheism is not present in people's minds from the beginning" (*GS* 19). A believer's own distorted concept of God and hypocritical lifestyle only strengthen the rise of atheism. There then follows a consideration of the atheistic assumptions found in forms of existentialism, as well as of Marxism, which "looks to people's economic and social emancipation for their liberation" (*GS* 20). In deference to the authenticity of atheism's search for meaning, the document responds that "everybody remains a question to themselves, one that is dimly perceived and left unanswered. . . . God alone, who calls people to deeper thought and to more humble probing, can fully and with complete certainty supply an answer to this questioning" (*GS* 21). Rejecting atheism, *Gaudium et Spes* nonetheless encourages believers and unbelievers alike to engage in a "sincere and prudent dialogue" in order to build a better world, an official call to cooperate with the intellectual conversation already begun by European Marxists and Catholic leftists.

Ultimately, the document proclaims Christ as the "New Man," the fullest expression of what is in store for humanity (GS 22). The influence of Teilhard de Chardin and the theologian Karl Rahner are most evident in this discourse. Teilhard, whose work was published only after his death in 1955 because Vatican censors suspected him of heresy, tried to bridge the divide between natural science and religious faith. Greene, owning a biography of Teilhard and copies of his works, wrote of his admiration of Teilhard's vision in his personal letters to Mary Pritchett, his friend and literary agent in the United States (herself a convert to Catholicism).[31] Teilhard's evolutionary theological vision helped to articulate for Catholic intellectuals a way to engage science and modernity, bemoaning that "Christian" and "human" no longer coincided with one another. He held that only a new recasting of theology could heal the rift. His notion of Christ as "Cosmic" imagines human participation in the Incarnation as ultimately an ongoing extension of Christ into the whole universe, a gradual consummation of all creation, so that "human action can be related to Christ, and can cooperate in the fulfillment of Christ, not only by the intention, . . . but also by the actual material content of the work done. All progress, whether in organic life or in scientific knowledge, in aesthetic faculties or in social consciousness, can therefore be made Christian." This is Christ-Omega, "the Christ who animates and gathers up all the biological and spiritual energies developed by the universe . . . Christ the evolver."[32] Humanity becomes for God the "pillars" of evolution: "Until now, the Christian has been brought up under the impression that he had to leave all in order to attain God. What he is now discovering is that he cannot be saved except through and as an extension of the Universe." Teilhard's use of the titles "Cosmic Christ" and "Christ-Omega" conveys the meeting of a vertical and horizontal relationship to God: "The synthesis of the God of the Above and the God of the Ahead: this is the only God whom we shall in the future be able to adore in spirit and in truth."[33] Teilhard brings a Catholic reading to evolutionary theory, whereby the doctrine of the Incarnation becomes the linchpin in uniting secular notions of human progress and utopian ideals.[34]

There is no evidence that Greene knew anything of Karl Rahner, but Rahner's perspective is seen everywhere in Catholic theology during the time of the Council. If Teilhard gave standing to a Catholic response to science and evolution, Rahner offered a Catholic response to modern secularization and atheism, echoed throughout *Gaudium et Spes*. Rahner's "Transcendental" Thomism posits that since human beings are by their very nature self-transcendent, God is the endpoint of that human drive toward self-transcendence. The pursuit of knowledge, goodness, and love are essentially directed toward a "horizon" of infinite mystery. Human beings thus first encounter God as the infinite mystery that calls forth truth, goodness, and love—and only through proclamation as the unsurpassably revealed person of Jesus Christ. Rahner redefines the experience of God, thereby circumventing the usual arguments for rational proof of God's existence. Everyone, even the atheist, who experiences self-transcendence can be said to be oriented to God in a nonthematized, uncategorical way, for if God is the infinite mystery behind every attraction toward the good, every act of goodness points to this mystery even when it may never be called so by name. Rahner proposed the term "anonymous Christian" to mean "the condition of a man who lives on the one hand in a state of grace and justification, and yet on the other hand has not come into contact with the explicit preaching of the Gospel and is consequently not in a position to call himself a Christian."[35]

Rahner's contribution to the Council was his ability to reframe the dogmatic formulas of Catholicism so that their tenor was radically reinterpreted in a more inclusive and ecumenical manner even as the scholastic language of formal orthodoxy was maintained. This is true most especially in the doctrine of "no salvation outside the Church," which is now transformed by the whole church as the "people of God" before any distinction is made among the various Christian churches.[36] Recast by Rahner, there is the possibility that Christ not only saves other Christians outside the Catholic fold but perhaps the "anonymous Christian" as well. It is the most profound example of Christian humanism that comes out of the theological reflection of the Council.

Catholic theologians afterward endeavored to recognize the roots of secularization as a neutral byproduct of a Christian civilization, neutral because secularization does not by necessity have to be opposed to religious faith.[37] During the 1960s and 1970s the Belgian Dominican theologian Edward Schillebeeckx spoke of this engagement as a new hermeneutical moment for the church: "We are not addressed by a *nuda vox Dei*, a word from God without alloy coming down to us, as it were, vertically in a purely divine statement. God's word is given to us within the already interpretive response to it in the Old and New Testaments. . . . The God of salvation was made the subject of *a conversation between men*—it was in this way that God's word was addressed to us."[38] The "horizontal creatural network," Schillebeeckx suggests, calls for a reinterpretation of Christian ways of speaking of God and humanity: "If religion has its irreplaceable word to say, this must be a religion concerned for human beings in the world. . . . Can there be any other humanism than the humanism of God himself, a God concerned for humanity, who wants people to be concerned for humanity as well?"[39] Schillebeeckx and others argued that nonreligious humanism and secularity was deeply indebted to Christian thought and behavior, in effect the "children" of a Western Christian heritage, so that the "building up of the world into a community of persons in justice and love appears on closer reflection—or more precisely, in a 'disclosure situation'—to coincide with acceptance of God and, in the concrete, even with faith in God."[40]

The postwar Protestant movement of radical theology—often referred to as "death of God" theology—protested that God's *transcendence* really meant God's *absence* from the world, that the process of secularization had killed the "God of religion." They pleaded for a "definitive silence about God . . . or a provisional waiting silence about God."[41] Catholic theologians countered that this stress on the *absence* of God was merely the emptiness of rationalist and utopian constructs surrounding modern religious awareness. Echoing the Catholic mystical language of John of the Cross and the *via negativa*, Schillebeeckx claimed that the modern experience of God's absence is in fact a moment of *metanoia*, the transcendence of God experienced as human surrender to mystery, where "the believer knows that God is present, but he experiences this presence only in the painful experience of absence, which nonetheless betrays a very intimate nearness and thus keeps hope alive." Not only does God's *absence* point to an original *presence*, but also that absence is eschatologically orientated: "For someone who lives in time, God's transcendence is not only memory and not only, here and now, a painfully experienced 'absence,' he is also the God who is to come, who goes ahead of us towards a future. . . . Transcendence thus tends to acquire a special affinity with what is called, in our temporality, 'future.' "[42] Küng goes even further in this regard, redefining the term "transcendence" from its metaphysical and existential notions to a more temporal understanding as "God before us, God behind the one regular flow of coming to be and passing away of past, present and future, as well as the future reality, the one who is to come, who bestows hope."[43] A renewed stress on God's eschatological Kingdom is the key transcendental reality that structures the meaning of ongoing human development and incarnates the "working of the Spirit." Thus, if Catholic scholastic discourse understood transcendence and salvation of one's soul as primarily a private affair of piety and good works, theologians after the Council reframed the notion to include God's immanent workings in human history. In the midst of claiming humanism as a Christian, even Catholic reality, the Council situated itself within a conversation with Protestants, Marxists, and positivists while never abandoning its critical stance toward them. A reinvigorated Christian humanism was put forth by the Church to show its relationship to secularism and to prevent political and philosophical systems from imposing any system that sacrificed the individual's religious freedom for the sake of an ideology that claimed to destroy it in order to bring about a better world.[44]

The long-term effects of the Council's desire to meet the historical-critical methods of modernity and still stay rooted in its own Catholic humanistic tradition changed the boundaries, and hence the nature, of the Catholic faith experience. Catholic identity, once so clearly marked and substantiated by the scholastic, Tridentine tradition, had now to be negotiated in a dialectic that affirmed the more personal and closed vertical dimension of religious faith, as well as the more socially engaged, horizontal dimension of human progress. This negotiation into a "modern" Catholic identity was made more difficult by the vast cultural shifts of the 1970s, a period that became more explicitly pessimistic in its critique of modernity. If the years during and directly after the Council seemed fixated on the "joy and hope" proclaimed in the first sentence of *Gaudium et Spes*, the later decades seemed focused on the "grief and anguish" about the future. Nevertheless, in the midst of the paradigmatic shift inaugurated by the Council, there are theological "markers" for a post–Vatican II Catholic imagination, found most clearly in the theological developments in Christology, liturgy, the sacraments, priesthood, and a concern for a faith that does justice in the world.

Of all these Catholic discourses that gave shape to Greene's post–Vatican II imagination, none is more central than liberation theology and social justice. Because of its importance, it will be discussed fully in the next chapter in its relationship to Greene's understanding and embodiment of Catholic *difference* in his late novels. In terms of Christology, liturgy, and the sacraments, Greene was most familiar with the work of Küng and Schillebeeckx, who were among the theologians who stretched the boundaries of traditional Catholic thought. My discussion necessarily examines their texts when they make a contribution in shaping the discourse surrounding these issues. Considered controversial and certainly the most progressive of European Catholic theologians, they provided interpretive lenses that proved important for Greene's continued identity as a Catholic in the last decades of his life.

Catholic Theology from Above *and* Below

A Catholic understanding of Christology before Vatican II stressed Christ's divinity, the preexistent Word of God in heaven who comes down to earth to take on human flesh and redeems the world in his Passion and Resurrection. From there, much of the attention in Catholic Christology concerned interpretations of Thomas Aquinas, whose Christological themes focused on Christ's inner makeup as the divine/human person and his relationship to the Trinity. In this classical metaphysical analysis of Christology, the humanity of Jesus was rarely brought to bear, save for a consideration of the Incarnation (the divine become human flesh) and the Crucifixion (the divine suffering human death). The medieval Christology of Aquinas and the theology manuals of the early twentieth century survived as the premiere christological foundation before the Council.

The Dominican historian Robert A. Burns notes that a distinction between a "Christology from above" and a "Christology from below" became part of Catholic discourse when Karl Rahner explicitly defined it in a lecture given in Munich in 1971.[45] If Christology from above begins with the divinity of Christ and descends into concerns of human existence, Christology from below begins with the historical Jesus proclaiming his commitment to the "Kingdom of God" and rises to the dogmatic formulas of the early Christian church. *Gaudium et Spes* explicitly highlighted the humanity of Jesus, noting that "human nature, by the very fact it was assumed, not absorbed," means that Jesus "has in a certain way united himself with each individual. He worked with human hands, he thought with a human mind. He acted with a human will, and with a human heart he loved" (*GS* 22). The Council was responding to a century of Protestant biblical scholarship, as well as to the impetus of Pope Pius XII's 1943 encyclical *Divino Afflante Spiritu*, which encouraged Catholic scholars to use the tools of modern scholarship in their research. The preaching and parables of the historical Jesus were thus placed within the context of the social, political, and economic realities of the period in which they were written. Catholic theologians began using critical methods to reexamine the radical quality of Jesus' preaching and the historical dimensions of his death and Resurrection.

This "perspective from below" was the hallmark of Küng's text, *On Being a Christian*, and Schillebeeckx's Christological investigation in his monumental volumes *Jesus* and *Christ*. Their works in Christology were well known in Europe, and Greene, an avid reader of Küng, also kept abreast of the controversy surrounding Schillebeeckx's work after the Council.[46] Using the critical methods of German biblical scholarship, Küng describes Jesus as an itinerant preacher indifferent to Jewish traditions and institutions, preaching the Kingdom of God as a universal concern for the well-being of humanity. Jesus speaks and acts in God's name and addresses God as *Abba* (Father). In considering the spiritual equality of each individual—Pharisees and tax collectors, Jews and Samaritans—as the focus of God's Kingdom, Jesus relativized Jewish institutions, laws, and cults of his time, which in turn made him a political and religious threat to the powerful and elite. Küng argues that Jesus felt truly forsaken by God at his death, but afterward his disciples experienced him as alive, so Jesus himself became the content of the disciples' proclamation of the Kingdom. Küng's Christology places the Crucifixion at the heart of that proclamation, the distinctive event that sets Christianity and faith in its Lord apart from other religious ideologies. The Crucifixion is "the permanent signature of the living Christ,"[47] keeping faith in the Resurrection firmly grounded in the liberating words and actions of the historical Jesus. In the midst of the historical exegesis that makes up the bulk of his text, Küng asserts that the doctrinal claims of the preexistent Word, the Incarnation, and the Trinity are the product of Greek metaphysical speculation that developed much later.[48] In arguing this, he does not deny that they have significance and value, but they are secondary to being a Christian. Indeed, for Küng these doctrines often divert attention from the Jesus of history, whose Crucifixion-Resurrection is the event that separates Christian faith from unbelief and superstition.[49]

Schillebeeckx begins his Christological investigation not with a Jesus who comes down from heaven but with the man from Nazareth, the prophet of the Kingdom of God whose life and death put into practice what such a kingdom might mean for humanity. He argues that the historical Jesus had a unique experience of transformation through his encounter with his *Abba*, and this became the basis for his ministry and mission. Jesus brought no new doctrine or religious system with him as he preached and lived a life of service to others, which for Schillebeeckx means that any metaphysical investigation into how Jesus can be both the form and aspect of a divine person must be abandoned because it is "a mystery theoretically unfathomable beyond this point."[50] Without denying the reality of Jesus' Resurrection, he insists that it should be understood "experientially" as an event that happened to the disciples, so that the Kingdom of God preached by Jesus becomes associated with the life and death of Jesus himself.[51] The early church becomes the ongoing sacrament of Jesus, historically mediating the practice of the Kingdom of God as a work of service: "Thus it is in the power of Jesus' Spirit that the Church mediates the manner in which God is concerned with all human beings."[52] It is the practice of the Kingdom—what Schillebeeckx calls orthopraxis (literally, "right practice")—that gives the church authority to work for justice and the liberation of the oppressed.

Both Küng and Schillebeeckx offered contemporary Catholics an understanding of Christ that brought together modernity's historical and political consciousness with evolutionary and interpretive modes of thinking. Christ is accessible neither as the omniscient God of traditional Catholic piety nor as merely the morally elevated human being of Protestant piety, standing as an exemplar for humanity. Christ is a human encounter that reveals a transcendent reality; he is a person grounded in history but transhistorical in significance. Neither theologian denies the divinity of Christ or the traditional Christologies "from above," but they would argue that such belief could not be verified by the methods they apply. What can be verified are those things that are *rationally* in accord with an understanding of Scripture as a document of the Church's faith in Jesus. Implied in their approach to Christology is a certain amount of methodological agnosticism, a wariness to make doctrinal truth-claims based on the Hellenistic philosophy that accrued over the centuries of Christian thought. Their perspective investigates historical evidence, contextualizing faith in Jesus from a series of epistemological claims and rational conclusions. For them, one's belief in Jesus as more than just a human reality (i.e., revealed as divine) ultimately comes from being drawn to Jesus' unique proclamation of God as *Abba*, an encounter with his radical humanism (love of enemies instead of their destruction, unconditional forgiveness instead of retaliation, and readiness to suffer instead of using force), and the testimony of the New Testament communities who proclaimed his Resurrection. The Church becomes the community united by the Spirit that gives witness to the ongoing work of God's salvation in Jesus.

Greene's personal library of Küng's books contains many marked passages and some marginalia. Greene was most taken by Küng's desire to articulate what it means to be a Christian in the simplest terms, free from dogmatic formulae. His approach resonated with Greene's own adverse reaction to theological abstraction. Writing critically of neoscholastic theology, Küng says that "the biblical profession of faith in Father, Son, and Spirit had turned into a higher conceptual mathematics, and the message of the Christ Jesus into a bloodless Christ-theory."[53] The metaphorical phrase "higher conceptual mathematics" is one often used by Greene in his personal dislike for the Catholic propensity for theological speculation. Indeed, the phrase appears in the dialogue sequences of both *The Honorary Consul* (1973) and *Monsignor Quixote* (1982), as well as in many of Greene's late interviews that touched on his religious belief. Greene's own absorption of this phrase is evident in the following passages marked in his copy of Küng's text, passages that describe Greene's own sense of religious belief:

> Faith is a free decision which presupposes open-mindedness, a readiness to believe. The more banal the truth, the greater the certainty. The more significant the truth, (for instance, aesthetic, moral, religious truth by comparison with arithmetical), the slighter the certainty. For the deeper the truth is for me, so much more open-

mindedness, so much more readiness, is required, even though
faith itself is by no means a blind and irrational, but justified and
intelligent faith.

The Church too—and this is what we all are—has every reason to
ask continually whether it accords with faith in Jesus Christ,
whether it lives by his justice, whether it takes account of the judgment that has been passed.[54]

Greene's understanding of Christ and his reading of Küng and Schillebeeckx come together in the 1983 book-length interview with Marie Françoise
Allain, when he is asked about belief in God, Jesus Christ, and the new theology
after the council. His response to the question of what God is like for him is
that it is "a mystery, an inexplicable force. That's why when one prays one
shouldn't, in my opinion, address oneself to this inexplicable and mysterious
force but to His intermediary, Christ. . . . It is easier to pray to Christ than to
an abstract entity."[55] When asked about the Vatican's investigation of Küng and
Schillebeeckx's works, Greene echoes their Christological premises and methodology, even critically commenting on their effect on him:

> I must admire Hans Küng, especially for his book *On Being a Chris-*
> *tian.* Schillebeeckx is a great and very learned, very estimable theolo-
> gian; but, as a barely practicing Catholic, I find it very disagreeable
> when a historical event like the Crucifixion is turned into some
> wooly sort of symbol . . . if one considers oneself a Catholic, there is
> a certain number of facts which have to be accepted. On the other
> hand if I were told that for some reason or other they had got it
> wrong about the Virgin Mary, or that the Trinity was no longer an
> article of faith, that would barely disturb my faith. The Trinity, for
> example, is nothing to me but a mathematical symbol for a mystery.
> . . . Catholicism has to remain human. A man lived: Christ. He lived
> in history. Why turn him into a concept, fit only for a handful of
> visionaries? This debate shows that the Church is still on the move,
> that we're a long way from the Inquisition. . . . [Yet paradoxically]
> while Fr. Schillebeeckx's declarations [on the resurrection of Jesus]
> were intended to make the unbelievable credible, they have had the
> opposite effect on me—they have suddenly revived in me a deep
> faith in the inexplicable, in the mystery of Christ's resurrection.[56]

He ends the same interview by noting his differences with theological
speculation, making a typically scholastic distinction between faith and belief:

"Faith is above belief. . . . I keep my faith while enduring long periods of disbelief. At such moments I shrug my shoulders and tell myself I'm wrong—as though a brilliant mathematician had come and told me that my solution of an equation was wrong. My faith remains in the background, but it remains."[57] These exchanges illustrate just how involved Greene was in his own struggle to affirm his faith in spite of his doubt. Belief for Greene has narrowed to conceptualization and argumentation about God, whereas faith is a primary affirmation of the mystery of God's revelation in Jesus. In the midst of such modern, historical-critical methodologies used by Küng and Schillebeeckx, Greene suggests both his affinity to their project (their emphasis on the humanity of Jesus and their attempt to clarify the essential qualities of being a Christian) and his wariness (their purported need to explain the Resurrection in a way that diminishes the historicity of the biblical narrative). There is thus an abiding religious faith in Greene during this period of his life that is still framed in more traditional conceptions than the postmodern investigations of Schillebeeckx and Küng. All of this is to say that Greene's Catholic imagination is very much attuned to the complicated Christological concerns that stem from the post–Vatican II era.

The developments that were stressing the humanity of Jesus affected the understanding of the sacramental character of Catholic worship. No text did more to influence Catholic thought on this matter than Schillebeeckx's *Christ the Sacrament of the Encounter with God*, published in 1960 and widely translated and read by Catholic scholars prior to the Council. Schillebeeckx's assertion that the Church itself is a basic sacrament was ultimately accepted by the Church's bishops and found its expression in many of the Council documents.[58] Catholic tradition is grounded by a belief in mediation, that an experience of God can occur only insofar as God adapts to human materiality. The embodiment of the spiritual in the material and the communication of God through the material is what Catholic theology calls the "sacramental principle." If the Church traditionally defined a sacrament as "a visible sign of an invisible reality instituted by Christ to give grace," Schillebeeckx asserts that the humanity of Jesus is the sacrament of God's grace, forgiveness, love, and presence to humankind; likewise, the Church is the basic sacrament of God's saving reality in history (namely, Jesus) for all the world. Schillebeeckx begins his section on "Christ the primordial sacrament" by saying that "the second person of the most holy Trinity is personally man; and this man is personally God. Therefore Christ is God in a human way, and man in a divine way."[59] Given this foundation, the sacrament of Jesus' humanity follows: "The man Jesus, as the personal visible realization of the divine grace of redemption, is *the* sacrament, the primordial sacrament, because this man, the Son of God himself, is intended by the Father to be in his humanity the only way to the actuality of redemption."[60]

Jesus' total human, historical existence—his poor and humble way of life; his healing miracles; his persecution, which included arrest and trial; his rejection by both Jewish and Roman leaders; his dying on the cross—is a sacrament of God's forgiving grace. In his life and death, Jesus is the visible sign of God's redemption. Yet, since Jesus is no longer visible and tangible after the Resurrection, Schillebeeckx concludes that the Church begins to function as the sacrament of Jesus, the historical community that mediates God's saving action in Jesus:

> The earthly Church is the visible realization of this saving reality in history. The Church is a visible communion of grace. . . . The fact must be emphasized that not only the hierarchical Church but also the community of the faithful belong to this grace-giving sign that is the Church. As much in its hierarchy as in the laity the community of the Church is the realization in historical form of the victory achieved by Christ. The inward communion in grace with God in Christ becomes visible in and is realized through the outward social sign . . . the final goal of grace achieved by Christ becomes visibly present in the whole Church as a visible society.[61]

The Church is thus the "earthly Body of the Lord," which points to and participates in God's salvation of the world.

The seven sacraments of Catholic worship flow out of this fundamental sacrament and are reinterpreted as the sevenfold "ecclesial" realizations of the sacrament of salvation in and through Christ. The meaning of the sacraments is understood only in and through the charismatic counsels of Jesus' preaching and healing. Schillebeeckx's explication of the sacraments transcends the traditional scholastic dichotomy of "sign" and "causality" (the relationship between God's grace and the effect of good works) for the more existential term "encounter," by which he means "the tangible pledge of [Christ's] willing readiness to enter upon an encounter with man."[62] The grace of the sacraments is not an isolated event in the life of the individual but an ongoing dialectic of encountering the sacred in the profane, played out throughout one's lifetime. In reframing the discourse, sacramental grace is seen as an extension of the life of Christ in the world (and not solely in the individual), so that the encounter with Christ in the sacraments "must show a real love for our fellow men, and this love must truly be the sacrament of our love for God."[63] Post–Vatican II sacramental theology thus reorients the sacramental principle from

God's vertical intervention from on high to a horizontal celebration of God's continuous action in the life of the Church.

The renewal in sacramental theology greatly affected the way in which Catholics thought about the Church's sacraments. No longer was baptism described as washing away "original sin" but rather as an initiation into the eucharistic community, where the life, death, and Resurrection of Jesus is reenacted. Confession was renamed the sacrament of Reconciliation to stress not the guilty person but God's (and the Church's) reconciliation with that person through Jesus. This reorientation was most pronounced in the celebration of the Eucharist in the Catholic liturgy, the first and most obvious change felt by Catholics after the Council. The vernacular Mass and the revised sacramental rites dramatically shifted the participatory nature of the liturgy. Though the Eucharist is still understood as a "divine sacrifice" and remains the "source and summit" of Catholic worship, Vatican II also describes it as a sacred meal in which the community shares. It is in the Catholic doctrine of the "real presence" in the Eucharist that the Council offered a nuanced development that is a consequence of the sacramentality discussed above.

Traditional Catholic teaching uses the term "transubstantiation" to define the real presence of Christ in the consecrated elements of bread and wine: the substance of bread and wine is forever changed into the body and blood of Christ, even though the form of bread and wine remains.[64] This absolute presence made the Host an object of worship, preserved in the altar's tabernacle or worshipped in benediction rites. In contrast to Protestant reformers who denied such devotional status to the Host, Catholic attachment to the real presence in the Eucharist became a defining mark of Catholic belief and ritual. The Second Vatican Council determined, moreover, that Christ's presence is not confined to and isolated in the consecrated elements but is also present in the community gathered together, in the person of the presiding minister, and in the proclamation of Scripture.[65] Hence, the emphasis that was once exclusively on the ordained priest was broadened to include the participation of all those present at the celebration. The Council situated the celebration of the Eucharist in the more horizontal perspective of the whole Church as the People of God, a communal celebration (indeed, the documents declare communal Mass preferable to the individual Masses said by priests prior to the council). Vatican II insisted that the laity participate in the Eucharist not as spectators to the actions of the priest but along with him, even if their function is not the same.[66] The action of grace in the sacrament is no longer discussed as if it is solely in the cultic role of the priesthood but is diffused throughout the church in those assembled for worship.

The development in the Catholic understanding of priesthood is closely aligned with the celebration of the Eucharist. The counterreformation concept of priesthood linked its very definition almost exclusively to the power to consecrate the Eucharist, and thus it gave priests special status in the community. Vatican II tended to relativize the priesthood by placing it within a context that emphasized the ministry of all Christians who are participating in the priesthood of Christ. Although the priesthood of ordination and the priesthood of the baptized differ "in essence and not only in degree," priests nonetheless share with all baptized persons a ministry to be "priest, prophet, and king."[67] The ministerial priest is thus understood to be not only a mediator between people and God but also a representative of the People of God, who experience Christ among them. New emphasis was placed on preaching the Gospel, tying priests' function to the ministry and preaching of Jesus' Kingdom of justice. Vatican II insisted that the ordained priesthood is essentially different from the common priesthood of the faithful but never clearly spelled out the precise nature of that difference. What remains is that the role of the ordained priest is seen to exist more in a common vocation with the laity than in the past.

This new conception of the priesthood had profound effects on the Church after the council, especially in Europe and America. Directly after the Council, large numbers of priests and religious left the priesthood, sometimes for very different reasons. Some priests left because of their decreased status within a Catholic culture that was being assimilated into an ever more secular society. The cultural and structural changes in society for these priests—between the pre–Vatican II Catholic milieu in which they had been ordained and the Council's engagement with the modern world—proved to be too difficult to negotiate. Still others caught up in the optimism of the Council's reforms left the priesthood because they interpreted the understanding of "vocation" to broaden beyond the ministerial call to the religious life. Their desire for "serving God" no longer necessitated their need to become ordained ministers. Yet as the role and status of priesthood suffered through this crisis in the Church, Greene's imagination paradoxically became more drawn to it. It is interesting to note that *The Power and the Glory* is the only novel from his Catholic cycle with a priest as its central character. Later Greene would write two novels, *The Honorary Consul* and *Monsignor Quixote*, in which priests become major characters and in which he investigates the function and condition of Catholicism in the aftermath of the Council.

The Greene-ing of a Post–Vatican II Catholic

> You report (7 September) that in an appeal for harmony in the Ro-
> man Catholic Church Bishop Harris said: "Christ came to recon-
> cile." Isn't this rather unorthodox? In my copy of the New Testa-
> ment Christ said: "I came not to bring peace but a sword," and
> spoke of new wine having to be put in fresh wineskins and cursed
> Capharnaum. If Christ had come to reconcile would he have been
> crucified?
>
> —Greene, *The (London) Times*,
> 10 September 1971[68]

Greene's letter to the editor perhaps speaks tongue-in-cheek about the
changes in the perception of how he understood Catholicism and its critical
role in the modern world. Like many British converts in the early twentieth
century, Greene had a sense that being part of the Catholic Church was as
much an ideological stand as a religious one, a way to oppose a culture grown
unprecedently secular. Catholics were differentiated from the comfortable agnosticism of modern England and offered a visible and conscious separation
from mainstream British culture by bringing "not peace but a sword" to the
discourse of an easy, bourgeois religiosity. The Council's dialogue with the
intellectual and ideological currents of the postwar years challenged some of
the very reasons many converted. Greene, 61 years old at the Council's end, is
representative of the general population of Catholics who were trying to think
through and negotiate this reform movement in the Church. The effect of such
a "reorientation" in theology, morality, liturgical practice, and ecumenism became a kind of "disorientation." Beyond his close reading of Teilhard, Küng,
and Schillebeeckx, it is important to summarize just how Greene experienced
and appropriated these theological developments—both positively and negatively—because it places Greene well within the mainstream of Catholic opinion after the Council.

Though he welcomed the ecumenical spirit of the Council and its consequent stress on faith and justice, his Catholic identity was much tested by
his personal distaste for the vernacular liturgy. Greene felt there was a di-
minishment of the supreme power, aura, and aesthetic beauty that the liturgy had traditionally played in the imagination of Catholics. In this respect
he agreed with other, more traditional English converts concerning the liturgical changes begun by Vatican II. In 1967 Greene was asked by the International Committee on English in the Liturgy to critique and offer sugges-

tions on the translations of the Mass. He dutifully did so but expressed his profound disappointment if the Latin Mass were ever lost in the process.[69] By 1971 Greene had signed with other Catholic artists and intellectuals an appeal sent to the Vatican, asking that the Tridentine Mass be preserved in both language and structure.[70] He complained in interviews about not being able to follow the vernacular Mass in the many places he traveled, his annoyance with "the freedom given to priests to introduce endless prayers—for the astronauts or what have you," and his grief over the abolition of the reading from John's Gospel that used to end the Tridentine liturgy.[71] As late as 1988 Greene was still commenting on the liturgy, writing to *The Tablet* that he feels "like many others a certain uneasiness at changing references to God in the Liturgy from He to She. Would it be a possible compromise . . . if in the Liturgy we call God It (of course with a capital I)? After all there is a hint of the indefinable and inexplicable in the word 'it.' "[72] Without a doubt Greene felt the loss of a formative experience of his conversion. He confessed in his last extended interview before his death that he was grateful to attend the Tridentine Mass in the last decades of his life whenever his friend, the Spanish priest Father Leopoldo Duran, was with him: "[He] has permission from his bishop to say the Mass in Latin and say it anywhere, so if he comes here he says it at that table. And if I'm traveling with him, he'll say Mass in the hotel room."[73] That the liturgical changes affected him will be seen more thoroughly in *The Honorary Consul* and *Monsignor Quixote*, for at the same time that Greene noted his dissatisfaction with the vernacular rite, his Catholic literary imagination actually becomes more "liturgical" in these texts. He creatively sets the celebration of the liturgy at climactic moments in order to discern and question God's presence in what is traditionally a Catholic manifestation.

Likewise, Greene's attraction to the priesthood remained constant throughout his life. His many friendships and correspondences with priests before and after the council are remarkable.[74] Vatican II reframed the ecclesiology of the Church in broader terms so that a priest was less a mediator and more a representative of the Church to the community. Greene continued to regard priesthood as the *extreme* representative of the Christian life, especially in areas where the Church played a crucial role in fighting poverty and injustice. He does not so much resist Vatican II conceptions of the priesthood as highlight priests' role as identifiable witnesses to religious faith, especially if suffering political persecution. Thus, by its very nature priesthood remains dialectical in Greene's imagination, a worthy vocation of adventure that demands a countercultural break with the normal routine of modern life:

I think that for many people, especially the young, the priesthood must have the attraction of a crack unit. It's an organization which has to train for combat, one which demands self-sacrifice. I've nothing in particular against priests marrying, . . . but I'm convinced that the drop in vocations has to do with the fact that we don't put across clearly enough the attraction to be found in a difficult and dangerous calling. One enlists in a venture which is total. People are attracted to the Church where there's danger.[75]

Greene's portrayal of the priest as an ontologically different category of human being is retained in both *The Honorary Consul* and *Monsignor Quixote*, but what is significant is that these priest characters are assailed not only by their own self-doubts about their ability to live up to their vocation but also by their self-doubts about the state of the postconciliar Church in which they minister. They battle on two fronts now, negotiating their earliest inspiration to become a priest in the pre–Vatican II era with the contingencies of the political and cultural changes of the present. Through it all Greene's imagination remains gripped by the cultic function of the Catholic liturgy and its priests who serve the Church; together, they embodied the essential legacy of Catholic difference.

Besides his enduring love of the Tridentine Latin Mass and his admiration for the priesthood, Greene was very much immersed in the larger institutional life of his faith and took a more progressive stance on many of the controversial issues that followed in the wake of the Council. His reading of Küng's theology was instrumental in helping him come to terms with his distrust of logical arguments for religious belief. Even in the midst of his persistent faith, Greene's rational disbelief about *how* and *why* God exists was affirmed in Küng's approach to the question. By centering the argument not on challenging the atheistic turns of modern rationality (the anthropological turn of Feuerbach, the social-political reasons of Marx, and the psychoanalytic approach of Freud), Küng asserted that belief in God is ultimately a justified fundamental trust in reality within the uncertain reality of the world.[76] The affirmation of reality is the ground of this trust, which grows and develops into a trust in God, thanks to God's Revelation. For Küng, like Greene, faith in God is grounded in human reality. Greene notes in a series of letters to Mary Pritchett that he accepted the title of an "agnostic" Catholic after careful reading of Küng's theological arguments. He found in his perspective a viable place to stand on questions of modern religious belief and Christian humanism.[77]

Greene, like many Catholics, opposed the Church's position on birth control, often citing the positive vote for contraception by the Vatican Commission formed by Paul VI in 1966 as the evidence that "proved that [birth control] couldn't be an intrinsic evil." He abhorred abortion but found it "nothing but the result of an absence of contraception."[78] He writes intriguingly of Pope John Paul II as an impressive man who helped to shake up the political geography of communist Europe but nevertheless was "proving unsatisfactory in everything except politics."[79] Even this positive assessment is tempered in his late interviews and letters to the editor, noting with regret the pope's condemnation of the political activity of priests in the Sandanista government of Nicaragua. Most significantly, liberation theology, social justice, and commitment to human rights galvanized Greene's post–Vatican II Catholic imagination. Latin America became for him "the sphere of activity in which he thought the Church showed its very best side."[80] Just how important it is for Greene's faith and his literary inspiration will be investigated more fully in the following chapter.

Finally, it is one thing to observe how truly immersed Greene was in Catholicism throughout the last 25 years of his life; it is quite another to claim that his later works continue to embody what I have been consistently calling a "Catholic literary imagination." Against those critics who have announced Greene as a "post-Catholic" artist, it might be more accurate to contend that his Catholicism becomes even more important to him after the Council than in the years just preceding it. That Catholicism is no longer envisioned as a bulwark that resists modernity does not mean that it depletes those Catholic symbols and images that make it a qualitatively distinctive faith. And to those who claim the Catholic novel a dead genre in the wake of the Second Vatican Council, Greene's late novels can perhaps offer a new paradigm in which to investigate the quality and effect of Catholicism in literature. To that end, the next chapters chart a literary path in Green's post–Vatican II novels, examining the themes of faith and belief, grace and its sacramental mediation, theological aesthetics, and liberation theology.

4

New Threads in an
Old Pattern

Greene's Catholic Imagination in The Honorary
Consul *and* The Human Factor

Civilizations are born, develop and die. But humanity is advancing
along the path of history like the waves of a rising tide encroaching
on the shore. . . . There are certainly situations whose injustice cries
to heaven. When whole populations destitute of necessities live in a
state of subjection barring them from all initiative and responsibility,
and from all opportunity to advance culturally and to share in social
and political life, men are easily led to have recourse to violence as a
means to right these wrongs to human dignity.

—Pope Paul VI, *Populorum Progressio* (1967)

The faithful do not have a vocation to be martyrs. When they fall in
the struggle, they fall with simplicity and without posing. . . . Life
ought to be given by working, not by dying. Away with the slogans
that create a cult of death. . . . The revolution calls for human beings
who are lucidly conscious; realists who have ideals. And if the day
comes when they must give their lives, they will do it with the simplicity of someone who is carrying out one more task, without melodramatic gestures.

—Luis Espinal[1]

I paint Christ as one of us, a man, that is to say a *compañero gueril-
lero* who comes out of the mountains and is taken by the enemy.

—Father Ernesto Cardenal[2]

We certainly see Christianity [in Latin America] as it always should have been—with the Church actively involved in the struggle for justice. . . . If it means that priests are allowed to play their part in politics in defense of the poor then I am all for it.

—Graham Greene

Revisiting Catholic Territories

During the last three decades of his life, Graham Greene continued to write and publish at a prolific pace. Critical reception of these late works often focused on an appreciation of the technical mastery of his texts that nonetheless offered little new of thematic interest to Greene's development as a writer.[3] Yet there is something more than the perfection of style in Greene's late novels: he continually returns to old territories—the tension between loyalty and betrayal, innocence and corruption, and religious faith and political commitment—but with a perceptive sense of the changes that have occurred both in Catholicism and in global politics during the last part of the century. Greene treats his characters with a new sense of comic detachment; his authorial voice is that of an uninvolved but acute observer. Though the tragic tension of his viewpoint is slackened, it nevertheless conveys a fresh imaginative vantage point in which to engage his literary and religious concerns.

Greene admits in his autobiography that the 1960s were a difficult decade for him, not only because of his move from England to France, but also because of his experience as a writer. He remarks that the psychological intensity of writing *A Burnt-Out Case* (1961) left him in such a depressive state that he felt certain it would be his last work of fiction. Soon after, however, his experience of Haiti and the repressive regime of Papa Doc compelled him to write *The Comedians* (1966). Both of these novels are indeed dark portraits, the first skeptical about the value of religious belief, the second about political action. In *A Burnt-Out Case* Catholic religious belief is put on trial; in *The Comedians* commitment to political and economic justice takes the stand. Both novels end with nearly the same verdict. As Greene's most existential novels, each focuses on the absurdity of life, with only hints of a meaningful transcendent referent.[4] So it was to Greene's own surprise that his response to his existential despair led him to write his first true comedy, *Travels with My Aunt* (1969), three years later. Greene remarked that he had written a novel "for the fun of it," which looked at old age and death as "a suitable subject to tackle at the age of sixty-five."[5] A picaresque story that portrays "laughter in the shadow of the gallows," Greene thought it one of his best books after *The Power and the Glory* because it was "a serious and sad book which happens to be funny."[6] He notes that it was the first time when humor and comedy won out over his penchant for tragedy: "I felt, above all, that I had broken for good or ill with the past."[7] Part of that accomplishment was perhaps due to the fact that Catholicism had always been the most profound reference point for Greene's sense of the tragic, and in this novel he felt there was no obvious Catholic thread woven into the narrative. Even so, the comedy of *Travels with My Aunt* is painted on a familiar Greene landscape. In a novel whose characters include Nazi collaborators of the past and violent dictators of the present, Greene stresses the extreme moral situations of human life amid such a world, although always muted by a surface of comic juxtaposition and laughter. Readers and critics alike thought the novel a major literary achievement for Greene, and the effect of writing it renewed his creative urge.

It is thus interesting that if *Travels with My Aunt* has no direct religious sensibility, its last pages point to Greene's return to a more intense exploration of writing about religious faith and political commitment. The novel ends humorously enough, with the protagonist, Henry Pulling, living in a Paraguayan border town with his Aunt Augusta while, with noted irony, he reads to his future bride the following lines from Robert Browning: "God's in his Heaven—/All's right with the world!"[8] If this optimistic stand seemed a natural end to Greene's developing thematic maturity, then *The Honorary Consul* (1973), written over the next few years, probingly picks up where *Travels with My Aunt* concluded: the central character, Dr. Plarr, is in another border town, this time gazing over the river into Paraguay from Argentina, and the novel (and to some extent, all the rest of Greene's novels) offers a thorough vetting of Browning's closing verse on whether God is indeed in his heaven and all is indeed right with the world. Questions of belief in God, religious and political revolution, and the unique way in which Catholicism and its clergy embody such questions return Greene more forcefully to the Catholic pattern in his carpet. *The Honorary Consul* is situated in a culture still imbued with its Catholic heritage, and the novel explicitly exhibits a religious theme embodied in Catholic terms; *The Human Factor* (1978), an espionage novel that followed five years later, subtly traces the complete loss of such a religious pattern in European cold-war politics. The greater part of this chapter examines a post–Vatican II discourse in *The Honorary Consul* and ends with a consideration of the political allegorization of his religious sensibility in *The Human Factor*.

The Honorary Consul narrates the tyranny, corruption, terrorism, and overwhelming poverty that are part of the Latin American political world at the end of the twentieth century. In its character development and plot, the novel embodies what has come to be known as liberation theology, anticipating its entrance on the theological stage. It is not mere coincidence that Gustavo Gutierrez's English edition of *A Theology of Liberation* was published in the same year as Greene's novel. Gutierrez called for a new kind of theology that spoke to the Latin American postcolonial situation, emphasizing the need for liberation from the structures of unjust economic exploitation and political domination. Although Greene denied having read Gutierrez or other liberation theology texts, he did experience at firsthand the Latin American situation that produced it, namely, the terrible poverty and oppression of the region, as well as the Catholic Church's involvement on both sides of the struggle.

The dialectical tendencies of Greene's religious imagination—his stand against injustice, his continual resistance to easy accommodation with political ideologies, and his focus on a living faith over a rote belief—found a home in these Latin American theological movements. Animated by the developments in Catholicism after the Second Vatican Council, Greene's texts exemplify the difficulty of interpreting a post–Vatican II Catholicism for third world nations. From his personal correspondence and friendship with many liberationist priests who were working among the poor and his own observations from his travels to the region, he was acutely aware of the great effort that religious and political activists had made in defending themselves from both the theological concerns of a cautious Vatican and the conservative political establishments of first world governments. Conservative critics within both camps had vociferously rejected liberation theology as Marxist at worst and utopian at best. *The Honorary Consul* enacts a historical and theological reading of such signs of the times. There is much complementarity between liberation theology and Greene's own sense of Catholic *difference* that suggests his deeper immersion into new modes of Catholic discourse.

Liberation Theology in Greeneland

Following the closing of the Second Vatican Council and the promulgation of Pope Paul VI's 1967 encyclical *Populorum Progressio (On the Development of Peoples)*, the bishops of Latin America held their own conference in Medellín, Colombia, to interpret and correlate the documents to the specific situation of Central and South America. *Populorum Progressio* focused on the international order among nations, reflecting on the relations of rich countries to poor ones and the struggle for economic and human development. In 1968 the Medellín conference spoke of Latin America as undergoing just such a development. The continent, it professed, was on the "threshold of a new epoch . . . a time of zeal for full emancipation, of liberation from every form of servitude, of personal maturity and of collective integration."⁹ The *locus theologicus* of what was to be called liberation theology would be the particular experience of the poor of this region and the structures that enforce such poverty and oppression among them.

Many Latin American theologians, educated in European theological centers during the 1960s and familiar with Continental philosophy and political theology, began to read their own situation as different from the Anglo-European experience. They asserted that the central question of theology's dialogue with the modern world was not primarily religious faith versus atheism but human dignity versus the subhuman conditions of the majority of Latin American peoples. By beginning with the historical reality of the poor, they departed from the traditional starting place of much of European-based theology of the time. As Gustavo Gutierrez notes:

> Much contemporary theology seems to start from the challenge of
> the non-believer [who] questions our religious world. . . . This chal-
> lenge in a continent like Latin America does not come primarily
> from the man who does not believe, but from the man who is not a
> man, who is not recognized as such by the existing social order: he
> is in the ranks of the poor, the exploited. . . . His challenge is not
> aimed first at our religious world, but at our economic, social, politi-
> cal and cultural world; therefore it is an appeal for the revolutionary
> transformation of the very basis of a dehumanized society.¹⁰

Gutierrez concludes that solidarity with the dehumanized poor means to enter deliberately the arena of historical confrontation between countries and between social classes. Salvation in Christ is expressed as liberation from those societal and multinational structures that perpetuate injustice. Gutierrez articulates three levels of such liberation: a sociopolitical liberation from the conflict of economic, social, and political processes between the oppressed and the powerful nations and classes; a reading of history as the conscious action of humanity's quest for freedom; and a biblical discourse on God's action in Jesus Christ who liberates humanity from sin and oppression.¹¹ Biblical notions of creation, exile, liberation, conversion, and eschatological promise imaginatively shape the meaning of salvation in the historical struggles for human dignity and justice. Focus is placed both on the sayings of Jesus as proclamations of God's Kingdom to the poor and on a reading of the cross and the death of Jesus as the central paradigms of persecution and suffering made present in the dehumanized peoples of Latin America.¹²

This reconfiguration of theological reflection—from religious belief/un-belief to notions of justice and freedom—moves one directly into political consciousness: "To become aware of the conflictual nature of the political sphere should not mean to become complacent. On the contrary, it should mean struggling—with courage and clarity, deceiving neither oneself nor others—for the establishment of peace and justice among all people."[13] Using Marxist analysis, Gutierrez argues that Latin American countries are kept in neocolonial relationships of underdevelopment with capitalist nations of Europe and North America,[14] and religious institutions are at times coopted into supporting these oppressive social orders: "The whole 'Christian set-up' is made to play a part inside the dominant ideology, which helps to strengthen and affirm a society divided into antagonistic classes. Conservative sectors in fact frequently appeal to Christian ideas to justify the social order which serves their interests and maintains their privileges."[15]

Gutierrez defends liberation theology against those who see it as a variant form of Marxism. He and others repeatedly argue that liberation theology merely employs the contemporary tools of the social sciences that use elements of Marxist analysis to provide a theoretical explanation for the existence of injustice: "Neither the social sciences generally nor the Latin American contribution to them can be reduced to the Marxist version . . . these two options—an atheistic ideology and a totalitarian vision—are to be discarded and rejected."[16] Rather, liberation theology highlights the centrality of "praxis," not Marxist analysis, as the real meeting place between theology and the social sciences.[17] It involves not so much putting theory into practice as putting the Christian message into practice as a stimulant for theological reflection. If orthodoxy refers to the "correct beliefs" that traditionally function as normative for Christians, liberation theology stresses the importance of orthopraxis, or "correct action," as the most basic norm of Christian faith. Orthopraxis, Gutierrez argues, is a liberating praxis for justice, a biblical and theological demand to construct a different social order in which the poor—the *other* of Latin American society—are freed from the objectification of harsh economic systems.[18]

Liberation theology demands personal witness to the practice of justice, and such a call was answered by many priests, nuns, and lay catechists who served the poor of the region. Often subjected to censure by conservative prelates and death threats by the political Right, adherents to liberationist movements were placed at the tenuous center in the struggle for justice. Pope Paul VI's famous slogan, "a faith that does justice," implied that the two could not be discussed or practiced in isolation, so practical faith was a direct call to work in creating a better world for the poor. Christian praxis was interpreted through the lens of biblical patterns of justice—the narratives of slavery, exile, and liberation—so that the hierarchical relationship between God and the world is horizontalized: God—and God's people—fight alongside men and women of different views to bring an end to oppression. This renewed emphasis on Christian action had an analogous relationship with the Marxist hope for bringing about a just economic and political system. Furthermore, in both Christian and Marxist terms, there is the fundamental belief that the political struggle is a communal event that has soteriological ramifications. Liberation at either the individual or the collective level is a type of ultimate liberation for all who practice justice and mercy in the here and now. The Nicaraguan priest-poet and government minister Ernesto Cardenal (quoted in one of the epigraphs for this chapter) can thus make the imaginative claim in his poetry that Christ sacrifices himself on the cross in the struggle for the liberation of his people, just as the revolutionary guerilla is caught and tortured by the power elite of corrupt governments.

It is perhaps obvious that Graham Greene's theological imagination found inspiration in this movement within Catholicism. It was in Mexico in the 1930s, after all, that Greene's own Catholic faith coalesced into a committed intellectual and emotional experience: "I had observed for myself how courage and the sense of responsibility had revived with persecution—I had seen the devotion of peasants praying in priestless churches and I had attended Masses in upper rooms where the Sanctus bell could not sound for fear of the police."[19] This found imaginative shape in *The Power and the Glory* and contributed to Greene's enduring focus on Catholic-Marxist tensions. Latin America would always be an important touchstone for his understanding of his Catholic faith and the place where he profoundly hoped for some détente between a Christian vision of socialism and the ideology of Marxism.

Greene visited Central and South America often in the last decades of his life and used his identity as a Catholic novelist as a privileged credential to investigate the postcolonial situation there. The articles and editorials from his travels highlight the central role that religion was playing in these economically poor and oppressed nations. Greene witnessed the possibility of Catholicism's cultural and ritual significance becoming a vehicle for authentic political change. He was in Chile in 1971 during the short-lived government of the Marxist president, Dr. Salvador Allende. He optimistically writes about his experience there in a lengthy article published shortly before General Pinochet's military coup: "Eighty priests, nearly all of whom are working in the slums, have signed a declaration in support of socialism." He recounts being present at an ecumenical service in the Chilean cathedral attended by the archbishop, President Allende, and representatives from communist embassies, all listening intently as the priest urged "everyone to expel the Cain inside him. Humility is necessary to recognize the homicide inside us. It is easier to declare that the aggressors are outside."[20] Greene found the Church's role in such a Catholic country exceedingly important in any attempt to revolutionize Latin American economic and social life.

Greene visited Panama five times in the late 1970s and early 1980s as the personal guest of General Omar Torrijos Herrera, the charismatic general who had assumed power in 1968, ending the right-wing dictatorship of then President Arias. Greene considered the general a great friend, and in 1984 he published a memoir of their many conversations and travels. His extensive tours gave him an exceptional perspective on the situation in Nicaragua and El Salvador, where he met the political players and religious communities that worked there. Greene visited Nicaragua in 1983 as the personal guest of Fathers Cardenal and D'Escoto, both cabinet ministers in the Sandinista government:

> After seeing the priests of the center I drove to a town renamed Ciudad Sandino to visit two American nuns who belonged, like Father D'Escoto, to the Maryknoll order. The town consisted of about 60,000 very poor inhabitants. The nuns lived in the same conditions as the poor—a tin-roofed hut and a standing pipe for water in the yard. One of the two, quite a young woman, particularly impressed me. She had lived for ten years in the town so that she had experienced the dictatorship of Somoza and the whole civil war.[21]

Greene's engagement with Nicaragua grew stronger. He wrote editorials in support of the Sandinista government and against the U.S.–sponsored Contra aggression. He offered a nuanced reading of Pope John Paul II's difficulty with priests who were serving in the Sandinista government, claiming that the pope did not realize that the priests' presence freed the government from much of the heavy Marxist ideology:

> I think [the Pope] made a mistaken parallel between Nicaragua and Poland. . . . The priests' presence in the government of Nicaragua is a kind of guarantee against a completely Marxist state. . . . Unlike Poland there had been a civil war. It was more like the position in France at the end of the war when Catholic and Communist resistants who had been working together were both represented in De Gaulle's government. It is desirable that they should continue to work together. That dreadful scene on television when the Pope waved aside Father Cardenal as he knelt to kiss his hand shows that he does not realize Father Cardenal's importance to his people. He is not only a priest, he is their greatest poet. No wonder there were disturbances at [the pope's] Mass.[22]

Greene insightfully saw what liberation theology brought to the fore: in an area such as Latin America, the religious and the political could interpenetrate one another to effect a humanizing change precisely because they were overwhelmingly Catholic countries, fighting not so much the ideological battle against atheism but the battle for economic and social justice.

Greene's literary imagination touches liberation theology in other ways besides the geographical. The metaphor of exile, an important biblical theme for Gutierrez and liberation theologians, has always been a fixture in Greene's fiction. Liberation theology's stress on the political and religious ramifications of the biblical stories of exile intersects well with Greene's own sense of his position as an artist on the boundaries of his professed faith. Greene continues to set his late novels on geographical borders between nations and ideologies, where characters are involved in physical and personal claims that transgress the lines of a single race, nation, religion, or political affiliation. As a descendent of a decaying British Empire, Greene frequently draws his existential outcasts from both sides of the border, the colonial oppressed and the colonial remnant left behind. His exiles live in a space between two worlds that is often portrayed in stereotypical fashion: on the one hand, the world of coercive power and empty affluence presented by European-American modernity and, on the other hand, the world of the familial, religious, premodern "third world." The crisis for Greene's characters stems in part from their acute awareness that the modern world of affluence and power has already begun to absorb, even wipe away, the premodern, Catholic world.[23] The metaphor of exile becomes a complex thematic thread in *The Honorary Consul* and *The Human Factor*, binding together the issues of faith, love, loyalty, and human agency in a postcolonial world manipulated by first world political games.

To a considerable extent Greene's late religious vision mirrors liberation theology's focus on orthopraxis as the normative standard of authentic faith. In his late texts Greene consistently suggests that "correct belief" plays a subordinate role in the faith of his characters and that "correct practice" is what distinguishes the religious from the nonreligious person.[24] It is the practice of ritual worship and the active engagement of service to others—not intellectual assent to formulaic doctrine or pious devotions—that guarantee the continuity of God's presence. Greene's own pursuit of a sociopolitical system of right action has always transcended the too easily reduced ideologies of both a dogmatic Church and an authoritarian State. Like liberation theologians, Greene's support of Marxism is always articulated in terms of its practical effect in helping to overthrow repressive dictatorships and create a more just distribution of wealth and human services. He explicitly invokes the spirit of dialogue and understanding at the Second Vatican Council in a letter to the *Times* (London) in 1984: "Unlike John XXIII [John Paul II] seems to take a political and partisan line. To him, as to President Reagan, Marxism is the great enemy, black against white, and the word Marxist becomes more and more a vague term of abuse. Is anyone completely a Marxist any more than any one is completely Christian?"[25]

All the same, Greene remained skeptical of Marxist ideological excesses, noting in a late interview that "Marxists do not believe in persuasion or dialogue. As for the famous Marxist optimism, it just makes me laugh; few men have distrusted their fellows more completely."[26] For Greene Marxist economic theory could too easily be subsumed into an ideological battle that expounded an antitranscendent materialism. Greene saw firsthand that the church's soteriological claims and its ritual communal practices could help humanize and spiritualize the struggle for liberation. Religious faith could provide a viable form of engagement in the midst of revolution and assess the worthiness of social action.

Greene's personal visits to the region brought him into direct contact with oppression, economic disparity, undernourishment, violence, and the sinister shadow of superpower interference—all which had been unknown or ignored by much of his first world readership and critics. Yet, throughout the 1970s and 1980s Greene's complex political-religious vision made him suspect to the political and literary Left, as well as to the Catholic Right. Not fitting into easy categories, his hope for a fruitful meeting of Marxist and Catholic practice was dismissed as too Marxist, too Catholic, or just too simplistic. When articulated in such novels as *The Honorary Consul* and, to a lesser extent, *The Human Factor*, Greene's vision was taken to task by critics for retreating from the realism that marked his earlier work into a romantic idealism that was thought untenable and naive during the political ferment of the cold war.

Thus, an intriguing parallel can be seen in Greene's embodiment of a Catholic literary imagination as it developed in his texts. During the critical reception of Greene's earlier Catholic cycle, he was often questioned about the orthodoxy of his theological vision. In response, he consistently called on the work of Cardinal Newman as his theological defense in such debates. The criticism of the late novels, however, often questioned Greene's political-religious construction of the human person; in response, Greene called on his experience of liberation theology in the Latin American church to offer evidence in his defense. His characterization of the religious sense in his novels after the council grows from merely *orthodox* considerations of a character's personal salvation to a reflection on *orthopraxis*, the right practice of a character's service to others as a manifestation of religious faith in whatever expression one is able to render it. Greene's sense of Catholicism is reinvigorated after the Second Vatican Council not only by his reading and appreciation of the theological developments that succeeded the council but perhaps more profoundly by the orthopraxis of Catholicism that he witnessed in the Latin American Church.

The Liberating Dialogue of *The Honorary Consul*

The Honorary Consul is a subtle and accomplished variation of Greene's continuing theme, the pursuit of personal salvation, but enacted in a more sophisticated landscape through the many points of view that the novel tries to engage. On the surface it is a mystery plot about adultery, betrayal, political kidnapping, and a brutal shoot-out.[27] The reader returns forcefully to the geography of Greeneland but with an awareness of the text's playful presentation of the author's greater thematic concerns. The status of religious faith and the many nuances of belief, disbelief, and unbelief characterize much of the novel's concern, but here the religious matrix has a decidedly different feel. It is more diffuse and tentative, less explicit and monolithic, a religious journey set in a mutual dialogue with the social and political realities of the time.

Greene presents differing ideological visions of salvation through the discourse of three main characters: Eduardo Plarr, a doctor who helps the poor; León Rivas, a revolutionary ex-priest; and Charlie Fortnum, the mistakenly abducted honorary British consul. All three of them are modern-day exiles in search of an identity that is at once personal, political, and religious. Their pursuit is shaped within the context of their familial relationships, their experience of political repression, the cultural machismo of Latin America, and post–Vatican II theological debate. In having three protagonists give voice to their search for authentic existence, Greene structures a complex plot and narrative dialogue that explores the gap, the slippage, between official ideologies and their practical consequences toward individuals. Each of the characters is a variation of Greene's antiheroes, fumblers and failures more aware of their own flaws than their accomplishments. Yet for all their failings, a pattern begins to emerge that places each of them at the crossroads of a theological and political world that is as much post–Vatican II as it is postcolonial.

Eduardo Plarr is a doctor living in both physical and psychological exile in a border town in Argentina. Plarr's heritage is itself a mix of cultures and geographies, the Old World and the New, half British from his father and half Spanish-Paraguayan from his mother. His father was a native Englishman who had become so devoted to revolutionary politics in Paraguay that he sent his wife and 14-year-old son to Argentina for safekeeping. Plarr venerates his father's memory and nurtures the hope that he is still alive in a Paraguayan prison. He feels compromised in his middle-class comfort and, as a way of honoring his father, devotes his medical service to the poor: "In the barrio of the poor I am aware of doing something he would have liked to see me do."[28] Apart from this one act of solidarity, Plarr is emotionally cut off; he involves himself in a series of loveless relationships with married women, but he is divorced from any community and without any form of political or religious belief.

His self-absorbed peace is shattered when he becomes an accomplice in a political kidnapping. A group of rebels from Paraguay plan to abduct the visiting American ambassador and hold him hostage in exchange for political prisoners. Plarr agrees to help them, in part because two of the rebels are childhood friends who assure him that his father is one of the bargained-for releases and in part because he supposes that little will come from a scheme planned by such novices. They end up kidnapping the wrong man, Charley Fortnum, who is an unimportant, honorary British consul traveling with the American ambassador. Fortnum is also the cuckold whose young wife, Clara, a former prostitute at the local bordello, is pregnant with Plarr's child. Thus, what begins as a simple farce for Plarr soon turns into an awkward and ultimately horrifying reality. As Plarr tries to find a way out of the debacle for all involved, he is shot and killed by the military police.

Plarr resembles a type of character that ubiquitously populates Greene's later novels—the jaded rationalist who casts an ironic glance at the wasteland of modern life. Not able to understand why his heart is in conflict with itself, Plarr simply dismisses life as an absurdity. He fears the "cord of love," claiming that love "is not a word in my vocabulary" (224). Only through his conversations with both León Rivas, the lapsed priest who leads the rebels, and Charley Fortnum, the wounded hostage whom Plarr tries to save, does he gradually learn that his lack of love is itself a sickness that he has failed to diagnose correctly. By the end of the novel, love becomes for Plarr not so much an expression of sentiment as an act of courage. He discovers that pain and fear are more than medical and emotional problems to be conquered but are essential aspects of one's humanity. Plarr submits in the end to the demands of his heart. In a heroic act to bring about a nonviolent resolution, he risks and loses his life to end the standoff.

Though Plarr considers his Catholicism a historical footnote of his Jesuit education, he is given the time and space in the rebel hideout to discover that faith might not be such an absurdity. Having given himself solely to the reasoning power of medical science, he ridicules the religion of his childhood, tormenting his friend León with metaphysical questions about his exotic theological views. Yet he realizes that what his loss of faith has really effected in him is a loss of hope in a more just future. The conversation with the former priest forces him to face the realization that "I can no longer mock a man for his beliefs, however absurd. I can only envy them" (275). As he envies León's commitment to a political-religious vision, he is equally envious of Charley Fortnum's genuine love for his wife, Clara, especially after Charley learns that she is carrying Plarr's child. Plarr sees Charley overcome his anger for the sake of Clara and the baby. Charley's commitment to love gradually permits Plarr to imagine the existence of God in the world, though a God whose mysterious actions are more like "a great joker somewhere who likes to give a twist to things" (249).

Consequently, Plarr discovers within himself a renewal of genuine love for Clara and the baby she carries. Having become involved with her as a way to meet his sexual needs, Plarr first considers the pregnancy to be the result of his carelessness. He hopes to abort the child as "a useless part of Clara like her appendix, perhaps a diseased appendix which ought to be removed." Yet his cold medical assessment of the child soon becomes more reflective: "The poor little bastard, if only I could have made some sort of arrangement for it" (265). In the course of his thoughts the child slowly becomes invested with a familial past, present, and hoped-for future. By the end of his interior monologue, the child has developed into a real human being, socially and biologically situated in the ties that bind it:

> He thought of the tangle of its ancestry, and for the first time in the
> complexity of that tangle the child became real to him. . . . It joined
> the child to two very different grandfathers—a cane-cutter in Tucu-
> mán and an old English liberal who had been shot dead in the yard
> of a police station in Paraguay. The cord joined it to a father who
> was a provincial doctor, to a mother from a brothel. . . . He would
> have liked the little bastard to believe in something, but he was not
> the kind of father who could transmit belief in a god or a cause.[29]
> (225)

Plarr wishes to leave a legacy of belief to his child, something he belatedly comes to desire for himself. Forced to prepare for his death while trapped with the rebels and discovering the capacity for such love and involvement in others, he realizes that human commitment is not to some abstract cause but to the practical demands of human affection and justice. His final attempt to broker peace between the rebels and the police takes on a consecrated gravity, indi-cating he has truly learned to live. It is in the practice of this virtue that Plarr reflects an orthodox religious vision of the transcendent power of love.

If Doctor Plarr is Greene's incarnation of the doubting cynic thrust into conversion from unbelief to tentative belief, Father León Rivas is the postcolonial descendent of Greene's whiskey priest of *The Power and the Glory*. The flawed pacifist priest of the persecuted church of 1930s Mexico is transformed into the liberationist priest who preaches a gospel of freedom from the tyranny of the institutional Church, as well as from its alliances with capitalism and despotic regimes. Reared in upper middle-class comfort in Paraguay, León rebels against his own politically compromised father as he searches for identity as a priest of the poor and the oppressed. Despairing of the church and of his own effectiveness as a priest, he marries a peasant woman named Marta and becomes an amateur revolutionary. In Father Rivas, Greene captures the religious upheaval in Latin America and the development of liberation theology that occurred after the Second Vatican Council.[30]

As with the whiskey priest, Greene continues to convey an ontological character in León's priesthood, for even though he has exiled himself from the church, he is still very much a priest in the eyes of most people, even his wife. Unaware that his captor is an ex-priest, Charley Fortnum observes his kidnapper cooking a breakfast of eggs, noting that "as he held two half shells over the pan there was something in the position of his fingers which reminded Fortnum of that moment at the altar when a priest breaks the Host over the chalice" (135). When a blind man goes searching for a priest in the barrio where the rebels are hiding, he hears "a priest's voice" among the group. After the blind man leaves, León's common-law wife chides him: "I think you should have gone with the poor man, Father. His wife is dead and there is no priest to help him" (242). As much as León corrects his wife and tries to wear the mask of a revolutionary, he is still confronted with the aesthetic and ontological apprehension of his vocation as priest. In this respect, Greene's Catholic imagination remains rooted in a pre–Vatican II understanding of the nature of priesthood. At the same time, the text seems to be investigating the validity of such an ontological understanding, for Greene's liberationist priest doubts the truth of such claims, something his whiskey priest of 30 years ago takes for granted. The whiskey priest can state with complete conviction that even if he is "a damned man putting God in the mouths of men," he nonetheless is God's instrument. Léon Rivas, on the other hand, "half-believes" this, questioning both the validity of his priesthood and his ability to mediate God's presence.

Like Doctor Plarr, whose final heroic act is the sign of his personal salvation, it is León's final act of pastoral care for those around him that signifies the orthopraxis of his religious faith, once again echoing Greene's theme of the priority of religious practice over rational belief. As Gutierrez asserts, "Liberation theology would say that God is first contemplated and practiced, and only then thought about. What we mean by this is that worshiping God and doing his will are the necessary condition for thinking about him."[31] Greene's priests dramatize the privileged place that the practice of faith has over the sometimes unorthodox articulations of that faith. Because the motivations and commitments of Greene's priests often coincide with the prophetic witness of Jesus in Scripture, the authority of their theological speculations are granted an aura of truth over the orthodoxy of the perfunctory priests and clergy who populate the margins of his narratives. Such is the case with León's theology. He admits that he was "at the bottom in most of my classes," yet he tries to defend his articulation of faith from Plarr's deprecations and Marta's fears: "The catechism is not the faith, Marta. It is a sort of times two table. There is nothing I have said which your catechism denies" (241). Greene plays on Hans Küng's complaint—that modern faith is often expressed as a "higher conceptual mathematics"—by treating León's revolutionary discourse on faith as a commitment to the Jesus of liberation, devoid of the dogmatic formulas that can overshadow the radical claims of the Gospel.[32]

León's effort to come to terms with the church's duplicity in a culture of acute social injustice reflects the tensions that arose post–Vatican II in imagining how Catholic faith could help transform the Latin American political landscape. León voices liberation theology's dialectical starting point, the contradiction between the liberating word of the Gospel and the confining status quo of both the ecclesiastical establishment and the political government. In a long conversation with Charley Fortnum, León confides:

> She [the church] is a sort of person too . . . they claim she is Christ
> on earth—I still half believe it even now. Someone like you—*un
> Inglés*—you are not able to understand how ashamed I felt of the
> things they made me read to the people. I was a priest in the poor
> part of Asuncion near the river. Have you noticed how all the poor
> always cling close to the river? They do it here too, as though they
> plan one day to swim away, but they have no idea how to swim and
> there is nowhere to swim for any of them. On Sunday I read to
> them out of the Gospels . . . 'Sell all and give to the poor'—I had to
> read that out to them while the old Archbishop we had in those days
> was eating a fine fish from Iguazù and drinking a French wine with
> the General. Of course the people were not actually starving—you
> can keep them from starving on mandioca, and malnutrition is
> much safer for the rich than starvation. Starvation makes a man
> desperate. Malnutrition makes him too tired to raise a fist. (132)

The complicity of the ecclesiastical authorities in the repressive structures of the state provokes León to leave his priesthood, if not his faith. Yet the text implies that León's theological focus on orthopraxis is the normative standard for authentic faith. Greene proposes that his correct practice is a noble response, the distinguishing characteristic between the religious and the non-religious person.

Charley Fortnum, the undefeated failure, rounds out the cast of Greene's main characters, beginning as a comic caricature and developing into a fully realized character by the novel's end. With Dr. Plarr and the English teacher, Humphries, Charley is one of the remnants of the British colony in that part of Argentina. He, too, is a lapsed Catholic, though unlike Dr. Plarr he retains an elegiac bond with his childhood faith. He lives mostly in a drunken stupor, chattering about the "proper measure" of whiskey; boasting about his jeep, Fortnum's Pride; and stressing over Clara, his young bride from Señora Sanchez's brothel. His cowardly nature, stemming from childhood memories of his abusive father, contrasts nicely with the machismo of Argentine culture. In the midst of such humor, Greene draws out Charley's growing stature in the text.

Charley's thoughts and comments are often profoundly transparent statements, whether they are about himself or others. Being sober for the first time that he meets Dr. Plarr, Charley perceptively notes Plarr's tough demeanor: "You sound a hard man, Ted. Haven't you ever loved anyone?" (64). Charley, on the other hand, who longs to find someone to love, thinks he has found it in Clara: "Do you know I never touched Clara for months? Not until I was sure she loved me a little . . . it was real love, not brothel love I wanted." Shocked by Plarr's dismissal of love, Charley, with a "paternal anxiety in his voice," asks him, "Has no woman loved you Ted?" (84–85).

In a text whose characters are in search of absent fathers, Charley is more and more imbued with the positive signification of fatherhood. The question of fatherhood is a central theme of the novel: the missing fathers of the protagonists, the questionable fatherhood of Plarr and Charley Fortnum, the fatherhood of priesthood, the fatherhood of God. When Plarr thinks aloud of his own father's situation, he is surprised: "Strangely the face he conjured up when he spoke was not his father's but Charley Fortnum's" (180). And León treats Charley with a touch of filial respect, transferring a priestly cast onto him. When León writes a last letter to Clara for him, Charley observes: "In the situation I'm in, I suppose you think I ought to find some way to forgive. Even my father" (215). Greene suggests that fatherhood is intimately linked with the ability to forgive, and Charley manifests such ability: he forgives his own father's abuse, Dr. Plarr's betrayal with Clara, Father León's actions, and finally

Clara's adultery. When he witnesses Clara's tears the day of Plarr's funeral, Charley consoles her: "There's nothing wrong in love, Clara. It happens. It doesn't much matter who with. We get caught up . . . we get kidnapped . . . by mistake." As they talk of the child, he utters: "I think we will call him Eduardo. You see I loved Eduardo in a way. He was young enough to be my son" (279–280). Charley's practice of love becomes a supreme example in the text because it flows out of a suffering that needs forgiveness and healing.

It is not only Greene's heightened sense of "faith as orthopraxis" that correlates well to a post–Vatican II religious vision; other discourses in the novel play with Catholic forms of religious expression. In terms of the primacy of a sacramental mediation, Father León, like his forebear the whiskey priest, stands isolated from both sacred and secular authorities. Yet whereas the whiskey priest could claim some certitude in his defined role as an anointed intermediary of sacramental grace, Rivas at first understands his priesthood only as a consecration of service to the poor, becoming a revolutionary leader for their sake. As León realizes that he will be forced to kill his hostage, the sacramental role of his priesthood comes back into focus. Marta begs him to celebrate a final Mass for them as a final ultimatum is heard over the loudspeakers, and he acquiesces to the request. The placement of the liturgical drama of the Mass within the larger drama of violence draws out a symbolic and linguistic space in the text where Greene suggests God's presence is ritually made present.

That Greene wanted the Catholic liturgy to be a critical lens to intensify the theological stakes in the many discourses of the novel can be argued by considering his first two unpublished drafts. Unlike the final text, where Charley Fortnum declines the offer to be present at the Mass, Greene in his earlier drafts has all the characters present at the liturgy, with Plarr helping Charley into the next room and holding him steady. The two paragraphs excised from the final text describe Leon's ritual movements interposed by key liturgical prayers and interior responses by Plarr. León voices the words, "As often as you do these things you shall do them in memory of me," to which Plarr immediately reflects, "How many acts in one's life were done thus in memory . . . this thing I do in memory of you, Father."[33] In the final version, Greene removes the lines that make explicit the critical relationship between the liturgical action of the praying church and the personal action of all those present. In excising this section, Greene seems to want the conflictual nature of faith and political commitment kept in a more ambiguous tension between characters until the very end of the novel.

If priesthood is still a principal conduit of God's grace, a vertical descent into the sacramental functions of priestly service, it is no longer the only conduit. Greene's theological imagination broadens the ways in which the presence of God is mediated, yet in a very Greene-like manner: he diffuses the priestly function into the three main characters of the novel, performing the role of priest for one another. Eduardo Plarr, León Rivas, and Charley Fortnum, all disenfranchised or disinterested Catholics, realize to their surprise that their conversations and actions with one another have a priestlike cast. When Charley questions Father León about why he married, the text points to the inversion of sacramental functions: "[León] said in a low voice (he might have been kneeling in the confessional box himself), 'I think it was anger and loneliness, Señor Fortnum'" (132). Charley notes the irony of the priest's acting "as though it were the penitent [León] who stood now by the coffin" (135). As the execution time nears, Father León urges Charley to receive the sacrament of confession, inadvertently also confessing his sins to Charley. He gives Charley absolution, to which Charley replies, "I'm a lot luckier than you are. There's no one to give *you* absolution" (259). And Greene draws a profoundly ironic implication of this shared ministry when Plarr and Father León meet their death. Plarr, the cynical man of science who has just risked his life for the sake of others, is drawn into the discursive orbit of the practice of the priesthood. In their final words to each other, they perform the Catholic formula of contrition and absolution, each voicing the other's role, so that Father León is penitent and Plarr is minister:

> "Lie still," Doctor Plarr said. "If they see either of us move they may shoot again. Don't speak."
> "I am sorry . . . I beg pardon . . ." [said León].
> "*Ego te absolvo*," Doctor Plarr whispered in a flash of memory."
> (264)

León finally gets his absolution in the last moments of his life. For both León and Plarr, their words intimate a sharing in the mediation of God's grace, a perhaps ironic portrayal of the "priesthood of all people," which was a central theme of the documents of Vatican II. God's grace is thus surprisingly manifested on both the vertical plane of a cultic priesthood and the horizontal plane of a "priestly people" who are showing care for and forgiveness of each other.

The doctrine of Christ was imaginatively understood in *The Power and the Glory* as a theological aesthetic of transformation into an *alter Christus*, a high Christology in which one is lifted up into the divine form of Christ. As the whiskey priest begins to see the hidden beauty of God's love in the poor and seeks to identify with them, he begins his own ascent into participation with Christ, who sacrifices himself for love's sake. This Catholic aesthetic is present at some level in all of Greene's novels about priests, and León, too, sees God in the horror and ugliness of life: "I have always wanted to understand what you call the horror and why I cannot stop loving it. Just like the parents who loved the poor bloody torso [of a child born without hands and feet]. Oh he seems ugly enough I grant you, but then I am ugly too and yet Marta loves me" (239). Yet in the late novels, other forms of discourse mute the aesthetic focus on Christ. In *The Honorary Consul*, the doctrine of Christ is rendered more in terms of the human struggle for justice. A low Christology is given precedence, which is the theological perspective of Küng, Schillebeeckx, and the general Christological emphasis of liberation theology. León asserts to Plarr that "Christ was a man, even if some of us believe that he was God as well. It was not the God the Romans killed, but a man. A carpenter from Nazareth" (232). Both the memory and practice of Jesus become the standard in which one's faith is practiced in this world and hoped for in the next.

A Vatican II Christological and ecclesiological discourse is most clearly expressed in the formalized dialogue between Father León and Dr. Plarr. León explains to Plarr that he had followed his conscience against the outright hypocrisy and complicity of the institutional Church. Yet he is still a man of some religious faith: "I never left the Church. Mine is only a separation, Eduardo, a separation by mutual consent, not a divorce. I shall never belong wholly to anyone else. Not even to Marta" (232). With a bit of fatalism, León states a profound understanding of the church as Sacrament, echoing the sacramental developments proposed by Schillebeeckx and adopted at Vatican II: "How can I leave the Church? The Church is the world. The Church is this *barrio*, this room" (213). Far from being diminished and absent, the Church is made radically present and tangible in the ordinariness of life, integral to the salvation of the world.

If Plarr is trapped in his memory of a lost father and cynical about any future hope in finding him, León sees the historical movement of the Church and revolutionary politics as reason for hope. Merging a Marxist analysis of history with his faith in Christ, he claims: "The Church lives in time too . . . I think sometimes the memory of that man, that carpenter, can lift a few people out of the temporary Church of these terrible years, when the Archbishop sits down to dinner with the General, into the great Church beyond our time and place" (233). It is the memory of "that man," the human face of Jesus, who is proclaiming a Kingdom of justice, that becomes the focus of León's faith and hope. The evolutionary spirit of Pierre Teilhard de Chardin hovers around this theological speculation, for León believes that the temporal Church is situated in a developmental process that moves toward "the great Church beyond."[34]

As the kidnappers' situation gets more desperate, León is further questioned about his religious motives, forcing him to speculate on the relationship of God to humanity in unorthodox dualisms. In doing so, he misappropriates the understanding of the *Imago Dei* as an *Imago Huminis*: in León's view, the dialectical struggle of good and evil in human nature is reflected ontologically in God the Father, so that there must come about "the redemption of God as well as of Man . . . God suffering the same evolution that we are, but perhaps with more pain" (240). Léon argues his position first from analogy: "He [God] made us in His image—and so our evil is His evil too. How could I love God if He were not like me? Divided like me? Tempted like me?" (239). Since God, according to the priest's Manichean reduction, has a "day-side" of goodness and a "night-side" of evil, God needs humanity in order to evolve into complete goodness. But in a subversive claim that checks the Manichean implications that he espouses, León offers a deeper incarnational insight into God's immanent proximity: "God is joined to us in a sort of blood transfusion. His good blood is in our veins, and our tainted blood runs through His" (241). León's argument once again echoes Teilhard, for human actions and God's activity are linked: "The evolution of God depends on our evolution. Every evil act of ours strengthens His night-side, and every good one helps His day-side. We belong to Him and He belongs to us. But now at least we can be sure where evolution will end one day—it will end in a goodness like Christ's" (240). The theme of God's suffering, so prevalent in the French Catholic revival that Greene appropriated, continues to ground Greene's religious imagination in the novel. The image of a suffering God implicated in evil seems to be the only image the priest can find that brings God close enough to give people courage in a revolutionary situation.

And yet León's theology of revolution and violence ultimately collapses when he refuses to kill the innocent honorary consul for the sake of the revolution.[35] His theological image of a God of divine goodness and human evil proves to be an idol, for as David Leigh argues in his analysis of the novel, the text indicates that God in the person of the Son, Jesus Christ, is embodied in an already suffering body—the poor of the *barrio*—in the midst of evil.[36] León realizes that violence cannot overcome evil; only committed, nonviolent love does so. In the priest's final hour of action—his own "orthopraxis"—he actually draws out a more orthodox theological vision that squares with the Catholic notion of the Church as the Mystical Body of Christ. León's personal, political, and religious identity is merged in the practical, tangible act of making faith in God present for himself and for others in his role as priest. He knows the powerful pull of communal worship, for when asked by Plarr why he is afraid to celebrate Mass in their final hour, he declares, "You see, if I took the Host I would still half believe I was taking His body" (237). León grasps that the practice of the Mass brings one into an encounter of "half-belief," an experience on the borderland of rationality and mysterious faith.

Greene suggests that it is precisely as a Catholic priest that León brings a worthy contribution to the revolution, fostering religious faith embodied in the popular religious rituals of the poor and of the celebration of the sacraments. The practice of the faith of the poor is the ideological check on any overtly atheistic/Marxist ideology. León celebrates the Mass in the final hour before the police storm the hideout. Ironically, Father Rivas utters the words *Ite missa est* ("the Mass is ended, go you are sent") just before he meets his own death. Plarr's attempt to mediate a truce between the rebels and the police ends with a bullet in the leg by a military sniper. León crawls out after him in one last priestly act to minister to Plarr and is killed. This final act between them is at once an acceptance and affirmation of León's vocation as a sign of God's presence and of Plarr's commitment to those he loves.

The end of the novel offers a nuanced criticism of liberation theology, for if its goal is to effect positive political transformation for the benefit of the poor, Greene's text refuses such a possibility. Politically, nothing has changed in the final pages of the novel; superficially, that both Plarr and León die points to the futility of such worthy dreams of justice and liberation. But if the novel's political geography has not changed, the religious landscape has undergone a subtle transformation. Plarr's religious imagination is galvanized by his exposure to Father León's commitment and Charley Fortnum's selfless love for his wife; likewise, León's identity as an effective witness to a just society is disclosed finally in his ministry as priest. The end of the novel emphasizes two places in which the religious and the political imagination intersect: hope and love. Human hope can ground political belief only when it is experienced in a personal commitment to others, and human love has a stake not only in creating communities of commitment but also in the evolutionary union of humanity with God. Indeed, love is the transcendent signifier in the novel that keeps human action focused on correct practice.

In this way Greene weaves together Catholicism and Marxism as interpretive discourses to understand the human factor in the struggle for liberation. Two of Greene's lifelong thematic concerns are brought together: the question of faith and belief in an alienating bourgeois society and the experience of exploitation by the social, political, and even religious structures of nations. In Eduardo Plarr, Charley Fortnum, and Father León Rivas, Greene creates a dialogical novel, in Mikhail Bakhtin's sense of the term, that explores the convergence of contemporary struggles with faith, hope, and love, using the contours of a post–Vatican II Catholicism as the textual space in which this occurs.

The epigraph of the novel, taken from Thomas Hardy, hints at a Teilhardian convergence through history: "All things merge with one another—good into evil, generosity into justice, religion into politics." By creating characters that journey toward this convergence, Greene offers his own variation of the competing ideologies of salvation. In the end, the experience of selfless love is Greene's hermeneutical standard that defines human beings, reflected and refracted through the lens of a Catholic imagination contextualized in the situation of Latin America.

Greene's theological perception is, in the end, a similar reading of the means and ends of liberation theology. Gutierrez asserts that "only through concrete acts of love and solidarity will our encounter be effective with the poor . . . our denial of love and solidarity will be a rejection of Christ."[37] And for Gutierrez, this concrete act of love finds its substance, its power, and its hermeneutical standard in the ritual celebration of the Mass:

> In Latin America even those who try to struggle against the ruling injustice face threats from different sources. . . . This is why we cele-
> brate the Eucharist, the prime task of the ecclesial community. In the breaking of bread we bring to mind the love and faithfulness of Jesus which brought him to his death, and the confirmation of his mission to the poor through the resurrection. . . . In it we express deep communion in human suffering—so often brought on by lack of bread—and recognize, in joy, the Risen Lord who gives life and raises the hopes of the people brought together by His actions and His word.[38]

The dramatic narrative of Christ's death and Resurrection in the Mass reframes the tragic death of Plarr and León into religious terms, a participation in the Christian story of hope and love. León is inexorably led back to the celebration of this meal by those who love him, and at the end of the novel this breaking of the bread gives substance, power, and a new interpretation to the kind of love and hope that authentic liberation must entail. For Greene, as well as for Gutierrez, it is in the practice of such faith that authentic hope emerges.

The *Honorary Consul* bears witness to the development of Greene's religious imagination. The novel's setting—in an overwhelmingly Catholic cultural context—allows an explicit embodiment of theological references to become visible thematic threads. The novel dramatizes the pilgrim nature of the Church with the modern political world in the dialogue between characters; it strongly emphasizes the humanity of Christ in the doctrine of the Incarnation as motivation for faith and hope; it subversively plays with the notion of a "priesthood of all people"; and it continues to develop more emphatically

Greene's belief in the supremacy of orthopraxis over orthodoxy in judging the veracity of religious faith.

Catholicizing the Human in *The Human Factor*

Five years after *The Honorary Consul,* Greene published *The Human Factor,* an espionage novel that he had begun to write in 1967. He stopped working on the novel over halfway through it because of his personal association with Kim Philby, a spy for the Soviet Union who had been Greene's superior in the British Secret Service during the war years. The discovery of Philby's real-life espionage and his defection to Moscow threatened to make Greene's novel a timely roman à clef.[39] After 11 years, Greene felt compelled to return to the novel and finally published it in 1978. Set in greater London, with an epilogue set in Moscow, *The Human Factor* explores the virtue in disloyalty to and betrayal of the state secret service apparatus. Greene focuses the novel not on the public diplomacy between nations but on the ambiguous alliances of the cold war.[40] What little explicit religious thread there is in the text is often expressed in elegiac terms—characters mourning a bygone era, when faith and belief might have once made a difference, or searching for a moral consensus that had once informed and analyzed the actions of institutions and governments. Yet faith and belief—whether in God or humanity—are the traces that linger on the edge of the text, implicating the post-Christian political order of both the Western powers and communist Russia. The search for a stable "factor"— the human factor of the title—is uneasily negotiated in a universe denied and deprived of Greene's usual recourse to explicit Catholic images and beliefs.

In exploring *The Human Factor* at the end of this chapter on Greene's embodiment of a post–Vatican II Catholic imagination, I am proposing that his use of the espionage genre allows for a political allegorization of his religious concerns.[41] However, my primary interest here is to read the text not so much as an excavation of religious themes that lie underneath the political issues but more as an investigation of how Greene's Catholic imagination still helps to structure and inform the human factor of his characters. To that end, I want to look at how the political wasteland of espionage dramatizes the religious vacuum in late twentieth-century political realities and then examine specifically how Greene continues to inscribe his secular characters with a particularly Catholic aura.

Maurice Castle is a 62-year-old Englishman who is working in the British secret service and is a Russian agent. Castle had worked in South Africa years before and had fallen in love with one of his agents, a black woman named

Sarah; he had married her even though she had already become pregnant by a man of her own race. Because their love was criminal under apartheid, and the South African security forces were pursuing them, Castle enlists a communist named Carson to help him get Sarah and her son, Sam, out of the country. When Sarah is deported he follows her to England, moves them into the security of a suburban home in Berkhamsted, and gets himself established at the Ministry of Intelligence, MI 6. Out of a sense of gratitude for Carson's help, Castle agrees to be a double agent for Russia, but only in African affairs. When a leak is discovered in Castle's section, his superiors attempt to quietly hunt down the culprit and secretly eliminate him before word leaks to the press. Castle's unambitious and dull demeanor makes him appear so harmless that attention turns to his assistant, Arthur Davis, who is suspected because of his love for flashy sports cars, expensive port, and *Penthouse* magazines. The sinister Dr. Percival is called in to help Colonel Daintry, the chief of internal security, with the ongoing investigation. Percival takes matters into his own hands and gives Davis a lethal dose of an untested toxic substance in order to disguise his death as the result of liver disease. Daintry, himself an unhappy man, is outraged at Percival's actions but feels helpless to do anything. Castle realizes that Davis's unfortunate end should have been his own, and he informs his contact that he is finished as a double agent. The moment of crisis, however, comes after the arrival of Castle's old enemy, Cornelius Muller, the chief of security in South Africa. Muller and his apartheid government are now working in conjunction with the British. As a sign of the détente between them, Muller gives Castle some notes on Operation Uncle Remus, an American program for nuclear military operations to keep South Africa from the communists. With Castle's pro-African sympathies—he calls himself a "naturalized black"—he makes the decision to save innocent African lives by sending a final report to Russia, even if it means blowing his cover. He sets his defection in motion, leaving behind Sarah and Sam at his mother's house with the hope of their joining him later in Moscow. In a cold apartment, Castle bides his time. After losing his temper with his Russian hosts, he gets connected on the phone to his wife, who is being kept in England by the vengeful Dr. Percival, who threatens to separate Sarah from her son if she attempts to flee. On the phone, Castle tells Sarah of his hopes of their coming to Russia, but he never hears her reply—"Maurice, Maurice, please go on hoping"—because the connection has been cut. Greene's novel ends on this pessimistic note, with the possibility of hope reduced to its narrowest margins.

Greene places his religious concerns within this secular context, allowing him to enlarge the scope of the spy genre by focusing on the moral questions that underlie human actions. Paul O'Prey notes that the novel "is about people who happen to be spies rather than about spying per se."[42] In this way Greene humanizes the thriller form by advancing the worth of each individual in a nexus of relationships that either nourish human love or make a claim on it. In the absence of actual war, the cold war becomes the ultimate power game. God has become a refugee, and belief in God seems hopeless in a world where professionals from the national intelligence agencies decide the fate of individuals. In this political climate, Greene relocates Newman's "original calamity" in the actions, methods, and philosophy of security organizations, for under the guise of English manners they empower, as well as conceal, the immorality of the political system. Liberation theology's articulation of the systemic structural reality of sin is echoed in the corruption, coercion, and will to power that fuel the world in which Greene situates his characters. Apartheid becomes a metaphor not only for the injustice in South Africa but also for the laws and rules that isolate and perpetuate the "apartness" of human life in larger, existential terms.

Emmanuel Percival most embodies Greene's man of "perfect evil walking the world where perfect good can never walk again." Though Percival respects the law as the necessary rules of engagement, he is a man without ideals or conscience. For him the law has little to do with justice or morality, and Greene skillfully makes this point when Percival attends Davis's funeral. He hears the vicar proclaim, "Behold I show you a mystery," to which he wryly wonders, is this "the mystery of whether I killed the right man?" And hearing the proclamation "The sting of death is sin, and the strength of sin is the law," Percival cynically responds that it sounded like a mathematical proposition: "Q.E.D. ["what was to be demonstrated"] seems a more suitable response to what the Vicar was saying than Amen."[43] He is open about his motives to his friend Sir John Hargreaves, the chief of British intelligence, asserting that power is the game of destiny: "I want to be on the side most likely to win during my lifetime. . . . I don't pretend to be an enthusiast for God or Marx. Beware of people who believe. They aren't reliable players" (147). And in a much discussed passage, Percival instructs Colonel Daintry on playing the espionage game by using an abstract painting to make his point:

> "Take a look at that Nicholson. Such a clever balance. Squares of different color. And yet living so happily together. No clash. The man has a wonderful eye. Change just one of the colors—even the size of the square, and it would be no good at all." Percival pointed at a yellow square. "There's your Section 6. That's your square from now on. You don't need to worry about the blue and the red. All you have to do is pinpoint our man and then tell me. You've no responsibility

for what happens in the blue or red squares. In fact not even in the yellow. You just report. No bad conscience. No guilt. (29)

Percival claims that living in such squares is the normal condition of the world, that human isolation is the ideal. He becomes the perfect foil to Castle, whose love for Sarah and Sam and hatred of apartheid transgress the colors and squares of Percival's clinical logic.

The text makes explicit a moral vacuity by Greene's employment of a Nazi-laden discourse. When Percival enthusiastically describes his scientific research on aflatoxin—the chemical that will quietly eliminate Davis—he tells Hargreaves that he is rather happy with his "neat little *solution* to our problem" (70). And Cornelius Muller calls his plan for the defense of South Africa the "Final Solution," a strategy to use nuclear devices on black South African townships as a way to fight any communist insurgency. Significantly, Muller not only gets the consent of the British intelligence agencies but travels to his German counterparts as well.[44] The familiar word "solution" serves as a euphemism for murder, and the text raises the specter of collusion between security operatives who are supposed to be political enemies. Daphna Erdinast-Vulcan's study of the novel succinctly argues the point:

> The striking resemblance between Dr. Percival and Cornelius Muller, who ostensibly do not belong to the same camp, blurs out the distinction between "our" side and "their" side, a distinction which is a pre-condition of loyalty . . . the insidious banality of evil is personified in the novel [by them], and the reader who comes to share Castle's vision of the horrors that might be inflicted on the world by these ordinary law-abiding citizens, cannot but become an accessory to Castle's "disloyalty."[45]

The reader understands Castle's betrayal of his organization and country as justified. Betrayal becomes an absurd notion because the amoral system is devoid of either a transcendent, ideal vision or a concern for the particularity and uniqueness of human beings. Indeed, Sarah voices the human factor that justifies such a reading. When Castle finally tells her that he is a traitor, she responds, "Who cares. . . . We have our own country. You and I and Sam. You've never betrayed that country, Maurice" (171).

The novel ends with Castle in Moscow, and the text is as critical of the totalitarian state as it is of the security games of Western democracies. The description of the Moscow winter describes Castle's desolation: "This was a merciless, interminable, annihilating snow, a snow in which one could expect the world to end" (231). His hope for a new spring in the cold winds of Moscow are dashed as he learns to deal with the drab and isolated reality of exile. Thus behind the chesslike political game of espionage and betrayal that the cold war fosters lurks Greene's religious concern: political life without any referent that respects the human individual becomes a deadly game, played with a deceptively simple belief in the ultimate efficacy of power.

To say all this is in keeping with the general—and I think accurate—reading of the religious undertones of the novel. Yet does Greene further embody his Catholic imagination in the text, beyond the moral correlation to politics? Do his characters become secularized versions of his Catholic saints and sinners? One can understand Maurice Castle as the sanctified sinner, the spiritual descendent of the whiskey priest and the spiritual contemporary of his Latin American counterparts, Eduardo Plarr and Father León Rivas. Castle, too, has little time for ideology, but in contrast to Percival's rejection of any belief in God or Marx, Castle struggles on the borders of half-belief in both political and religious terms, tenuously trying to hold on to a stable sense of duty and responsibility to those he loves. His care for individual people is his primary concern, and it comes from the human connections he makes: the love for his wife and son and the personal responsibility he has for them, the sense of pity he has for those less fortunate, and the gratitude he has for those who have helped Sarah and Sam escape imprisonment in South Africa. Castle's love and his commitment to his conscience become the unnamed spiritual ground of the novel.

It is new to Greene's characters that Castle and Sarah are *happily* married and very much in love. This representation of married love differs sharply from Greene's earlier Catholic cycle. I suggest that it is not only Greene's age and wisdom that inform this new conception of marriage in his texts but also his appreciation of the developing Catholic discourses on such issues. Sexual tension between lovers and spouses had been the typical mark of his characters' spiritual suffering, whereby the temptations or corruptions of the flesh signified either the paralysis or the *metanoia* in a character's spiritual development.[46] This once normative pattern of the Catholic literary revival was challenged by post–Vatican II theological discourse: the body-soul dualisms and the Jansenistic dread of anything sexual were abandoned for a more holistic, incarnational understanding of married love as a reflection on the divine image in human relationships. Beginning perhaps with Clara and Charley at the end of *The Honorary Consul*, Greene's late novels offer glimpses of married love as the new *Imago Dei*, the only divine-human factor that visibly makes a claim over all the isms and abstractions of contemporary life. In a world where God seems absent, married love becomes God's trace, the gleam of hope in an otherwise dark world, the text's tenuous transcendent signifier. Love is held up as a realistic ideal, yet the text resists romanticizing such an ideal, for Castle notes that the last year in South Africa had taught him "the age-old lesson that fear and love are indivisible" (83). The power that commits one to another subverts the rules of ideological sides, engendering fear and concern for the fragility of such a commitment. Even though Castle clings to Sarah and Sam as his peace and security, he fears that his political treachery, his compensation to Carson for making his love possible, will be discovered. He realizes that "a man in love walks through the world like an anarchist, carrying a time bomb" (125), a violent sanctification of the power of love amid a world of political power. Without any other religious referent in the text to engage such perversions of power, Greene seems to turn to married love as the transcendent standard.

Castle is also Greene's secular saint in his self-proclaimed half-belief. Though Castle is not a Catholic, he ponders Christ as "that legendary figure whom he would have liked to believe in" (131). He tells Sarah he is not a religious man but admits to her that he has met religious men in the past whose convictions were so great that he was convinced by their lives. His thoughts turn to a particular priest in Africa, as well as his communist friend, Carson: "For a while I half-believed in his God, like I half-believed in Carson's. Perhaps I was born to be a half-believer" (94). Castle's half-belief tragically undermines the possibility for any peace of mind and generates the metaphysical anxiety that fuels his crisis. All the same, Castle reflects on life in a familiarly Catholic, Greene-like manner:

> "Why are some of us, he wondered, unable to love success or power or great beauty? Because we feel unworthy of them, because we feel more at home with failure? He didn't believe that was the reason. Perhaps one wanted the right balance, just as Christ had. . . . 'Come unto me all ye that travail and are heavy laden.' [Perhaps] he was there to right the balance. That was all." (131)

Castle thinks he rights the balance in the world, participating in the balance that Christ is supposed to have brought in his radical proclamation of love to the powerless.[47] Castle half believes that his actions mirror—indeed, mediate—Christ's actions.

Though Castle's belief is narrowed, he doesn't lose the habit of many of Greene's characters of visiting a church's dim confessional in moments of crisis. Under the weight of Castle's years of secrecy, the desire to confess to someone overpowers him. But the confessional scene in this text is a far cry from those in his earlier novels. In previous works the priest's words would often exacerbate the extreme spiritual torment of the penitent by voicing the Church's orthodox take on the consequences of their actions. Now even the ability to communicate in religious terms is made absurd. Greene presents a subtle criticism of the therapeutic paradigm of the post-Christian world that is displacing the spiritual, confessional mode of religious faith. Castle goes to the confessional box as if "a patient who is visiting a psychiatrist for the first time with trepidation," telling the priest, "I want to talk to you" (167). The priest responds, "You are here to talk to God, not me," and Castle snaps back, "No, I'm not, I'm just here to talk . . . I want to talk, that's all." When the priest discovers that Castle is not a Catholic, much less a man of faith, he angrily retorts, "Then I think what you need is a doctor" (168). The text suggests an ambiguous tension in Greene—as well as in post–Vatican II Catholicism— between the psychological and the spiritual in the late twentieth century. The text implies that the priest's literal-minded orthodoxy betrays his authentic call as a priest to help others, at the same time that it indicts Castle's misappropriation of the form and function of the confessional to assuage his betrayal.

Yet in a text that is ostensibly about the players in a game of espionage, Greene discursively embodies a Catholic imagination in Castle's situation as a double agent by his constant reference to Catholic analogies and images. The interface between spying and Catholicism is not new to Greene, for he began to refer to this connection early in his career. Usually it was in reference to the historical struggle that Catholics underwent during state oppression. In a 1948 address, he exhorts Christians to become "the spies of God" if the world "succumb to a totalitarian and atheistic regime."[48] In a 1951 article on the publication of the spiritual journal of the Elizabethan Jesuit martyr John Gerard, he notes how Gerard's narrow escapes and final capture have been "enacted in many countries during our half-century since Father Pro landed at Vera Cruz . . . but in Gerard's narrative, it is happening in our own Norfolk, to us."[49] What is unusual in *The Human Factor* is that with the lack of a Catholic culture and explicitly religious interiority in his characters, Greene ironically inscribes the communist apparatus with a religious aura. Boris, the Russian contact, is very much a priest-confessor for Castle: "There's no one in the world with whom I can talk of everything, except this man Boris. . . . A control was a bit like a priest must be to a Catholic—a man who received one's confession whatever it might be without emotion" (104). And after Castle's defection to Moscow, a young assistant who follows an elderly K.G.B. (the Soviet secret service) agent is described as if "an acolyte attending a priest of his faith, and in spite of the heavy moustache there was something priestly about the old man, about his kindly smile and the hand he extended like a blessing" (230). Castle, in the matrix of Greene's Catholic imagination, is the displaced religious person who searches for surrogate priests who can assist him with kindness through the crises of his life.

Greene's fascination with Catholic priesthood draws its most explicit textual analogy in the description and actions of Castle. He is what one critic calls "a priest without a Church."[50] Throughout the novel Castle intuitively aligns himself with the weak, the innocent, and the miserable. He accepts Sam as his own son, consenting to take on the responsibility of fatherhood. He reminisces from his own childhood about a girl whom he had loved because she was shy and ugly and "he wanted her to feel that she was loved by someone and so he began to love her himself" (131). He agrees to accompany Colonel Daintry to his daughter's marriage because "he could seldom resist a call of distress, however it was encoded" (113). Once again there is a latent theological aesthetic at work that reflects Greene's Catholic cycle of novels: Castle does not see himself in a priestlike way, but most others do. While discussing the security check, for example, Davis tells Castle: "You take risks—like they say priests have to do. If I really leaked something—without meaning to, of course—I'd come to you for confession . . . expecting a little justice," to which Castle amusingly responds: "I would always absolve the people I like" (114). Castle is indeed ready to absolve any person by virtue of his or her humanity. As Daphna Erdinast-Vulcan suggests, "Like the whisky priest, Castle projects his private, personal, fatherly love and responsibility upon the world at large . . . the suffering and death of the innocents is not a theoretical or ideological question for him; it is as real and close as the suffering of his own child."[51] Castle's dilemma is a matter of conscience, born out of his particular experience of love and sympathy for others.

Under the shadow of Catholicism Greene conceives a fundamental, ontological reality to Castle's human relationships. This relationality correlates well to a Catholic anthropology of personhood (the *Imago Dei*), in which a person's being is in direct proportion and relationship to the Absolute Being of God. In Castle's secularized humanism the "self," the "soul," and the "spirit" are shown to be grounded in a Catholic epistemology of identity and ontology of being. Castle's identity is stabilized in his moral agency toward particular persons and peoples, not in political, sexual, economic, or scientific constructions of the self. Both communism and blind patriotism in various ways ignore the claims of human dignity and agency. The text secularizes Greene's constant dialogical overlay of the humanistic and the religious concerns that had become the hallmark of his theological reading in the last years of his life. As Castle searches for an existential truth that can balance his life, he interprets the possibilities and consequences of his actions in the hope that this balance can be achieved.

Greene's "game" metaphor becomes the "inhuman" factor in a culture unmoored from the Judeo-Christian cultural constructions of the self. Maurice and Sarah Castle stand opposed to the contemporary politicization of the human person, where human love is only a pawn in the discourses of power. Their marriage is the redeeming sacrament in which their love embodies its own reward, a radical and, in Greene's religious imagination, a prophetic stance. The end of the novel suggests that though Castle is spatially and socially cut off from Sarah, their human connection remains intact and immutable. When they speak on the telephone between Moscow and London, "the line was so clear that he might have been speaking from the next room" (242). As one critic notes, in the midst of the spiritual apartheid that informs the text, the novel's closing pages repeat the words "when the spring comes" four times.[52] Castle may lose a great deal in sacrificing himself for others, but he saves his humanity, and in doing so he points to a spring, a victory, a transcendence that reaches beyond the text.

Such sacrifice makes Maurice Castle an *imitatio Christi*, incarnating the *human* in an inhuman world, for Castle's world is devoid of the human factor, much like the postcolonial world of Latin America. Just as do Greene's characters in *The Honorary Consul*, Castle's life and exile embody the humanization of individuals in a dehumanizing world. The reader understands that in losing everything Castle is not spiritually lost because his motives have been pure: he is saved by love. Although his actions look foolish from inside the game of political espionage and its construction of the self, they look familiar from inside Greene's religious imagination. Indeed, the Catholic sensibility of the novel impinges on the text. Catholic images and allusions still inform the reader's understanding of Castle as a priest "without a Church," who in the end offers his peace and comfort on behalf of those threatened in a deadly game of power. As a pilgrim bereft of any vital cultural signs of religious signification, Castle embodies in his commitments and in his actions an ontological understanding of the human person, an emphasis of orthopraxis over systems of belief and a sanctification of the efficacy of moral agency, all inspired by Greene's continuing interaction with his Catholic faith.

5

The Pattern Completed

*The Final Greene/ing of the Catholic Imagination
in* Dr. Fischer of Geneva *and* Monsignor
Quixote

Unfortunately St. Paul gives a definition of love which includes
hope. And many of us today find hope even more difficult than love.
There is an English hymn which I have always liked, 'Abide with
me,' and I always misquote one line. The hymn reads, 'Help of the
helpless, O abide with me', but I always find myself saying, 'Hope
of the hopeless'.

> —Graham Greene, letter to Father Duran
> (5 February 1984)

To believe in God is, in a certain sense, to create Him, even though
He creates us beforehand. It is He who is continually creating Himself in us . . . we do not hope because we believe, but rather we believe because we hope.

> —Miguel de Unamuno, *The Tragic Sense of Life*

The trouble is I don't believe my unbelief.

> —Graham Greene to Father Duran (8 July 1987)

Not in a metaphorical sense but in a physical sense, the Energy of
Incarnation was to flow into, and so illuminate and give warmth to,
even wider and more tightly encircling forms of embrace. . . . Thus I
reached the Heart of the universalized Christ coinciding with the
heart of Amorized Matter.

> —Pierre Teilhard de Chardin,
> *The Heart of Matter* (1950)

Greene's writing during the last decade of his life continued unabated, inter-rupted at times by his involvement in Central America and, closer to home, by his political involvement along the French Riviera.[1] Greene's publications included newly edited collections of short stories, letters to the press, and oc-casional articles, the culmination of his 50 years as a novelist and man of letters. Two major works of fiction published in the 1980s, *Doctor Fischer of Geneva, or the Bomb Party* (1980) and *Monsignor Quixote* (1982), showed Greene's surprising stylistic turn to fablelike compositions: the stark realism of his narrative style was fused with romantic idioms that heightened the sym-bolic weight of his characters.[2] As Greene approached his ninth decade, his writing profoundly embodied Catholic discourses and imagery. The critic A. A. DeVitis compares Greene's late work with the last plays of Shakespeare, for both artists turn away from the previous heroic forms of tragedy to explore broader aspects of Christian humanism.[3] Like *The Tempest* and *The Winter's Tale*, there is something allegorical and even mystical in the spare and focused development of these two novels. They reverberate with a startling complex signification: characters search for meaningful ways to affirm the existence of beauty, love, and goodness, as they witness and reflect on the tragedies of life. Stylistically and thematically, these texts go beyond the existential or merely humanistic constructions that have so defined the critical reading of his work since his Catholic cycle of novels.

The central aspects of Greene's Catholic literary imagination—those orig-inating in the classic themes of the Catholic literary revival and reconstituted in terms of post–Vatican II developments—find a culminating expression in these two late works. Characters persist in voicing often subversive theological speculations on the relationship between God and humanity while struggling to understand the paradoxical claims that are made on them by others. Like-wise, the texts employ a Catholic sacramentality uneasily situated within the corrupt and decadent descriptions of modern life. And Greene continues to offer an incarnational and evolutionary theological vision of history at work, still very much informed by his appreciation of Cardinal Newman, Teilhard de Chardin, and liberation theology. If none of this is new to Greene's religious sensibility, it finds a fresh and clearly focused culmination in these texts. These late works place Greene's religious vision well within a broader Catholicism at the end of the twentieth century, illustrating both the maturation of Greene's literary imagination and its fecund distillation of the interplay between his faith and his fiction.

The Carnivalesque Catholicism in *Doctor Fischer*

The title of this novella immediately announces the dialogical quality of the work.[4] *Doctor Fischer of Geneva, or the Bomb Party* suggests to the reader two possible significations: the life and death story of Doctor Fischer or a tale of the macabre and grotesque "bomb party." In many tones of voice Greene manages to exploit a mixture of genres—allegory, fable, thriller, detective story—to propose various possible ways of reading the text. Georg Gaston, for example, briefly summarizes the following ways in which the novel can be read: "a parabolic study of the nature of evil; a dialectic on the distinction between hating and despising; a commentary on the sickness of greed, an existential love story, or even as an ironic presentation of the strengths and weaknesses of a novelist's self-created world and mind."[5] Yet Gaston misses an important reading of the text: in explicit ways, the tale is a carnivalesque play on the major themes of Greene's religious imagination. Catholic ritual, tropes, and images are turned upside down or are transgressed throughout the text in order to display the macabre effects of jealousy and greed on love. The novella assumes a highly religious quality, subordinating Greene's usual realistic narrative style to a symbolism that points to more epic and metaphysical dramatic structures.

The story is told in the first person by Alfred Jones, a British man in his 50s employed at a large Swiss chocolate factory as a translator for the company's foreign correspondence. He had lost his parents and his own left hand during the London blitz of World War II 30 years earlier; 10 years after that, he had lost his pregnant first wife and unborn child. In what he calls a "near-miracle," Jones meets a young girl of 20, Anna-Luise, and they fall instantly in love. Anna-Luise is the only daughter of the extremely rich widower, Dr. Fischer, who made his fortune by inventing a toothpaste called *Dentophil Bouquet*. She is estranged from her father because of his terrible treatment of her mother. Dr. Fischer is described in diabolical terms as a jealous, proud, and vengeful man. In his effort to discover how far human avarice can go, he inflicts sadistic humiliations on greedy friends (called "Toads" instead of toadies in Anna-Luise's broken English) as the price for an expensive gift. Against Anna-Luise's wish, Jones attends one of these parties—as an observer more than a guest—and his disgust at the humiliation and the groveling of the Toads actually earn him a small level of respect from Dr. Fischer. Jones and Anna-Luise marry and have an idyllic few months of happiness before she dies in a fatal ski accident, caused by trying to swerve around a young boy who had fallen on the slope. Doctor Fischer, who did not attend his daughter's marriage, does not attend her funeral either.

Jones, sick with despair over the loss of his wife (he has unsuccessfully tried to kill himself with an overdose of aspirin) and full of resentment at Dr. Fischer, accepts an invitation to the doctor's final party—the "Bomb Party." It takes place on the snow-covered lawn of Fischer's great white mansion, lit with huge bonfires. After a sumptuous meal, each guest is promised a gift of 2 million francs, which is to be found in a Christmas cracker placed in a bran tub away from the table. They are warned that one of the crackers contains a small bomb that will explode when the cracker is pulled. Fischer gloatingly watches as his guests' greed overcomes their fear of death. Jones wants to die in order to be with his lost love, but when he pulls the final three crackers, he learns that there is no bomb. Even more embittered at the doctor after this ruse, Jones desperately walks away. On the lawn he meets a man named Steiner, whom Doctor Fischer had hounded into poverty because of jealousy: Steiner had secretly shared an intimate love for music with his wife many years ago. Fischer, now frustrated by Jones, meets up with both of these men, the only two (unless one counts Anna-Luise) who had failed to be compromised by Fischer's humiliating games. When Jones and Steiner tell Fischer that he must despise himself for the way he acts, the doctor agrees, and the story ends with Dr. Fischer walking off and shooting himself in the head. Jones looks at Fischer's body, that "bit of rubbish I had once compared in my mind with Jehovah and Satan,"[6] and returns to his solitary life, a chastened man whose dead wife's few effects are now his only treasures.

The fablelike structure of the novella pushes the religious signification to the fore. Dr. Fischer is described as one who "looks very much like Satan," who "mocks others but none mocks him." The carnivalesque aspect of Dr. Fischer's last party suggests a bonfire of the vanities, a ridiculous if deadly satire of the hollowness and hypocrisy of the rich. The party is a subtly staged religious ritual, where the Christian liturgical drama is subverted. Gaston points out, that "Fischer holds his last party in his snow-covered garden (antithetically edenic) and serves his guests with a final banquet (or last supper) before he offers them (communion-like) Christmas crackers, all but one containing a bomb (or the final risk of punishment)."[7] As a parody of Christ presiding over the Last Supper, the party becomes a dramatic performance of a dark morality play. The performative nature of the party is made explicit when one of the Toads, Richard Deane, an alcoholic film actor, objects to being thought of as a mere pawn in a director's drama. Fischer responds: "Are you so sure of that? Haven't you all played your parts for my amusement and your profit? Deane, you for one must have felt quite at home taking my orders" (120). Fischer directs these performances to make present (in the Catholic, theological sense) the primacy of greed in his distorted and hollow understanding of the human person.

The allegorical quality of the text allows for a reading of Dr. Fischer not only as a perversion of Christ but also as a satanic parody of "God the Almighty." Fischer is compared to both Jehovah and Satan, a dangerous presence who hates the whole human race. His own daughter considers him the incarnation of hell (18) and advises Jones not to "let him [Fischer] take you into a high place and show you all the kingdoms of the world" (33). Fischer's hatred for others, the reader finds out, actually began in the seeds of his jealousy: he found his wife enjoying the private company of the poor clerk, Steiner. Fischer was hurt because their clandestine meetings were a "region into which he couldn't follow" (40). He felt betrayed and humiliated by her choice of such a poor and unworthy man, and his hurt pride becomes a disease in which he despises first his wife (who, to escape him, wills herself to die) and, after her death, the Toads, whom he uses to act out his revenge. Yet Fischer claims he is a man who despises more than he hates, and with malevolent logic he corrects Jones on the semantic use of the word:

> To despise comes out of a great disappointment. . . . When one despises, Jones, it's like a deep and incurable wound, the beginning of death. And one must revenge one's wound while there is still time. When the one who inflicted it is dead, one has to strike back others. Perhaps, if I believed in God, I would want to take my revenge on him for having made me capable of disappointment. I wonder by the way—it's a philosophical question—how one would revenge oneself on God. I suppose Christians would say by hurting his son. (105–106)

In the midst of this dialogue on metaphysical questions, the reader hears the voice of Milton's proud angel. Fischer wreaks vengeance on God by despising and inflicting humiliation upon all those around him. As Anna-Luise comments to Jones, "It was his pride, his infernal pride" (39) that made him want to humiliate his wife.

If Dr. Fischer and his Toads portray the ascendancy of avarice and hatred as the essential quality that fuels human actions, Jones and Anna-Luise counter this depiction. The text conveys Greene's most idyllic portrayal of love in his entire oeuvre, one that, like *The Human Factor*, serves here as Greene's transcendental dimension. Indeed, Jones calls their love a "near miracle." This miracle is even more remarkable because it is conceived and born within the affluence of Switzerland and the coercive power of Dr. Fischer's looming presence in their lives. Sarah and Maurice Castle's capacity for love in *The Human Factor* was ultimately thwarted by espionage and exile; Anna-Luise and Jones's love is freed from such political constraints but is nevertheless thwarted by the unpredictable—and meaningless—accidents of life. After Anna-Luise's death, Jones is drawn into Dr. Fischer's net (an apt subversion of Christ, the *Fisher* of men, netting his disciples), but he goes armed with his "memories of love" for his wife. Jones does not succumb to Fischer's game, for he has personally felt the bitterness that engenders Dr. Fischer's humiliations and recognizes that in a small way he carries in himself the same capacity for revenge that now overwhelms Dr. Fischer. With his memory of Anna-Luise and his own insight into himself, Jones brings Fischer face to face with hatred and despair— the final hatred that ultimately will lead to his suicide. "Fischer's suicide at his last supper suggests the despair of Judas, the death of the heart that has drawn inward . . . the biblical adage of winning the world and losing the soul."[8]

Greene further weaves explicitly Catholic discourses through this already deeply religious allegory. Though Jones and Anna-Luise are not Roman Catholics, they attend the Christmas midnight Mass at the nearby abbey because it was "the universal feast of childhood." They are surprised to see Dr. Fischer's Toads there, whose presence makes the Mass seem "as social as a cocktail party" (81). Later in bed, Jones begins a fanciful discussion about the human soul: "I think our souls develop from an embryo just as we do . . . and our embryo soul isn't yet a soul . . . perhaps that is why the Roman Catholic Church invented Limbo" (82). He thinks that he may have a soul, "shop-soiled but still there" and that Anna-Luise certainly does because of her suffering over the loss of her mother. They discuss whether each of the Toads has a soul (they conclude that only one might because "there's something unhappy about him") and then turn more serious in their judgment of Fischer: "He has a soul all right . . . but I think it may be a damned one" (83). Indeed, Dr. Fischer behaves like a lost soul, one that ultimately must be pitied more than hated, and that is exactly what happens at the end of the tale. On the night of the bomb party, Steiner comes to the mansion full of hatred for Dr. Fischer because of the ruin and humiliation he had caused him over the years. Wanting to spit in Fischer's face in one last defiant act, Steiner finds he cannot do it. When he finally confronts Fischer, he later tells Jones, he found that "you see—when it came to the point—I pitied him" (141).

The metaphysical dimension of the novel turns on theological speculation about the nature and image of God—familiar terrain in Greene's religious thought. Anna-Luise, Jones, and Steiner metaphorically declare that Dr. Fischer is like God, or at least aspires to the omnipotence of God. Fischer, too, regards himself in theological terms and thinks "theology an amusing intellectual game" (61). He assumes that his desire to humiliate his wealthy sycophants is very much like God's kind of greediness: "Believers and sentimentalists say that he [God] is greedy for our love. I prefer to think that, judging from the world he is supposed to have made, he can only be greedy for our humiliation, and *that* greed how could he ever exhaust? It's bottomless" (62). Fischer's view of the nature of God expresses more bitterness than even Father León Rivas's theology of the evolution of God's night-side and day-side in *The Honorary Consul.* In the judgment of Dr. Fischer, only the night-side of God reigns supreme because there is no Christ, no salvific Incarnation that places God in the material world. Fischer understands God only in terms of his own experience with his Toads: God thus becomes a giver of presents and bribes that keeps humanity abjectly begging for gratification through all the humiliations that he inflicts on them. The dark intensity of Fischer's image of himself as God takes on the aura of Christian sacrifice, but blasphemously inverted into a black Mass. He tries to explain to Jones:

> 'Yes, but my greed—I told you before—is of a different order. I
> want. . . . ' He raised the Christmas cracker rather as the priest at
> midnight Mass had raised the Host, as though he intended to make
> a statement of grave importance to a disciple—'This is my body.' He
> repeated: 'I want . . . ' and lowered the cracker again. (109)

The repeating ellipses after "I want . . ." suggests that Fischer's insatiable disappointment and his sense of betrayal points to a dissatisfaction that borders on religious obsession. His is a religious-inspired quest to make real—to rehearse through his humiliating parties—his vision upon the world.

Fischer's discourse on God and the continued reference to Fischer as a Godlike character has led some critics to judge the novella not only as Greene's most pessimistic theological speculation on the nature of belief but also as the truest revelation of his own unorthodox theological vision of God. Gaston, for example, argues that, "Dr. Fischer is used as an oblique or metaphorical reflection of Greene's beliefs. This is why, by considering Fischer carefully, one can come to a true understanding of Greene's final moral vision." Gaston oddly concludes that Fischer voices Greene's theological position: "Fischer comes to despise himself and kills himself. What can this mean in the allegorical sense? The answer seems to point directly at what has happened to Greene's religious faith. God no longer exists because for Greene he has committed suicide. To put it in a less exotic way, the idea of God has died in Greene's mind."[9] Fischer's thoughts and desires are thus understood as expressions of Greene's own post-Catholic, even anti-Christian fatalism. But such conclusions seem premature, for it is precisely the competing analogies to God's image embodied in characters that anchor the text's theological vision. Gaston's assessment would mean that Fischer, and not Jones, speaks for Greene, yet Jones's first person narration, and his continual claim that "there is something mad about Fischer," seem to suggest otherwise. By the end of the novella, Fischer's thoughts on God are proven inadequate, and Fischer admits as much to Jones and to Steiner.

In an orthodox and specifically Catholic manner, Greene has consistently created fictions in which the human construction of the self stands or falls on how well it is proportionate to the image of God revealed in the drama of Christ. The reader understands that Fischer's image of God is faulty, flawed by his own self-hatred and aggrandizement: "Don't I wish to humiliate? And they say he made us in his image. Perhaps he found he was a rather bad craftsman and he is disappointed in the result. One throws a faulty article into the dustbin" (62). It is also flawed because there is no mediating, incarnational reference to Christ as the aesthetic standard of the *Imago Dei*. Jones insists that Fischer acts as if he were God "the Almighty," an image of God solely constructed in terms of omnipotence and, in this case, a will to manipulate borne out of hatred. As to Christ, Jones claims that Fischer "would certainly have despised Christ for being the son of a carpenter, if the New Testament had not proved in time to be such a howling commercial success" (41). Fischer's materialistic assumptions of class and wealth occlude his comprehension of the mystery of the Incarnation.

If Fischer is allegorically related to an idea of a devilish God of omnipotence, surely Anna-Luise and Jones point to an idea of God that relates to Christ's suffering and love. Greene thus creates a discursive counterpart to Dr. Fischer's conceptualization in Anna-Luise and her relationship to Jones. The text suggests a human-divine image that does correlate to a more orthodox consideration: Anna-Luise is called "the living image" of her dead mother, the antithesis of her father. Fischer *sees* this in her physical appearance and rejects her for it because it reminds him of his wife; Steiner *sees* this image in her and faints because it reminds him of the happiest time in his life, with her mother; and Jones *sees* this in her and holds her image in his memory as he goes to one last battle at Fischer's party. The form of Anna-Luise's beautiful image as seen by these characters suggests a religious signification that appropriates a Catholic aesthetic of being drawn to Christ. If there is such a thing as a soul, Anna-Luise is said to have one because she has suffered the loss of her mother and has not succumbed to her father's temptations. And Anna-Luise's words to Jones echo Christ in the Gospel about the expansive claims of love on one another (Mark 3:33): "You're my lover and my father, my child and my mother; you're the whole family, the only family I want" (17). The love that the two have for one another is said to be miraculous, and its power liberates both of them from the oppressive orbit of greed and flattery that defines their surroundings. Yet even here Greene keeps this reading of romantic love from becoming too much like a fairytale; rather, love is real, embodied in the material world, and compromised by death. Life after the loss of such love is a painfully negotiated existence. Jones borders on despair as he uneasily negotiates the loss of love, a distinctly different kind of despair than the self-hatred of Dr. Fischer.

Jones's relationship to Anna-Luise takes on even greater religious significance through Greene's constant use of Catholic images that sacramentalize Anna-Luise's effects. This is found most clearly at two moments in the text. Jones had given Anna-Luise a white sweater for Christmas, which she wears on her ski trip. When a crowd forms around the accident victim, Jones was first relieved that it wasn't Anna-Luise because the woman "was wearing quite a different kind of sweater . . . a red sweater" (90), but a moment later he realizes that it was her white sweater stained through by blood. The sweater takes on an ontological weight for Jones—an object that makes Anna-Luise painfully present to him. Jones recalls the sweater when Dr. Fischer sends a message to him about the trust money left for Anna-Luise by her mother: "Perhaps [Fischer] gets the money—the blood money. I remembered her white Christmas sweater stained with blood" (102). And as he drives to Fischer's house to renounce the money, his memory goes back to the "all-red sweater on the stretcher" (103). Theologically, it suggests that the Christmas sweater becomes, in effect, a Good Friday sweater. For Jones, Anna-Luise's sweater acts as a mediating grace. She is not only a victim of circumstance but also a martyr, a sign for Jones of the destructive world that surrounds him in Dr. Fischer's presence.

With the death of Fischer, Jones's hatred of him also dies; at the same time his love for Anna-Luise lives on in his memory. The strong sacramental overtones in Jones's accounting of this memory only increase:

> As long as I lived I could at least remember her. I had two snap-
> shots of her and a note in her hand written to make an appointment
> before we lived together; there was the chair which she used to sit
> in, and the kitchen where she had jangled the plates before we
> bought the machine. All these were like the relics of bone they keep
> in Roman Catholic churches. (143)

Jones goes about his days in his memory of love. When he cooks himself a dish that Anna-Luise used to prepare for him, he notes. "I heard myself repeating a line which I had heard spoken by the priest at the midnight Mass at

St. Maurice: 'As often as you do these things you shall do them in memory of me'" (143). His memory of Anna-Luise and the relics of their life together become for Jones the closest claim to a kind of religious faith, captured in Catholic imagery and liturgical language. For Jones, the mystery of love defines the real, for he continues to discover that love beyond Anna-Luise's death.

With its constant reference to Catholic images and ideas, the fablelike structure of the novella indicates Greene's religious imagination at play. Yet the story resists any easy, monologic religious reading because, as David Lodge notes, "One glimpses here the possibility of accommodating the fable to orthodox Christian faith . . . but the premise that God exists remains a hypothesis in this book: there is not a single believer among the characters—only non-believers, ex-believers and would-be believers."[10] On the surface this is true, for Greene situates his dark tale in the affluent center of a post-Christian Europe, suffering from spiritual aridity. In the end, Jones feels abandoned, without belief and without hope. He discovers that death is "no longer an answer— it was an irrelevance." He muses after Anna-Luise's death that "only if I had believed in a God could I have dreamt that the two of us would ever have that *jour le plus long*. It was as if my small half-belief had somehow shriveled with the sight of Doctor Fischer's body." He states that "evil was as dead as a dog and why should goodness have more immortality than evil?" (142–143). Thus, if the tale correlates to Christian faith, it does so in the manner of dialectical language in Greene's religious imagination: it is a prophetic tale, more tragic than comic. The Catholic images and subversive theological speculations embedded in the tale serve as a "deconstructive therapy," revealing the fundamental delusions in contemporary interpretations of the human person. Chastened by such knowledge, Jones qualifies his agnosticism in the final words of his tale, noting that if his hatred dies with Dr. Fischer, the memory of his love for Anna-Luise lives on. It is a kind of memory that is informed by Christianity and made present through Catholic modes of thought and feeling. This same sense of the memory of love and its powerful trace in the midst of loss will be more fully articulated and religiously rendered as a transformative, grace-filled experience in Greene's next novel, *Monsignor Quixote*.

The *Quixotic* Heart of Vatican II Catholicism

In his next and last great novel, Greene's religious imagination becomes the central matrix through which his literary creativity takes form. *Monsignor Quixote* (1982) is a culminating work that explicitly refutes the division of his fiction into Catholic and non-Catholic or religious and political categories. Critics who divide Greene's works into such groupings have tried to come to terms with this novel in various ways. Maria Couto claims that it is "neither Catholic nor Communist, but essentially Christian and humanist, encompassing the ideals and values of both," whereas John Spurling considers it "a second coda to Greene's group of Catholic novels."[11] Contrary to these views, I would argue that *Monsignor Quixote* is overwhelmingly more Catholic than communist, more Christian than humanist, and more a new development—stylistically and thematically—than a mere coda to Greene's celebrated Catholic cycle. Indeed, Greene's Catholic imagination not only serves to frame plot and character but also becomes a principal theme, voiced in the text: "Perhaps we are all fictions, Father, in the mind of God."[12]

The novel was initially conceived as a short story to commemorate the deepening friendship between Greene and the Spanish priest Leopoldo Duran. Much of the novel's geographical description and theological conversation were taken from Greene's many summer vacations in which he and Duran would tour the Spanish countryside.[13] It began as a short story, published in the 1978 Christmas issue of the Catholic journal *The Tablet* as "How Father Quixote Became a Monsignor," and it became the first chapter of the novel.[14] Greene's overriding literary and religious concerns are brought together in a style that is as contemplative as it is comical, whereby the traditional realism of his technique is undercut by the transparency of his character's search for a viable way to understand the timeless problems of human life. The text is filled with self-referential humor (the monsignor fears he is becoming "a whiskey priest") and many intertextual discourses that inform the character's thoughts and actions (there are direct quotes from the writings of Marx, Augustine, Unamuno, Francis de Sales, Cervantes, the eighteenth-century spiritual writer Father Caussade, the Bible, the liturgical texts of the Latin Mass, and countless references to other persons and texts). In the midst of these various interpolations that thematically mark the narrative, Greene reduces the action to the barest picaresque form to create a novel that reverberates with metaphysical wonder.

Set in post-Franco Spain, the novel's plot humorously comments on Cervantes' *Don Quixote* by making the monsignor a "real" descendant of his fictional namesake.[15] Quixote, a gentle and modest parish priest of El Toboso, is quite by chance elevated to the rank of monsignor as a result of a hospitable encounter with a curial bishop from Rome. Encouraged to take a respite by his own unfriendly bishop, Quixote decides to travel with his friend, the town's communist ex-mayor whom he affectionately calls Sancho. Loaded with plenty of local wine and cheese, they take off in Quixote's car, appropriately named Rocinante, after the don's famous horse. In the comic journey that follows,

Quixote spends a night in a brothel, unwittingly views a pornographic film, hears a confession in a public toilet, and helps a thief escape from the police. These events are tied together by personal conversations amid wine, food, and fellowship, which deepen the bond between the two travelers. Though Quixote's motivations throughout all these encounters are innocent, his local bishop finds them scandalous, and he and his secretary, Father Herrera, succeed in having the monsignor captured and brought back to El Toboso. Suspected of madness and made a prisoner in his own home, he flees with Sancho's help. Their escape takes them to the region of Galicia, where they visit Señor Diego's winery and hear of an idolatrous Marian feast in which the priests of the district have sold places of honor in the procession and have allowed the statue of the Virgin to be covered with money. Outraged at this blasphemy, Quixote puts on his ecclesiastical regalia and goes into town, where he disrupts the procession and is hit on the head by an acolyte's censer. With the crowd calling for their arrest, Sancho and Quixote flee in Rocinante toward the Trappist monastery at Osera. The Guardia pursue them and shoot their tires, thereby causing a wreck in which the monsignor is injured. Taken into the monastery by a Father Leopoldo, Quixote is medicated and made to rest. At three in the morning he sleepwalks his way into the chapel with Sancho, Father Leopoldo, and a visiting American scholar in tow. In a dreamlike state, he performs an imaginary Mass before them, centered on the eucharistic narrative. Quixote consumes the imaginary host and wine and then turns to Sancho and says, "Compañero . . . you must kneel" (226), at which time the mayor falls to his knees and duly receives an imaginary host. Quixote then falls into the arms of Sancho and dies. The tale ends on the following day with a discussion among those who were present, each voicing a different opinion about the veracity of Quixote's Mass. Sancho leaves them, transformed as "the love which he had begun to feel for Father Quixote . . . seemed now to live and grow in spite of the final separation and final silence" (232).

Even those critics who argue that Greene's religious faith is idiosyncratic— that it is heretical at worst or humanist at best—recognize religious themes as the centerpiece of the novel, especially in terms of Greene's lifelong dialectic between faith and belief and in his hope for a constructive dialogue between Marxism and Catholicism. In almost ritual-like conversations, the monsignor and the mayor discuss the similarities and dissimilarities between their respective beliefs, one a Catholic, the other a Marxist.[16] Through their journey together, Quixote slowly comes to appreciate "how sharing a sense of doubt can bring men together perhaps even more than sharing a faith" (48). The uncertainty of any ideological claim becomes the neutral ground where understanding and friendship are possible. Yet doubt is not an end in itself but a beginning point of engagement, revealing a common claim for the necessity of negotiating and constructing meaning. Greene is certainly influenced here by the Spanish philosopher Miguel de Unamuno (1864–1937), whose fideism, inspired by Pascal and Kierkegaard, resonated with Greene in his own struggle to understand his faith.[17] Unamuno claimed that reason was the necessary enemy of faith, and the never-ending conflict between them engenders a doubt and uncertainty that bring forth a truer expression of faith. For Unamuno, it is ultimately a faith in a suffering God:

> Suffering tells us we exist; suffering tells us those who love exist; suffering tells us the world we live in exists, and suffering tells us that God exists and suffers; and this is the suffering of anguish, the anguish to survive and be eternal. It is anguish which reveals God to us and makes us place our love in Him. To believe in God means to love Him, and to love Him is to sense His suffering and have compassion for Him.[18]

In *Ways of Escape*, Greene admits that he had read Unamuno's *The Tragic Sense of Life* and *The Life of Don Quixote*. Unamuno's text "continued to work its way through the cellars of the unconscious," so that by the time he had completed writing *A Burnt-Out Case* (1961) he had found himself "in that tragi-comic region of La Mancha."[19]

Unamuno describes such a region of uncertainty, doubt, and distrust of theology as sacred because it allows for mystery once again to be at the heart of religious faith. This dialectic between faith and doubt runs through Greene's novel. The mayor, who is "rather afraid of mystery," admits to the monsignor: "You drew me to you because I thought you were the opposite of myself. . . . I was drawn to you because I thought you were a man without doubts" (184). Surprised by this the monsignor responds: "Doubt is not treachery as you communists seem to think. Doubt is human" (185). Sancho, committed to the materialist ideology of Marxism, sees reality as a hermetic interplay of biological and socioeconomic forces that can be known with rational certainty. For the monsignor, such certitude would destroy faith, and thus doubt is essential to fostering faith. In such an exacting world of science and positivism, doubt is a profoundly humanizing act precisely because it forces one to transcend the epistemologically narrow categories of what is real for metaphysical claims of what is true.

Moreover, the doubt that Quixote suffers from and that Greene seems to celebrate is not a doubt over the existence of a spiritual reality, as some critics seem to suggest;[20] rather, it is the religious doubt of Kierkegaard and Pascal, doubt of one's ability to fathom the attendant mysteries of human life. Quixote is frightened by the egotistical satisfaction and security that come from either ideological position, whether the materialism of Marx or the triumphant scholasticism of the Catholic Church. Yet that is not to say that Quixote doubts the underlying dramatic movement of the Christian story. Indeed, he considers the foundation of his faith to be "in a historic fact—that Christ died on the Cross and rose again" (74). As John Desmond points out in his insightful study of the novel, "While Quixote lives in the typical Greenean paradox in which doubt guarantees mystery, he does not doubt the essence of Christianity, the Incarnation and the Resurrection of Christ, which for him is the true reality."[21] Doubt thus serves a dialectical purpose in Quixote's religious imagination, allowing him to see again a horizon of mystery beyond the reductive certitudes of human knowledge. Quixote understands that without doubt, there is no faith, and he is instinctively horrified, wondering to himself, "Can a man live without faith? . . . God forbid" (69). If mutual doubt is the common ground where the monsignor and the mayor meet, it is only to move first the monsignor and then the mayor onto more mysterious ground. Quixote prays that his friend be "saved by doubt" from the rigorous certitude and righteousness of the Marxist thesis.

Greene's reading of progressive Catholic theologians, his travels to Latin America, and not least of all, his growing bond with Father Leopoldo Duran brought his Catholic concerns to the foreground of the novel. Like *The Honorary Consul, Monsignor Quixote* presents religious discourses that exemplify post–Vatican II formulations. I will look first at those aspects of the text that illustrate the contradictory responses that Catholics—including Greene—continued to feel in the wake of the changing paradigms inaugurated by the Council. The more easily discernable traits in the novel are the dialogical exchanges about Marxism and Catholicism, moral theology, liturgical change, and ecclesiastical power. Second, and more important, I want to conclude with the ways in which I think the novel extends Greene's Catholic imagination and demonstrates the theological development in his overall literary project.

Unlike the extremely tense confrontations between ideological positions in *The Power and the Glory* and *The Honorary Consul*, the geography of post-Franco Spain allows the monsignor and the communist mayor a freer and more affirming exchange that mirrors the cooperative hopes of Vatican II. "Dialogue" is a key term of the council documents, and Greene creates a novel structured by theological and political dialogue, in which the conversations between differing positions reveal deeper affinities between characters. Quixote lends Sancho a book on moral theology and Sancho encourages Quixote to read *The Communist Manifesto*. Quixote reminds Sancho "how Marx defended the monastic orders of England and condemned Henry VIII" (41), as Sancho reminisces that, as a university student, Unamuno's religious faith kept him "in the Church with my half-belief" (98). Quixote reads Marx because he wants to understand Sancho, and he honors the idealism, if not the ideological suppositions, present in both Marx and his friend: "It's the work of a good man. A man as good as you are—and just as mistaken" (111).

Though critics often take the novel as Greene's assimilation of Catholicism and communism into some form of unidiomatic humanism, the text betrays such a reading. There is an affirmation of the positive intentions of communist theory in general, but Quixote's remarks consistently point out the "mistaken" assumptions of such an ideology. When the mayor endeavors a Marxist interpretation of the parable of the prodigal son, the result is more a sign of Marxism's failure to convince than an attempt at rendering such a reading plausible. Sancho's version of the parable begins with the prodigal son, "so disgusted by the bourgeois world in which he had been brought up that he got rid of his wealth in the quickest way possible—perhaps he even gave it away and in a Tolstoyan gesture he became a peasant" (50). Quixote playfully listens to Sancho's version but in the end claims that "your story begins to sound almost as dull as my breviary" (51). Sancho's revisionist reading feels forced and fanciful, an abstraction that in the end does not persuade. Peter Christensen argues that "Greene, for all the sympathy the novel seems to extend to Marxism, has written a narrative which virtually eschews economics and politics. . . . Greene's Spaniards seem less class-conscious than the Mayor's Prodigal Son. If they are class-conscious, the Mayor seems unable to point this out."[22] Quixote's sympathy with Sancho's beliefs at the level of personal intention and practical goals constitutes a variant form of the orthopraxis that Greene, like liberationist theologians, claims as the true, if only, meeting place between Marxism and Catholicism.

The humorous attacks on moral theology in the novel—especially the Church's stand on birth control—point to Greene's obvious engagement in Catholic theology since the Council. The monsignor's only currency with current theological developments comes from his monthly journal: "There were criticisms in it referring sometimes to dangerous ideas—spoken even by a cardinal, in Holland or Belgium, he forgot which—or written by a priest who had a Teutonic name" (16). These allusions to Edward Schillebeeckx and Hans Küng situate the exchanges on sex and birth control in the tensions that resulted after the promulgation of *Humane Vitae* by Pope Paul VI in 1968. As was shown in chapter 3, Greene's reasoned dissent on the issue of birth control is based on his theological reading, and his position is well documented in his personal letters and in a number of late interviews. Greene makes droll fun out of moral distinctions involving sex as Quixote and Sancho discuss the theology text by Father Heribert Jone, a standard presentation of the scholasticism of pre–Vatican II moral theology.[23] After a comical exchange over Jone's moral casuistry, Quixote tells his friend: "You may laugh at Father Jone, and I have laughed with you, God forgive me. But Sancho, moral theology is not the Church." Quixote clarifies his statement: "His [Jone's] book is only like a book of military regulations. Saint Francis De Sales wrote a book of eight hundred pages on the love of God. The word love doesn't come into Father Jone's rules and I think, perhaps I am wrong, that you won't find the phrase 'mortal sin' in Saint Francis' book" (79). Actions motivated by love and not law are the moral compass for Quixote's life and his ministry.

Quixote's understanding of moral theology honors motivation and intention over rules and regulations. As the two friends argue over who committed worse crimes, the Spanish Inquisitor Torquemada or Stalin, Sancho insists that "motives in men's minds are a mystery," which in Sancho's usage of the word implies a relativist position. Yet Quixote defends Torquemada precisely because of intentionality: "At least he thought he was leading his victims toward eternal happiness" (38). Later, when Sancho asks why the monsignor felt justified to hide a criminal in the trunk of Rocinante, he answers that moral judgments are complicated: "So much depends on motive, after all" (130). Contrary to his bishop and Father Herrera, Quixote ultimately grounds his moral vision on the primacy of conscience—"It is the law which was put into our hearts at birth" (87)—a position that echoes back through Cardinal Newman's writings and had gained a privileged status at the Second Vatican Council. Quixote finds sustenance in the formation of his conscience not in scholastic thought but in the Gospels and the spiritual writers of his faith—St. John of the Cross, Saint Theresa, and St. Francis de Sales. In conversation with Father Herrera, a doctor of moral theology, Quixote says that "another sound base is God's love," to which the young priest responds, "But we mustn't forget His justice either. . . . Jone makes a very clear distinction between love and justice" (31–32). When such a conflict between justice and mercy occurs, Quixote errs on the side of mercy: where conscience is troubled, Quixote relies on the practice of Christian love to guide his thoughts and actions.

Finally, the text plays subtly on two issues hotly contested in post–Vatican II Catholicism: liturgical renewal and ecclesiastical authority. As has been noted earlier, Greene found the postconciliar vernacular liturgy less than inspiring, an uneasy accommodation to the Protestant forms of worship that he left behind after his conversion. Greene's discomfort is reflected in the monsignor's love for the old Latin Mass. Quixote goes along with all the new liturgical changes but finds it a less satisfying rite. He personally offers the prayers that had been such an important part of his training as a priest, admitting to

Sancho that he continues to pray quietly to himself the words from John's gospel that ended the Latin Mass: "He was in the world, and the world was made by Him, and the world knew Him not" (25). The young Father Herrera stands in opposition to the monsignor not only in the dictates of moral theology but in liturgical practice as well. The changes in liturgy become a sign of the chasm that exists between the two churchmen. While at dinner together, Quixote realizes, "he could never communicate with Father Herrera on anything which touched the religion they were supposed to share. Father Herrera was in favor of the new Mass . . ." (62). At the climactic and unauthorized liturgy (the bishop has deprived him of his faculties), the monsignor celebrates in a dreamlike condition "the old Latin Mass, but it was in an oddly truncated form" (224).[24] The final Mass is highly personal, voicing only the most cherished parts of the rite as he races toward the moment when he consumes the Host and offers it to Sancho.

Quixote's preference for the Tridentine liturgy is as much about coercion by ecclesiastical authority as it is about the church's attempt at modernization, for Quixote feels the vernacular has been unjustly mandated from Rome. The theological emphasis on discipline and punishment, what Quixote calls "the Gospel of Fear," is linked both to the Council's liturgical reform at the same time that it is conflated with the authoritarianism of a curial Church bureaucracy. The post–Vatican II liturgy in the novel is always associated with figures of authority, implying that Greene's complaint is with the authoritarianism of the hierarchy. The text broadens this complaint by many references to the conservative lay organization Opus Dei, founded in 1928 in support of the ruthless dogmatism of Franco's Spain. When Quixote and Sancho arrive in Madrid at an ecclesiastical clothing store, the monsignor observes the attendant at the counter: "such a man was almost certainly a member of Opus Dei—that club of intellectual Catholic activists who he could not fault and yet who he could not trust" (58). And later a member of Opus Dei working for the Ministry of the Interior helps the bishop find Quixote and kidnap him back to El Toboso. Sancho voices Greene's oft-quoted charge that the Vatican curia is much like the Stalinist bureaucracy—more interested in its self-perpetuation than in its ideals: "He [Stalin] very nearly killed Communism . . . just as the Curia has killed the Catholic Church," but Quixote responds, "Not entirely, Sancho. Here beside you is at least one Catholic in spite of the Curia" (183). However provocative the comparison, Greene voices the complaint of many Catholics about the exercise of curial power after the Council. The humane and optimistic documents of Vatican II implied that the Church's hierarchy had become sensitive to balancing freedom and responsibility, renewal and tradition. Some Catholics, Greene included, thought that after the Council the Vatican Curia reverted to the entrenched pre–Vatican II paradigm of the Church as an organization of static perfection in which rules of conduct and Church discipline determined one's Catholic orthodoxy and one's influence in the Church.[25]

Much of the above analysis makes clear Greene's involvement with the changing paradigms of Vatican II theology in his literary imagination. But does the novel also show a Catholic milieu that does more than comment on the various developments in the Church? Does *Monsignor Quixote*, in effect, suggest a further dramatic and culminating development in the Catholic literary aesthetic in Greene's work? The following theological reading of the novel illustrates how it became Greene's most thorough investigation of the effects of the Incarnation on his literary imagination. Greene embeds the discourse of this Christian doctrine in a variety of ways: a Teilhardian understanding of the spiritualization of matter; a Christological, aesthetic apprehension of reality; an extended development of sacramentality in the Eucharist; and the discursive play between religious faith and the creation of literary fiction.

As has already been suggested, Greene's texts attribute an ontological significance to reality, in which metaphysical meaning can be found in and through the persons, events, and history of the characters. In *Monsignor Quixote* Greene comes closest to grounding this ontological position in the Incarnation of Christ, whereby the redemption of matter is part of the universal, dramatic, historical movement of divine love. Indeed, John Desmond argues that this novel is Greene's most Christological, maintaining that Greene "explicitly argues out the question of the 'meaning of matter' in the many debates between the Monsignor and the Communist Sancho."[26] Desmond reads the theological implications of the novel in light of William Lynch's claim for the analogical contours of a Catholic imagination, whereby the entry of Christ into history revolutionizes matter and thus revolutionizes a Christian view of what is real. In Desmond's reading of Lynch, the historical act of Christ's incarnation, death, and resurrection mysteriously transforms the possibilities of creation by constructing the analogical equation of God's relationship to matter in new terms, or what Lynch calls "a second or new creation." The dramatic form of Christ's life in human history gives new energy to the ontological significance of creation: all created beings share proportionately in the energy of Christ's divinity.[27] Lynch's thought echoes Teilhard de Chardin, for both propose a "Christic energy" at work in the material world:

> It is only progressively, after it has the unbreakable confidence that there is some essential Christic development in supernatural history, that the new imagination begins to assume the order of creation and lift it into its own vitality. Thus Christ is water, gold, butter, food, a

harp, a dove, the day, a house, merchant, fig, gate, stone, book,
wood, light, medicine, oil, bread, arrow, salt, turtle, risen sun, way,
and many things besides.[28]

The evolutionary views of Lynch and Teilhard complement one another in
arguing for a sacramentalized vision of reality: both assert that the unleashing
of the Incarnation upon the material world assumes an ever-increasing spiritual transformation of matter by the energy of love.

Monsignor Quixote enacts just such a spiritual process. Though the novel
is filled with a plethora of voices that suggest multiple ways in which to read
the text, the overwhelming majority of them come from the spiritual writers
who inform Quixote's understanding of his faith. On his journey he takes with
him St. Francis de Sales' *The Love of God* and randomly reads: "Among the
reflections and resolutions it is good to make use of colloquies, and speak
sometimes to our Lord, sometimes to the Angels, to the Saints, and to oneself,
to one's own heart, to sinners, and even to inanimate creatures" (93). The novel
is a series of colloquies in which the monsignor speaks with great love to God;
to Sancho; to his favorite saint, "Señorita Martin of Lisieux"; and to his car.
After reading this text Quixote immediately thinks of Rocinante and says, "Forgive me. I have driven you too hard" (93). Indeed, Rocinante is given a place
of honor throughout the novel, an inanimate creature worthy of Quixote's love
and care. Thinking of his car, Quixote asks the visiting Roman prelate, "Would
you consider it heretical to pray to God for the life of a horse?" (10). The bishop
replies that a prayer for the terrestrial life of a creature is allowable but not for
its eternal life: "It is true there is a movement in the Church which would
grant the possibility that a dog may have what one may call an embryo soul,
though personally I find the idea sentimental and dangerous. We mustn't open
unnecessary doors by imprudent speculation. If a dog has a soul, why not a
rhinoceros or a kangaroo?" Yet Quixote, "plunged far in his own thoughts,"
has extended the logical consequence of the mystery of the Incarnation onto
the salvation of all material being, even comically to his car. Noting Quixote's
contemplation, the bishop tells him, "These are great mysteries" (11).

Sancho, the materialist, will also be forced to reconsider the mystery in
matter during his discussions with Quixote. When Sancho wakes up to find
that the monsignor has been forcefully taken back to his parish in El Toboso,
he initially plans to make his way across the border to safety. Yet, as he later
confesses to his friend, "I nearly didn't come. . . . When I found you gone—I
thought, I'll borrow Rocinante and make for Portugal . . . [but] I looked at your
damn purple socks and your bib, and your new shoes which we had bought
in León, and I remembered suddenly the way you had blown up that balloon."[29]

Quixote responds, "They seem insufficient reasons," but Sancho reflects, "They were sufficient for me" (187–188). The finite material of socks, clerical bib, and shoes sufficiently makes present to Sancho his commitment to Quixote. When the mayor leaves the monastery after his friend's death, he passes by Rocinante smashed against the wall: "He insisted with a kind of ferocity on the likeness, fighting for a certainty: that the human being is also a machine. But Father Quixote had felt love for this machine" (231). In the end, Sancho's biological determinism and epistemological certainty are placed in doubt by his sharing in Quixote's mystical vision of the material world.

Quixote's faith professes that love is the mystery discovered in material reality. Another quote from St. Francis de Sales becomes a central metaphorical phrase in the text: "Iron has such a sympathy with Adamant that as soon as it is touched with the virtue thereof it turns toward it, it begins to stir and quiver with a little hopping . . . and thereupon it doth advance and bear itself towards the Adamant, striving by all means possible to be united to it" (124).[30] Quixote reads the text after viewing with Sancho a mildly pornographic film called *A Maiden's Prayer*. Thinking the film was about Mary, the mother of Jesus, Quixote is bewildered by the simulated sex: "They seemed to suffer such a lot. . . . They didn't seem to find it pleasurable—or perhaps they were bad actors. . . . They took it so seriously that I was really afraid to laugh" (123). Quixote understands human love in analogical terms—in proportion to the love of God, even if only the slightest measure of that love. He finds the sexual "hopping" in the film funny because it seems a farcical rendition of what he believes love to be: "Oh yes, he had seen a great deal of hopping, he thought, but he had not experienced the lively love" (124). The aesthetic standard for "lively love" is the movement of the Incarnation into the world of matter. Watching the actors unsuccessfully attempt to project an image of love on the screen and wondering if "perhaps he had even less capacity to love than a piece of iron," he questions his own humanity, praying silently, "O God, make me human, let me feel temptation. Save me from my indifference" (125). "The mechanical hopping of bodies," John Desmond notes, "is a travesty of love, a debasement of the human spirit into a totally physical exchange. Quixote's wish to experience sexual desire so that he can claim a fuller humanity is mistaken; the real temptation is to fail to find love in the workings of the physical world."[31] The temptation, then, is to become a materialist like Sancho, seeing the biological urges as the natural end of human desire.

The "hopping" metaphor is playfully related to the conversation about "jumping" into faith between Father Leopoldo and Professor Pilbeam at the Trappist monastery. Hopping is not only the aesthetic consequence of the divine embrace of matter but also a Pascalian wager in which one can willfully hop into faith. If logical belief fails to convince, one can choose to rely on the instincts of faith. When the monk, whose study of Descartes led him to faith, is asked by the professor why he chose a severe monastic order after his struggle with doubts, he answers that "when one has to jump it is so much safer to jump in deep water." The professor answers back, "I decided long ago that I was not a jumper" (215–216). Immediately after saying this, the two men jump as they hear a car smash into the monastery wall, bringing to a climax the text's most profound participation in this "hopping love." Quixote, sedated after the crash, tells Sancho in a strong voice, "By this hopping you can recognize love" (223).

This hopping action is dramatized in the celebration of the Eucharist, especially in the strangely shared communion between Quixote and Sancho. As the monsignor is about to place the imaginary communion wafer on Sancho's tongue, he twice intones, "by this hopping" before collapsing into Sancho's arms. The mayor is brought into the mysterious realm of love in and by his attachment to the monsignor. The spiritual force of their affection is textually consummated in a eucharistic rite that celebrates the exaltation of kenosis—self-emptying love—as the form of divine-human love. Now in the orbit of Quixote's love for him, Sancho moves into a state of doubt about what has just happened to him. Like Father Leopoldo, his uncertainty offers him the possibility of jumping, to wager his life on such mystery. Though he tells the monk that he still prefers Marxian certitude to mystery, the mayor nonetheless wonders "to what end" his love for the monsignor will lead him.

The standard for what is real is most strikingly signified in Quixote's faith in Christ. Quixote affirms that his belief is in a "historical fact," that Jesus was a real man who suffered, died, and rose from the dead. Early in the novel, he feels dread after waking from a dream in which Christ is triumphantly saved from the cross by a legion of angels. Christ gets down from the cross before death, acclaimed and worshipped as God by Roman soldiers and Jewish leaders alike. The dream sequence constitutes Greene's strongest textual claim that religious doubt plays a necessary role in nurturing authentic faith. Quixote's dread is indeed framed in terms of doubt, belief, and faith, but more important the dream shows the Manichean temptation to force an inadequate vision of the divine on reality. Quixote's dream subtly criticizes the Manichean imagination's inability to see the divine within the fallenness of material reality. If Christ does not die on the cross, then the dualistic vision of God persists: the Incarnation has not fully penetrated the ultimate experience of finite matter. Such is William Lynch's argument that the Christological imagination understands reality in an *adequate* way because the drama of Christian salvation takes human tragedy seriously: "This achievement of tragedy has always occurred when the dramatic text has allowed itself to move through human time to the very last point of human finitude and helplessness."[32] The tragic drama of Christ's death on the cross is necessary if God is both to respond to and embrace the finite particularity of human life. Participation in such tragedy brings a person to the experience of a deep beauty and exaltation, but not by the route of beauty and exaltation, which is inadequate to the full range of human experience. The exaltation in the Resurrection of Christ is experienced as hope: in terms of faith, it is God's promise to be present in the brokenness of human life. Christ's Incarnation, then, is participation in such beauty and exaltation, but by the way of the cross. Again, Lynch dynamically summarizes this Christological process: "Christ moved down into all the realities of man to get to his Father."[33] Part of Quixote's dread is that Christ would not have entered all the realities of human life. He prays, "God save me from such a belief" (65). Greene's text is making a very Catholic claim: it is the faith that God is in the reality of Good Friday that allows for the hope of Easter Sunday.

The drama of Christ's passion and death becomes, then, the supreme standard of what is real, grounding human identity in the image of Christ. Greene continues to portray Quixote's identity as a priest with his now well-refined Catholic literary aesthetic: the monsignor's journey of faith draws him into a greater participation into the form and image of Christ. He becomes an *alter Christus*, a sacrament who mediates God's spirit by conforming himself to the drama of Christ's life, death, and resurrection. Yet interesting and new to this novel is how those around Quixote challenge this Catholic aesthetic—the conformation of self to Christ—by trying to force the analogy of his identity out of the realm of faith and into the realm of fiction. Throughout the text the monsignor's claim to be the descendent of his fictional ancestor, Don Quixote, competes with his desire to be understood as a simple priest. All of the characters are aware of Cervantes's novel and constantly refer to it and even quote from it. The bishop, who is offered hospitality by Quixote, urges him "to go forth like your ancestor, Don Quixote, on the high roads of the world" (14). The mayor, affectionately taking on the fictional role of Sancho, continues to recall the parallels of their journey across Spain to that of the don's. Quixote's own bishop asks with incredulity, "How can he be descended from a fictional character? . . . A character in a novel by an overrated writer called Cervantes—a novel moreover with many disgusting passages which in the days of the Generalissimo would not even have passed the censor" (4). In fact, conflating Monsignor Quixote's life with Cervantes's story of the don more easily allows the bishop of El Toboso to condemn him as insane.[34] If the dramatic movement of Quixote's life can be defined merely in relationship to a fictionalized character, then those around him can dismiss his greater claim of a theological analogy to Christ and render him a mad man, like the fictional don. When brought back to El Toboso, Quixote refuses to admit that he is mad and escapes the fate of his ancestor's admission of defeat to the authorities.

The monsignor himself struggles with the analogy to the don. He begins to resist the comparison placed on him at a critical moment of conversation with Sancho:

> "Why are you always saddling me with my ancestor?"
>
> "I was only comparing—"
>
> "You talk about him at every opportunity, you pretend that my saints' books are like his books of chivalry, you compare our little adventures with his. Those Guardia were Guardia, not windmills. I am Father Quixote, and not Don Quixote. I tell you, I exist. My adventures are my own adventures, not his. I go my way—my way—not his. I have free will. I am not tethered to an ancestor who has been dead these four hundred years." (143)

Greene masterfully plays on the conventions of literary reality by having a fictional character voice a declaration that he exists. He draws on the fictive allusiveness of Cervantes's don to undermine and reverse the claim of fictive illusoriness of the monsignor. Quixote's revolt against such conflation is not only a claim for his own ontological status untethered from a 400-year fictional discourse; it is also a claim to found his factual status on his relationship to God. The monsignor immediately continues to defend himself to Sancho: "Oh, I know what you think. You think my God is an illusion like the windmills. But he exists, I tell you. I don't just believe in Him. I touch Him" (144). The assumptions about what is real and what is illusion, what is fact and what is fiction, are ultimately placed within a metaphysical framework. Transcending post-Enlightenment epistemological and materialist constructs, the real is given a theological status: the experience of love has both material and spiritual signification, revealing what is real *within* and yet *beyond* matter. Greene, in other words, is suggesting a sacramental understanding of the real in and through the power of love.

This profound incarnational aesthetic culminates in the final Eucharist celebrated by Quixote. As Edward Schillebeeckx maintains, the Eucharist is an "encounter," a tangible pledge of Christ's presence, par exellence. Quixote has claimed that he touches God in the Host when he celebrates the Mass,[35] echoing 40 years later the whiskey priest's claim to the atheist lieutenant that he can "put God into a man's mouth." Yet Greene pushes the sacramental language of sign and symbol further by the very absence of bread and wine at Quixote's dreamlike Mass. The classic theology of transubstantiation locates the divine reality in the presence of the consecrated bread and wine; here, Greene locates the divine reality in the encounter—the communion—of love between Quixote and Sancho as coconstitutive with the liturgical drama.[36] Greene renders a more dynamic and communal mediation of God's grace, reemphasizing the Eucharist as the incarnation of the divine in the bond of love between these two friends. After Quixote consecrates and consumes the imaginary bread and wine, he smiles upon Sancho: "Compañero . . . you must kneel" (226). The mayor knelt, and he "opened his mouth and *felt the fingers like a Host, on his tongue*" (227; my italics). In this liturgy, Quixote not only mediates God's love but also becomes that tactile presence himself, the "Christ form" that touches Sancho: he becomes, in effect, the Host, offering himself in love to his friend. If, according to von Balthasar's theological understanding, kenosis is the key to a Catholic aesthetic of divine presence in a fallen world, then Quixote enacts a final kenosis of himself in the very words of the liturgy that make Christ sacramentally present. Quixote's final Eucharist is his life, an incarnate sign of the spiritual energy of love.

Not since *The Power and the Glory* has Greene embodied such a profound sacramental aesthetic, now imbued with a post–Vatican II sensibility. The significance of their love and companionship is fully realized in this moment of touch. Quixote touches God in a supreme act of faith and then becomes the material action of God's touching of Sancho. But the movement of grace works in the other direction as well. Quixote's act of selfless love is itself a response to his compañero's gradual intensification of his commitment to him as both friend and priest. Only after Quixote is touched by their travel, conversation, and concern for one another is he finally prepared to recognize Sancho as his compañero. That bond is given a sacred signification in the concluding celebration of the Eucharist. In a condensed liturgy that steadily moves to the moment of Communion, the monsignor sees "the hopping love" between him and the mayor. Their mutual attraction and commitment to each other reveal the depths of true compañeros.[37] Both men mediate God's grace through their affection for one another, for as much as the monsignor hounds Sancho, Sancho also hounds the monsignor. As Michael Higgins rightly suggests, "Quixote's 'emptying' achieves perfect reciprocity: as Sancho rescued the monsignor, so has the monsignor rescued Sancho. Love, remembrance, Eucharist have replaced the ideological fixities and complacencies of the past, and certitude is never quite what it was."[38]

Three characters witness Quixote's final Mass, figuratively representing different philosophical positions that Greene has portrayed throughout his work. Sancho, an ex-Catholic (he was a seminarian at one time), exemplifies the person who has lost his earlier faith and has attempted to replace it with historical materialism. Father Leopoldo is the Catholic intellectual whose Cartesian skepticism has caused him to make "a greater leap than Descartes—a leap into the silent world of Osera" (214). Professor Pilbeam, the foremost scholar of Ignatius of Loyola, is the nominal Catholic who, though raised in the faith, no longer accepts it. Pilbeam calls himself a Catholic but has "not bothered to change the label that [he] was born with" (215). In many ways, the three represent the diverse state of Catholicism in the wake of Vatican II. Each comments on what "really" happened at Quixote's liturgy. Ironically, Pilbeam the nominal Catholic takes the most conservative position: "What we listened to last night could hardly be described as a Mass. . . . There was no Host and no wine" (229). Father Leopoldo, taking an approach that echoes a more liberal theological position, responds, "Do you think it's more difficult to turn empty air into wine than wine into blood? Can our limited sense decide a thing like that? We are faced by an infinite mystery." And Sancho, afraid of the power in such mystery, defensively retorts, "I prefer to think there was no Host" (230). Even though the conversation verges on the comical—almost as if Greene was poking fun at his lifelong themes—the reader is still left with a fundamentally changed Sancho. Despite his best efforts, he is progressively brought back to God through his participation in the life of his friend. When Quixote declares to him, "I don't offer you a governorship, Sancho. I offer you a kingdom. . . . Come with me and you will find the kingdom," Sancho instinctively responds, "I will never leave you, father. We have been on the road together too long for that" (223). Sancho's love "seemed now to live and grow in spite of the final separation and the final silence" (232). Love comes to define what is real because it grows beyond the death of matter: love continues to touch Sancho as a real presence.

The liturgical drama enacted in the text points to a truth about the real that Greene extends into the realm of fiction. The validity of the Mass centers on the mystery of fact versus fiction, or what Father Leopoldo consistently says to Professor Pilbeam: "Fact and fiction—in the end you can't distinguish between them—you just have to choose" (215). When Pilbeam exclaims, "Don Quixote had no descendants. How could he? He's a fictional character," the monk again emphasizes, "Fact and fiction . . . so difficult to distinguish" (217). Father Leopoldo repeats it twice more in the last pages of the text to underscore not so much the *fiction* of truth but the *truth* of fiction. His insight draws the reader into a consideration of how fact and fiction are related to religious belief. The novel intimates that one can come to some semblance of religious belief through rational argument, reasoned discernment, and even Newman's understanding of "accumulated probabilities." But, as Quixote himself says, "When I find that my belief is growing weak with age like my body, then I tell myself that I must be wrong. My faith tells me I must be wrong . . ." (184). Faith, then, must ultimately rest on something else beside rational belief: the novel suggests it rests on trust. The believer comes to trust in God's story of salvation, revealed and enacted ritually in the Catholic imagination through the liturgical life of the Church. The art of believing in such a story involves the affirmation of reality—a sacramental reality—made real in and by Christ's Incarnation into history. The leap of faith that Greene's texts embody is thus not so much from the natural to the supernatural, the real to the imaginary; rather, the leap of faith is more a negotiated trust in a story, a trust that such a story takes the individual somewhere adequate to the full range of human experience. Graham Holderness says something similar in his assessment of the novel:

> Monsignor Quixote's innocent trust in human love merges imper-
> ceptibly into his innocent trust in a loving God. To choose faith is
> ultimately no more difficult than to 'believe' in the truth of a novel.
> In a novel, where in the reader's surrender to the truth of fantasy
> fact and fiction become indistinguishable, there lies the possibility
> of imaginative conviction. In faith, where doubt and anxiety become
> subsumed into a voluntary, willed resignation to trust, there lies the
> possibility of salvation.[39]

Greene plays with the understanding that fiction very often reveals truth and, as such, functions very much like a fact, a datum of human experience. Greene seems to hold that fiction can make symbolically present (like a sacrament) the complex drama of human life, and do so in an adequate way if it takes seriously the creative mystery at the heart of every motivation and desire. Maurice Bendrix in *The End of the Affair* cynically mopes that God is like an omniscient author, imposing his plot upon us. *Monsignor Quixote*, on the other hand, offers the same image but encountered more optimistically. Quixote asks Sancho to trust the author of their story, to live in the mysterious evolution of character. In Greene's last great work, his Catholic imagination is fully engaged, making a case for faith over belief, hope over despair, love over hatred, and mystery over doubt.

Epilogue

Coloring Catholicism "Greene"

Graham Greene died in Vevey, Switzerland, the Wednesday after Easter, April 3, 1991. He had converted to Catholicism at the age of 21 and died 65 years later, still very much engaged with his faith. Father Leopoldo Duran, Greene's compañero during the final 20 years of his life, was called from Spain and celebrated the last sacraments with him. Greene died with the rites of the Church available to him—in what in Catholic parlance is called a "good death." Though he was buried in Switzerland, a memorial Mass was celebrated at Westminster Cathedral in London, with a packed congregation praying for this "novelist who happened to be a Catholic." The mystery and ritual of Catholicism that captured Greene's literary imagination throughout his life was, now in death, fully displayed for those who mourned his passing and honored his achievements.

Greene was a writer immersed in the political and religious events of the twentieth century. He came of age when the recognition of God in European culture was at best a discourse of nostalgia and at worst a myth to be discarded for newer, more secular varieties. In this regard, he stands in the company of T. S. Eliot, G. K. Chesterton, Edith Sitwell, Evelyn Waugh, W. H. Auden, and C. S. Lewis, to name just a few who resisted the trend toward atheism by converting to Rome or to a distinctly high church Anglicanism. Within the iconoclasms of high modernism, these artists held fast to a Catholic-Christian sensibility in their art, often as an attitude of moral and intellectual superiority over their peers. They demonstrated the personal apprehension and struggle to maintain faith in God in the midst of the events of the twentieth century. Though Greene shares this trajectory, he is unique among them because he continued to live and write well into the last half of the twentieth century. If he participated in the modernist turn toward institutional religion articulated by Eliot and embodied by the writers of the French literary revival, he also participated in the later postmodernist appropriations of cultural discourse that became part of Catholic experience after the Second Vatican Council.

I have traced the influences on Greene's religious imagination, correlating his own explicit references to theologians and Catholic artists throughout his life. His close reading of John Henry Newman, his deep friendship with priest intellectuals—Bede Jarrett in the 1920s and 1930s, C. C. Martindale in the 1940s and 1950s, and Leopoldo Duran in the 1970s and 1980s—and his constant immersion in the theological developments of his Catholic faith situates Greene in the mainstream of Catholic artists whose faith informed the metaphysical and moral claims of their works. His close analysis of the French revival and his personal friendship with François Mauriac helped to extend his literary vision to farther shores. Appropriating the thematic tensions of the French writers—Péguy's sinner at the heart of Christianity, the mystical substitutions of Bernanos, the divine pursuit of the erring soul in Mauriac, and the indictment of bourgeois materialism in Bloy—Greene was a celebrated master of what became the genre of the Catholic novel. His unique engagement with Catholic theological and literary texts helped to create such masterful works as *The Power and the Glory*, *The Heart of the Matter*, and *The End of the Affair*. These texts extended the boundaries of the English novel by offering a distinctly Catholic embodiment of the way in which characters imagine, judge, and understand the world.

If Greene's own identification as a practicing Catholic became tenuous in later years, his commitment to a Catholic vision of the world never wavered, as is evident from his avid reading of Vatican II theology, his personal support of liberationist movements in Latin America, and his attempt to be an agent of dialogue between Catholicism and Marxism. As the Council inspired theologians to develop and embrace new paradigms and metaphors to discuss the relationship of the Church and the modern world, so, too, did Greene represent a more nuanced Catholic ideological discourse in his late novels. There is a decidedly different feel to Greene's novels from this later period, a refashioning of the religious tensions of the classical Catholic genre. *The Honorary Consul* and *Monsignor Quixote* offer the most explicit examples of such theological development—the Teilhardian theology of evolutionary convergence, the historical significance of Jesus in evaluating moral agency, the dialogical nature of faith and belief, and the mediation of God on the horizontal plane of human affection and commitment—all amply portrayed. Both novels have climactic liturgical moments that imply an ultimate theological signification to the words and actions of the characters. With *The Human Factor* and *Doctor Fischer of Geneva*, Greene's Catholic imagination is more dialectical (prophetically so in *The Human Factor*), illustrating the dire effects of a post-Christian understanding of the human person, especially when the coercive power of political force or material wealth displaces the uniqueness of each individual person "made in the image and likeness of God."

Greene never liked being called a Catholic novelist; he was more comfortable with the title "Christian humanist." His fiction, like all good literature, tended to encourage readers to acknowledge and attend to the humanity of other human beings, to enter a fictional world in order to experience "the heart of the matter" about human life or "the human factor" in the mystery of political events. Yet many critics have questioned whether Greene's humanism is all that Catholic. They contend that he became more secularized later in life, arguing that his late novels reduce religious belief to such an extent that only the aura of belief remains. I hope this study has made clear how narrow and finally misleading an assessment this is of Greene's late work. Greene diminishes the institutional and rationalized side of Catholic belief, not to rid himself of it, but to make clear that it is the practice of faith, hope, and love—and primarily a faith, hope, and love that costs the individual something—that makes possible belief in a God present in the world. The whiskey priest, Father Rivas, and Monsignor Quixote lose the institutional trappings of their priesthood in order to gain participation in the drama of Christ's suffering. The unchurched Sarah Miles finds in her painful longing for the body of Maurice Bendrix the presence of the body of Christ on the crucifix. Sarah and Maurice Castle's agnostic search for a safe place to love one another free from the political games of the world is finally revealed as a love that endures suffering for the sake of others. And Alfred Jones discovers a presence in the lingering love for his dead wife that helps him to withstand the coercive effects of Dr. Fischer's spiteful games. In each case, Greene draws more than just the aura of Catholic belief: he offers a human encounter with religious mystery, embodied and articulated in Catholic claims of sacramentality.

I conclude by offering a few remarks on my reading of Graham Greene's Catholic imagination and post–Vatican II Catholicism in general. First, the Catholic novel in the early half of the twentieth century was an easily discernable genre because Catholicism was experienced more monolithically as a hermetic system of belief and practice. Whether or not it was the intent of the Council's deliberations, Vatican II again opened up multiple ways to embrace

Catholic belief and practice. After the council, Catholicism had in fact arrived at its own postmodern moment—Catholics began to situate their faith historically in the various social, political, and regional locations in which their faith was practiced. Although the Church's magisterium continues today to emphasize narrow orthodoxy and strict authority as the visible sign of Catholic faith, Vatican II Catholics have gone on to identify their adherence to their faith in a variety of ways. One has only to log on to Beliefnet.com on the World Wide Web to find a humorous, if accurate, account of the spectrum of Catholic identity in today's Church. Though stereotyped into simple categories, the web site lists five *kinds* of Catholics: traditionalist, neotraditionalist, liberal, progressive, and recovering. Interesting enough, Graham Greene is listed as the novelist who most captures the religious imagination of Catholic liberals, and Evelyn Waugh is the favorite novelist of traditionalists.[1] Catholic *difference*, it seems, is thus not only *ad extra* but also *ad intra*. Greene's late novels are a testament to the dialogical nature within Catholicism, for as much as Father León Rivas and Monsignor Quixote create a dialogue with agnostic or atheistic ideologies, they are struggling in effect for a kind of Catholic practice that they find missing in the institutional Church in which they serve.

Second, I insist that if there are kinds of Catholicism, then all of them still share some fundamental theological characteristics. I have argued that charting Greene's artistic engagement with Catholicism allows us to see some of these characteristics as the unifying thread of his literary genius. If Newman, Teilhard de Chardin, Lynch, von Balthasar, Schillebeeckx, and Küng have a common thread in their theology, it is a vision of reality that rests on the paradox of the Incarnation, the proximity of God made sacramentally present in one's participation in the central drama of Christ's life, death, and Resurrection. Whether one is a traditionalist, liberal, or recovering Catholic, the embodiment of God's spirit in creation stands at the center of Catholic faith. Each of Greene's novels discussed in this book places the Incarnation as central to religious faith or the lack thereof. The presence of God is to be found in the fallen nature of Greene's characters, discussed in theological dialogue and mediated in the Eucharistic liturgies that populate his texts.

Finally, I have suggested that criticism of Greene's works is advanced if a wider lens is used to understand his religious imagination, especially in relationship to their Catholic ideology and aesthetics, specifically the dialogical manner in which Greene's thematic concerns intersect with the theological concerns after the Second Vatican Council. Greene's developed literary aesthetic is not post-Catholic or post-Christian but Catholic and post–Vatican II, an ongoing artistic response to the political and religious upheavals of the twentieth century. His engagement elevates any fixed designation of the Catholic novel out of the rigid confines of its past. His late novels offer a fresh perspective in which to chart how the discourse of Catholicism adds a surplus of meaning beyond the merely political, economic, and cultural ideologies that pervade much of literary criticism. Likewise, these novels offer Catholic discourse a surplus of meaning beyond the emphasis of orthodoxy and authority that is such a part of the pre–Vatican II Church and, perhaps, beyond today's Vatican Curia. Greene portrays characters involved with personal and political struggles of power, influence, and equality, who in the final analysis point to and express choices and insights based on the reflective experience of committed love. The mysteriousness of such encounters intimate a moment of insight, transformation, or choice of action beyond the political and social reductionisms of ideology. In his theological reading of contemporary Catholic thinkers and in his focused fascination with exiles and priests, Greene creates an imaginative world in which theology and politics are in constant dialogue. His writing echoes the hopes and dreams of a religious faith creatively imagined in the midst of the real horrors of the twentieth century. To color Catholicism "Greene" is, in the end, a palette very much woven into the pattern of faith and belief today.

Notes

CHAPTER I

1. Marie-Françoise Allain, *The Other Man: Conversations with Graham Greene* (New York: Simon & Schuster, 1983), 159.

2. The designation of "Catholic" novel as a genre and the distinction of being named a "Catholic" author applied to many authors besides Greene, especially during the first half of the twentieth century. In England, Greene was usually paired with Evelyn Waugh and, later, with Muriel Spark. Sigrid Undset in Scandinavia and Gertrud von Le Fort and Elisabeth Langgässer in Germany were other Europeans who stood out as part of the Catholic literary revival. In the United States, the term applied to writers as diverse as Thomas Merton, Flannery O'Connor, J. F. Powers, and Walker Percy. Yet Greene's concentration of four novels in 12 years—what critics call his Catholic cycle—stand out as a singular achievement because of their intensity, popularity, and timing.

3. A. A. DeVitis, *Graham Greene*, rev. ed. (Boston: Twayne Publishers, 1986), 189; Anthony Burgess, *Urgent Copy: Literary Studies* (New York: W.W. Norton, 1968), 20; Satnam Kaur, *Graham Greene: An Existentialist Investigation* (Amristar, India: Guru Nanak Dev University, 1988), 32.

4. Graham Greene, "François Mauriac" *Collected Essays* (London: Penguin, [1945] 1969), 91.

5. Graham Greene, *Reflections* (Toronto: Lester & Orpen Dennys, 1990), 113.

6. Greene's four salutary articles on James demonstrate a unique perspective on James's "religious sense": "James spent his life working towards and round the Catholic Church, fascinated and repelled and absorbent"

(140); "the point which may have attracted James to the Church was its treatment of supernatural evil. The Anglican Church had almost relinquished Hell . . . but no day passed in a Catholic Church without prayers for deliverance from evil spirits 'wandering through the world for the ruin of souls.' This savage elementary belief found an echo in James's sophisticated mind, to which the evil of the world was very present. He faced it in his work with a religious intensity" (49); "James believed in the supernatural, but he saw evil as an equal force with good" (33). Greene's desire to portray James as a quasi-religious novelist perhaps says more about Greene's fixation than James's but nonetheless expresses the sense of his own literary affinity to the Master.

7. Robert Detweiler's *Breaking the Fall: Religious Readings of Contemporary Fiction* (San Francisco: Harper & Row, 1989) is an excellent example of this methodology. See also Robert Detweiler and David Jasper, eds., *Religion and Literature: A Reader* (Louisville, KY: John Knox Press, 2000), a compendium and resource that embodies and explicates this model of interdisciplinary work.

8. Paul Tillich, *Theology of Culture* (New York: Oxford University Press, 1959), gives a full exposition of this methodology. Tillich's cultural examples come mainly from the fine arts, especially painting: "Painting is a mute revealer and yet often speaks more perceptibly to the interpreting mind than concept-bearing words. For it impresses us with the irrefutable power of immediate intuition." *On Art and Architecture*, edited by John Dillenberger (New York: Crossroad, 1987), 58.

9. See Theodore P. Fraser's *The Modern Catholic Novel in Europe* (New York: Macmillan, 1994) for a succinct history of the origins of the Catholic novel (1–23). Fraser places great emphasis on Fyodor Dostoevsky's influence, claiming he was "the first European novelist to place the relationship of the individual and God at the heart of the novel" (5). For the political and cultural background of the Catholic literary revival in France, see Richard Griffiths, *The Reactionary Revolution: The Catholic Revival in French Literature, 1870–1914* (New York: Frederick Ungar, 1965).

10. Ellis Hanson, in *Decadence and Catholicism* (Cambridge, MA: Harvard University Press, 1997), notes that decadent texts are littered with Catholic conversions: "Catholicism was the odd disruption, the hysterical symptom, the mystical effusion, the medieval spectacle, the last hope of paganism, in an age of Victorian puritanism, Enlightenment rationalism, and bourgeois materialism" (26).

11. David Lodge, introduction to François Mauriac, *The Viper's Tangle*, translated by Gerard Hopkins (New York: Carroll & Graf, 1987). Quoted in Fraser, xiv.

12. Patrick Allit, *Catholic Converts: British and American Intellectuals Turn to Rome* (Ithaca, NY: Cornell University Press, 1997), gives a well-documented history of this revival. Allit notes that English converts treaded difficult terrain within both the Church and Protestant society. Because these converts were educated or well-known individuals, they were suspected by the church of having liberal or modernist tendencies, at the same time that they had to defend to their Protestant peers the idea that religious and intellectual freedom was an essential element of their newfound faith: "Converts, therefore, had to keep an eye on the authorities to their 'right' as well as the skeptical non-Catholic audience on their 'left'" (x).

13. Joseph Pearce, *Literary Converts* (San Francisco: Ignatius Press, 2000), offers short historical vignettes not only of these leading English converts of the early twentieth century but also of such luminaries as Maurice Baring, Robert Hugh Benson, Christopher Dawson, Compton MacKenzie, Alec Guiness, Muriel Spark, and Malcolm Muggeridge. Pearce's analysis of Greene is highly critical, claiming that his brand of Catholicism was "an enigma, a conversation piece—even a gimmick" (144). One senses that Pearce is upset that Greene never found great comfort or peace of mind by converting to Catholicism.

14. "Le pécheur est au coeur même de chrétienté . . . Nul n'est aussi competent que le pécheru en matière de chrétienté. Nul, si ce n'est le saint." Charles Péguy, *Oeuvres de Prose, 1909–1914* (Paris: Gallimard/Bibliothèque de la Pléiade, 1961), 1074.

15. Mary Gerhart, "What Ever Happened to the Catholic Genre?" in *Morphologies of Faith: Essays in Religion and Culture in Honor of Nathan A. Scott, Jr.*, edited by Mary Gerhart and Arthur C. Yu (Atlanta, GA: Scholars Press, 1990), 181–201.

16. Gene Kellogg, *The Vital Tradition: The Catholic Novel in a Period of Convergence* (Chicago: Loyola University Press, 1970), 1.

17. Albert Sonnenfeld, *Crossroads: Essays on the Catholic Novelists* (York, SC: French Literature Publications, 1982), viii.

18. David Pryce-Jones, *Graham Greene* (London: Oliver & Boyd, 1963), 100.

19. John Atkins, *Graham Greene* (London: Calder & Boyars [1957], 1966), ix.

20. Cates Baldridge, *Graham Greene's Fictions: The Virtues of Extremity* (Columbia: University of Missouri Press, 2000), 129.

21. Many other book-length commentaries on Greene's work imply this dichotomization: Neil McEwan, *Graham Greene* (London: Macmillan, 1988); Brian Thomas, *An Underground Fate: The Idiom of Romance in the Later Novels of Graham Greene* (Athens: University of Georgia Press, 1988); Roger Sharrock, *Saints, Sinners, and Comedians: The Novels of Graham Greene* (South Bend, IN: University of Notre Dame Press, 1984); Gwen R. Boardman, *Graham Greene: The Aesthetics of Exploration* (Gainesville: University of Florida Press, 1971).

22. David Tracy, *Plurality and Ambiguity: Hermeneutics, Religion, Hope* (Chicago: University of Chicago Press, 1987), 14.

23. David Tracy, *The Analogical Imagination: Christian Theology and the Culture of Pluralism* (New York: Crossroad, 1981), 376–398, 405–420.

24. Two of Greeley's recent books, *The Catholic Imagination* (Berkeley: University of California Press, 2000) and *Religion as Poetry* (New Brunswick, NJ: Transaction Publications, 1996), present a statistical case for such a difference in religious communities and cultures.

25. Three recent texts that reflect Lynch's resurgence as a critical lens are Francesca Aran Murphy's *Christ the Form of Beauty* (Edinburgh: T. & T. Clark, 1995), Gerald J. Bednar's *Faith as Imagination* (Kansas City: Sheed & Ward, 1996), and John Neary's *Like and Unlike God: Religious Imaginations in Modern and Contemporary Fiction* (Atlanta, GA: Scholars Press, 1999).

26. The term "ideology" is not meant in the narrow sense of Marxist thought. It is a more neutral term, denoting those unconscious traces of Catholic philosophy, aesthetics, and theological tendencies that have been overlooked or rejected as insignificant in the twentieth century by formalist criticism, as well as deconstructionist programs.

27. See, for instance, Georges Bataille, *Theory of Religion*, translated by Robert Hurley (New York: Zone, 1989), 10; Jean-François Lyotard, *The Postmodern Condition: A Report on Knowledge* (Minneapolis: University of Minnesota Press, 1984); Terry Eagleton, *The Ideology of the Aesthetic* (Oxford: Basil Blackwell, 1990).

28. Paul Giles, *American Catholic Arts and Fictions: Culture, Ideology, Aesthetics* (Cambridge: Cambridge University Press, 1992), 21–30.

29. Hanson, 7.

30. Greene, *Collected Essays*, 16–17.

31. In ancient shadows and twilights
    Where childhood had strayed,
    The World's great sorrows were born
    And its heroes were made.
    In the lost boyhood of Judas
    Christ was betrayed.

32. Graham Greene, *Ways of Escape* (New York: Simon & Schuster, 1980), 79.

33. A. F. Cassis, ed., *Graham Greene: Man of Paradox*, (Chicago: Loyola University Press, 1994), 277.

34. Greene, *Reflections*, 207.

35. Georg M. A. Gaston, *The Pursuit of Salvation: A Critical Guide to the Novels of Graham Greene* (New York: Whitston Publishing, 1984), 2–3.

36. John Henry Newman, *The Idea of a University* (London: Longmans, Green, 1912); quoted in Graham Greene, Introduction, *A Burnt-Out Case* (London: Penguin, 1974), xiv.

37. Allain, 150.

38. Evelyn Waugh, "Felix Culpa?" *The Tablet*, 191 (5 June, 1948); reprinted in Samuel Hynes, ed., *Graham Greene: A Collection of Critical Essays* (Englewood Cliffs, NJ: Prentice-Hall, 1973), 101.

39. Greene's novel *The Power and the Glory* was for a time on the Catholic Church's Index of Forbidden Books.

40. Sharrock, 14. Evelyn Waugh was one such critic. When asked to review *A Burnt-Out Case* for a newspaper, he refused, for he thought the novel showed either Greene's loss of faith or, at best, his exasperation at being labeled a Catholic writer. See *The Diaries of Evelyn Waugh*, edited by Michael Davies (Boston: Little, Brown, 1976), 774–776.

41. See Harold Bloom, ed., *Graham Greene: Modern Critical Views* (New York: Chelsea House, 1987), for some negative criticism of the Catholic novels. Frank Kermode laments the "neo-romantic" emphasis on Catholicism (38), and Bloom pontificates that Greene will be primarily remembered not for his religious novels but for his thrillers (4–8).

42. Robert Pendleton, *Graham Greene's Conradian Masterplot* (New York: St. Martin's, 1996), 5–7.

43. Baldridge, 4.

44. Jacques Maritain, *Art and Scholasticism* (London: Sheed & Ward, 1923).

45. J. C. Whitehouse, *Vertical Man: The Human Being in the Catholic Novels of Graham Greene, Sigrid Undset, and Georges Bernanos* (London: Saint Austin Press, 1999), 15.

46. The scholastic term *ex opere operato*, "by the work worked," claims that the sacraments bestow grace in virtue of the performance of the sacramental action. Positively, it expresses that Christ's commitment to the sacraments makes them efficacious; negatively, it upholds the idea that the gift of grace is therefore not dependent on either the sanctity of the minister or the faith of the recipient. Protestant reformers interpreted the concept as limiting God's freedom to work only through the sacraments, making God's grace both magical and seemingly automatic. Though this is a misunderstanding, the concept had wide currency in the popular belief of the Catholic Church prior to the Second Vatican Council, giving an aura to the mystery and power of sacramental rituals on the Catholic imagination. For a discussion of the term, see John Schanz, *The Sacraments of Life and Worship* (Milwaukee, WI: Bruce Publishing, 1966), 51–52; and Mark Jordan, ed., *The Church's Confession of Faith: A Catholic Catechism for Adults* (San Francisco: Ignatius Press, 1987), 265–266.

47. Austin Flannery, O.P., ed., *The Documents of Vatican II* (New York: Costello Publishing, 1996). See also Fraser's discussion of these post–Vatican II developments and their effect on the Catholic novel (143–151).

48. T. S. Eliot, *Essays Ancient and Modern* (London: Faber, 1934), 93.

49. For a discussion of Greene's friendship with Bede Jarrett, O.P., and Tom Burns, the Catholic layman and publisher of *The Tablet*, see W. J. West, *The Quest for Graham Greene* (New York: St. Martin's, 1997), 35–38, 60–61. Greene's correspondence with Frs. C. C. Martindale, Hans Küng, Ernesto Cardenal of Nicaragua, and many other priests, bishops, and theologians can be found in the Graham Greene Archives at the Burns Library, Boston College.

50. Greene's debt to Newman cannot be underestimated: "Newman has often influenced me. I read him before my conversion. I still read him frequently. I greatly admire him." "Table Talk with Graham Green," interview with Père Jauve and Marcel Moré; translated by Nancy Hargrave; in *Dieu Vivant*, 16 (1949), 129. In Newman he found both a theological lens and a ground for support for his ambivalent profession of faith, noting that "as a writer, I have often been criticized by the pious. Newman answers them." Interview with V. S. Prichett for the *London Times*, 18 March 1978, in Cassis, 287.

51. Terry Eagleton, "Reluctant Heroes: The Novels of Graham Greene," in *Graham Greene: Modern Critical Views*, edited by Harold Bloom (New York: Chelsea House, 1987), 114–115.

52. It is interesting to note that before the 1960s, almost every interview and important article written by Greene discussed the sense of sin in his novels. In 1949 he writes, "I have always been preoccupied with the mystery of sin. It is always the foun-

dation of my books" (*Dieu Vivant*, 127). After Vatican II, Greene denies the importance of sin in his work but argues the point from a theological perspective. In 1988 he states, "Original sin does not mean anything much to me any more than the Trinity does . . . once you try to explain a mystery you get things tabulated. But I certainly believe there is good and evil in the world." Quoted in Maria Couto, *Graham Greene: On the Frontier. Politics and Religion in the Novels* (New York: St. Martin's, 1988) 212. Whenever Greene comments on his novels and their relationship to his faith, he displays a remarkable theological logic, as when he is asked about hell: "I don't believe in hell: if God exists—I'm not convinced that he does—He is omniscient; if He is omniscient, I can't bring myself to imagine that a creature conceived by Him can be so evil as to merit eternal punishment. His grace must intervene at some point" (Allain, 151).

53. Graham Greene, *Yours, Etc: Letters to the Press, 1945–1989*, edited by Christopher Hawtree (New York: Penguin, 1989), 225.

54. Cassis, 334.

55. Paul Tillich, *Systematic Theology*, Vol. 3 (Chicago: University of Chicago Press, 1963), 245.

56. Allain, 168.

CHAPTER 2

1. Letters of Graham Greene to Vivien, found in Norman Sherry, *The Life of Graham Greene*, vol. 1 (New York: Penguin, 1989), 259, 260.

2. Greene, *The Lawless Roads* (London: Penguin [1939] 1982), 10–11.

3. "The Job of the Writer," *The Observer*, (15 Sept. 1957); quoted in Cassis, 123.

4. Letters dated 28 May 1927 and 14 June 1927; in Sherry, 352, 353.

5. Sherry postulates, in rather psychoanalytic fashion, that the characters Elizabeth and Andrews in *The Man Within* represent Greene's romantic sense of his early marriage to Vivien (372–375).

6. Bede Jarrett, O.P., *Mediaeval Socialism* (London: Burns Oates & Washbourne, [1913] 1935), 29–41, 80–90. Jarrett is mentioned often in Greene's letters during the 1920s and 1930s. He died at the age of 53 in 1937. The couple's friendship with Jarrett is well documented in West, 35–38, 60–61.

7. Greene owned the complete works of Newman, and his copy of Newman's *Apologia Pro Vita Sua* contains over 50 marginal notations, including large sections of the chapter "Position of My Mind since 1845." Greene's personal library is found in the Graham Greene Papers, Boston College.

8. Ian Ker, *The Catholic Revival in English Literature, 1845–1961* (South Bend, IN: University of Notre Dame Press, 2003), 13. Ker's chapter on Newman makes much of Newman's process of discovering in Roman Catholicism an objective reality that saved oneself from the egocentric subjectivism of romanticism.

9. John Henry Newman, *Apologia Pro Vita Sua* (New York: Penguin, 1994), 182.

10. Ibid., 31.

11. Ibid., 183.

12. Cassis, *Graham Greene*, 435.

13. Greene, *A Burnt-Out Case*, introduction.

14. Newman, *Apologia*, 130.

15. Newman, *An Essay in Aid of a Grammar of Assent* (Oxford: Clarendon Press, 1985), 253, 274, 313.

16. Newman, *Parochial and Plain Sermons*, 8 vol. (Oxford: Clarendon Press, 1987), vol. 3, 144–145; vol. 4, 22; vol. 5, 268.

17. Newman, "An Essay on the Development of Christian Doctrine," in *The Essential Newman*, edited by Vincent Ferrer Blehl (New York: Mentor-Omega Books, 1963), 123.

18. Nicholas Lash, in *Easter in Ordinary: Reflections on Human Experience and the Knowledge of God* (South Bend, IN: Notre Dame University Press, 1988), 139, writes of Newman's position via Hegel's dialectic: "As a historian [Newman] sees no prospect or guarantee of the interplay of [the philosophical, political, and the ritual elements of Christianity] finding stable resolution within the historical process which they constitute. If he retains his confidence that no one or two of the elements of religion will succeed in definitively crushing or obliterating the others, this is born of the conviction that, however fragile and unstable the pattern, that pattern is, nevertheless, the sacramental expression of the vector of God's action in human history. In that sense (even if in that sense alone) Newman's view of the matter is not unlike Hegel's belief that human history is an expression and obscure transcription of God's eternal self-movement."

19. Newman, *The Via Media of the Anglican Church* (Oxford: Clarendon Press, 1990), 147.

20. See Richard Griffiths, *The Reactionary Revolution. The Catholic Revival in French Literature 1870–1914* (New York: Frederick Ungar, 1965), 3–20, for a concise history of the major figures of this literary movement.

21. Kurt Reinhardt, *The Theological Novel of Modern Europe: An Analysis of Masterpieces by Eight Authors* (New York: Frederick Ungar, 1968), 77.

22. Léon Bloy, *L'Exégèse des Lieux Communs* (1902); quoted in E. T. Dubois, *Portrait of Leon Bloy* (New York: Sheed & Ward, 1951), 79.

23. Greene, *Collected Essays*, 103, 104.

24. Greene, *The Power and the Glory*, 210. This echoes Bloy's comment: "I could have been a saint, a worker of wonders. I have become a man of letters."

25. Greene, *Brighton Rock*, 246.

26. Greene, *The Lawless Roads*, 6; *Collected Essays*, 103.

27. Graham C. Jones, "Graham Greene and The Legend of Péguy," *Comparative Literature* 21 (1969), 140. Jones notes that Greene valorized for himself a heroic legend of Péguy as a renegade based more on the man's personality than on a complete picture of his writing (139). Jones argues that Greene's understanding of Péguy is selective.

28. Greene, *The Power and the Glory*, 82.

29. Hans Urs von Balthasar, *Bernanos: An Ecclesial Existence* (San Francisco: Ignatius Press, 1996), 352.

30. Ann M. Begley, "Georges Bernanos' Love Affair with God," *Religion and Literature* 33.3 (2001), 38.

31. Greene, *Collected Essays*, 96.

32. Ibid., 99.

33. Quoted in Phillip Stratford, *Faith and Fiction: Creative Process in Greene and Mauriac* (South Bend, IN: University of Notre Dame Press, 1964), x.

34. Ibid., 1–32.

35. François Mauriac, *God and Mammon* (London: Sheed & Ward, 1936), 20.

36. Mauriac shows his literary and theological appreciation of Pascal in his study *Les Pages Immortelles de Pascal: Choisies et Expliquées* (New York: Longmans, Green, 1941).

37. Fraser, 36.

38. The argument over the relationship between nature and grace was very much a part of the Catholic theological revival of the early twentieth century. Is nature opposed to the working of God's grace (Pascal's position) or does God's grace build on human nature (Thomas Aquinas's position)? For a short but dense summary of the argument, see Karl Rahner, *Theological Investigations*, vol. 1 (Baltimore: Helicon Press, 1961), 297–310. Rahner disputes the Pascalian view of the argument.

39. Greene, "François Mauriac," *Collected Essays*, 92, 94, 95–96.

40. Greene, "The Two Maritains," *New Statesman and Nation* 31 (26 January 1946); quoted in Stratford, 16.

41. Greene, "The Last Pope," *Reflections*, 113, translated from the French by Philip Stratford. Originally published as the lecture "La civilization chrétienne est-elle en péril?" in *Essais Catholiques* (Paris: Seuil, 1953).

42. Greene, "Message aux catholiques français," *Essais Catholiques*, 12–13. The original French text reads: "Il y a quelques mois à peine, j'eus l'occasion, à 5 heures et demie du matin, d'entendre la Messe dans une petite église franciscaine de l'Italie du Sud et de voir, lorsqu'une manche glissa, l'horrible blessure noircie des stigmates dont le Père Pio depuis un quart de siècle est marqué aux mains, aux pieds et au flanc. Or, dans la pénombre de cette heure très matinale, je me rappelai un autre spectacle dont je fus naguère le témoin privilégié. C'était en 1938, pendant la Semaine Sainte, et tout à la fin des persécutions mexicaines. . . . Acun prêtre n'avait le droit d'entrer dans une église, toutes les messes étaient dites secrètement dans des maisons privées; mais le Vendredi Saint, les Indiens descendirent de leurs montagnes et se répandirent en foule dans les èglises. Il y avait dix ans qu'ils n'avaient pas entendu de messe, ils ne savaient pas l'espagnol, et pour le latin il n'en est naturellement pas question. Mais ils s'appliquaient à reconstruire, en leurs idioms secrets qui diffèrent de village à village, la cérémonie de la Messe."

43. Mauriac, "Men I Hold Great," in Samuel Hynes, ed., *Graham Greene: A Collection of Critical Essays* (Englewood Cliffs, NJ: Prentice-Hall, 1973), 76.

44. Mauriac, quoted in Stratford, 237–238.

45. Greene constantly denied the charge of Jansenism and Manichaeism: "People who think they are getting at Jansenism in my novels usually do not know what Jansenism really means. They probably mean Manichaeism. This is because in the

Catholic novels I seem to believe in a supernatural evil. One gets so tired of people saying that my novels are about the opposition of Good and Evil. They are not about Good and Evil, but about human beings. After Hitler and Vietnam, one would have thought good and evil in people was more understandable"; interview with Gene Phillips in 1969 in Cassis, 208. Jansenism is often equated with Manichaeism, but there are great differences. Jansenism was a movement in the French church, founded by Bishop Cornelius Jansen (1585–1638), which rejected the Catholic notion of freedom to choose at any time between good or evil. The denial of freedom of the will made any resistance to Divine Grace impossible. Jansen further maintained that Christ died only for an elect few. Blaise Pascal, Mauriac's chief religious mentor, was among the greatest apologists of Jansenism. Manichaeism, on the other hand, stems from the third century and upholds the Persian doctrine of the "two principles": God/light/spirit eternally opposed to Satan/darkness/materiality. It thus rejects any notion of fallen humanity and consequently any conviction of personal sin. The Incarnation is necessarily rejected, for Christ could only manifest divinity. For a discussion of Jansenism, see Nigel Abercrombie, *The Origins of Jansenism* (Oxford: Clarendon Press, 1936), 161–220; for a discussion of Manichaeism, see Joan O'Grady, *Early Christian Heresies* (New York: Barnes & Noble Books, 1994), 64–72.

46. Stratford, 197–198.

47. William Lynch, *Christ and Apollo: The Dimensions of the Literary Imagination* (New York: Sheed & Ward, 1960), 66–67.

48. Greene, *The Power and the Glory*, 67. The page numbers of all future quotations will be parenthetically noted in the text.

49. The first American title of *The Power and the Glory* was *The Labyrinthine Way*.

50. Hans Urs von Balthasar, *The Glory of the Lord: A Theological Aesthetics*, vols. 1–7 (San Francisco: Ignatius Press, 1982–1988). For what follows, see the extensive introduction in vol. 1, *Seeing the Form*, 17–127.

51. Ibid., 124.

52. Ibid., 504.

53. For a further discussion, see Mark Bosco, "Seeing the Glory: Graham Greene's *The Power and the Glory* through the Lens of Hans Urs von Balthasar's Theological Aesthetics," *Logos: A Journal of Catholic Thought and Culture* 4.1 (2001), 34–53.

54. Jae Suck Choi, *Greene and Unamuno: Two Pilgrims to La Mancha* (New York: Peter Lang, 1990), 81; Baldridge, 71, 87–88. Daphna Erdinast-Valcan, *Graham Greene's Childless Fathers* (New York: St. Martin's, 1988), 2.

55. Lynch, *Christ and Apollo*, 233.

56. Elliot Malamet, *The World Remade: Graham Greene and the Art of Detection* (New York: Peter Lang, 1998), 37.

57. Ibid., 34.

58. Cates Baldridge argues differently, claiming that the Catholic understanding of Grace as mediated has little success in the text because of its absolutist and dialectical strain: "The priest, we are compelled to understand, is acceptable to God, but it

seems to be his very *isolation* from the body of his church that is the making of his worth in the eyes of the Divinity. . . . Green's thematic juxtaposition of the mediated and the absolute within *The Power and the Glory* would thus appear to paint all varieties of institutionalized religion as fatally inadequate in their self-proclaimed roles as mediator and conduit between the individual and God" (54, 57). Yet it can be argued that Greene sets up the tension in order to heighten the theological problem of modernity—a too easy appropriation of bourgeois culture in the life of the Church. It is the realm of Bloy, Péguy, and Mauriac, echoed here. The chasm between the priest and the pious allows Greene to fight any notion of pharisaism, allegorizing the prodigal son as the closest thing there is to an elect. Furthermore, the absolutism of living in persecution demands an absolute commitment: if there is an either/or choice, it is persecution or surrender. Finally, Baldrige's claim that the power of grace in the novel never has a good and lasting transformation on the world (62–64) misses the effect of a Catholic theological aesthetic. The priest engages a new vision: the world does not change; his vision—and by extension the reader's—changes.

59. Couto, 69.

60. Some critics suspect Greene of portraying Catholicism as an exclusive club, an elect that has a true understanding of the spiritual dimension of life. In contrast, J. C. Whitehouse argues, "For Greene, Catholicism is a club to which anyone can belong—Mexican Indians, British colonial officials, the wives of Whitehall civil servants, Vietnamese housewives, South American revolutionaries. It is for the poor and ignorant, the rich and sophisticated, the worldly and the naïve. Men and women of any ideological persuasion can find comfort in the knowledge that their ideas and feelings are shared by others. And whatever part of vanity or superiority there might be in the recognition of a supposed superior truth in those ideas and feelings may well be a tendency which is attributable to human beings in general. To attribute it solely to Catholics perhaps says as much about the unsympathetic critic as about Greene" (76). Though it is true that Greene's Catholic characters have a heightened sense of what is at stake in the world, Greene is actually much closer to James Joyce's definition of Catholicism—"Here comes everybody"—than any Gnostic, exclusionary form of Catholicism.

61. Ian Gregor, "The End of the Affair," in *The Moral and the Story* (London: Faber & Faber, 1962); author's italics.

62. Greene, *Ways of Escape*, 142.

63. See DeVitis, 94–97, and Stratford, 205–240, for a more thorough comparison.

64. Greene claimed that it is Sarah's story, but critics are sharply divided. A. A. DeVitis, Francis Kunkel, and Maria Couto claim that Sarah's journey is the principle theme of the novel, whereas Frank Kermode, David Pryce-Jones, Herbert Haber, and John Atkins regard it as Bendrix's story. See DeVitis, 95; Kunkel, *The Labryintine Ways of Graham Greene* (New York: Sheed & Ward 1959), 128–130; Couto, 83; Kermode, "Mr. Greene's Eggs and Crosses," in Hynes, 7; Pryce-Jones, 83–88; Haber, "The End of the Catholic Cycle: The Writer versus the Saint," in *Graham Greene: Some Critical Considerations*, edited by Robert O. Evans (Lexington: University of Kentucky Press, 1963), 130–132; and Atkins, 194–200.

65. Elliott Malamet notes that "the use of the diary in *The End of the Affair* leads to the displacement of Bendrix's version of the truth; this has much to do with one's perception of not only Bendrix and Sarah, but of the authenticity of the diary form, with its unspoken claims of honesty" (89–90). Malamet, among other critics, finds Sarah's diary to be less than sincere and not such an "artless" record of her "true" self.

66. As to the centrality of John of the Cross to the theological aesthetic at work, DeVitis notes, "If Greene relied on *The Waste Land* for the imagery of his earlier novels and entertainments, in *The End of the Affair* he relies as heavily on 'Ash Wednesday.' . . . Both Sarah and Bendrix, within broad outline, follow the pattern of spiritual awareness described in John's *La Noce Oscura.* . . . John describes, like Eliot, the penitent experiencing despair, rebellion, and drought in his ascent to heaven" (99).

67. *The End of the Affair*, 47. The page numbers of all further quotations are cited parenthetically in the text.

68. Stephen Schloesser, in "Really, Really Dark: Inventing the Catholic Novel," *Explore* 5.2 (Spring 2002), 9–17, notes that French Catholic revivalism begins with J.-K. Huysmans's realist presentation of "the hysteric" as the ambiguous, indeterminate body that can claim both a scientific, rationalist interpretation and a supernatural cause: "The devilish beauty of hysteria for Huysmans was that we can't prove which is which because we have no access to the underlying causes" (15). It is, in Schloesser's phrase, the Catholic Huysmans's "outgrotesquing the grotesque" realism of the antireligious, naturalist writers of the late nineteenth century. Sarah, whose diary refers to her sense of hysteria, becomes that indeterminate embodiment of divine grace.

69. The reader is reminded that Mauriac, in talking of his own religious formation, notes that the "inoculation of faith" took in him when it didn't in others.

70. Greene, *Ways of Escape*, 144.

71. Stratford, 212, notes that this analogy is quite similar to Mauriac's approach to the creation of character, another manner in which Greene's religious imagination was informed by his French Catholic contemporary.

72. J. C. Whitehouse argues that this does not mean that Sarah is somehow a representative of the predestined elect, a charge often made against the novel: "If one cannot assume that Greene's characters have freedom, the whole aesthetic structure of the novel collapses. . . . It is freedom and consciousness, to whatever degree they may be perceived and accepted, which for Greene are the preconditions of holiness. Sarah is not holy because she has behaved in prescribed ways or through prescribed thoughts, but because at some point in her life she has seen her true nature and has decided to live in what she sees as accordance with it. Apparently virtuous predetermined ways of thinking, habits and established patterns of behavior may in fact tend to exclude or at least diminish such freedom" (79–80).

CHAPTER 3

1. Unpublished letter dated 6 October 1979, from the Graham Greene Papers, John J. Burns Library, Boston College. Pritchett was Greene's friend and American literary agent.

2. Unpublished letter from Greene to Hans Küng, 24 October 1989; used with the permission of Hans Küng.

3. Quoted in Sherry, vol. 2, 257, 329. Sherry quotes many of these love letters that place Greene's sense of the affair in terms of God and his Catholic faith. For a thorough study of Greene's affair with Catherine Walston, see William Cash, *The Third Woman: The Secret Passion that Inspired* The End of the Affair (London: Little, Brown, 2000).

4. See Stratford, 243–280 for a religious analysis of Greene's plays, and see Greene's second collection, *Reflections* (1990), for his articles of the 1950s and 1960s that report on the situation of Catholics in Indochina, Poland, Northern Ireland, and India.

5. See West's biography of Greene, 198–205. West maintains that Greene's decision to leave England permanently ended his close association with many Catholic friends there, especially priests, as well as the Catholic psychiatrists that Greene had used for treatment during bouts of depression.

6. Vivien and Greene never divorced but discussed it in 1948, especially when Greene naively hoped Catherine Walston would divorce her husband and he could then marry her. Walston refused, and Greene and Vivian ultimately settled on a deed of separation. Besides the fact of their Catholicism, Sherry quotes Vivien Greene's concern over Graham's suicidal tendencies as a reason not to have a complete break (283–287).

7. Greene, *The Quiet American*, 189.

8. See V. V. B. Rama Rao, *Graham Greene's Comic Vision* (New Delhi, India: Reliance Publishing, 1990) for a discussion on the tragicomic in Greene. Rao illustrates the general progress of Greene's fiction from the stress on a tragic conflict between the human and divine to a more ironic "comedy in the tragedy of modern life" (15).

9. Peter Muford, *Graham Greene* (London: Northcote House, 1996), 45.

10. Greene, *A Burnt-Out Case*, 207.

11. Greene, *Ways of Escape*, 263.

12. *Ways of Escape*, 265. In a letter, Greene admits to Waugh that there is some of Querry in him but that "if people are so impetuous as to regard this book as a recantation of faith I cannot help it. Perhaps they will be surprised to see me at Mass" (264).

13. François Mauriac claimed that Greene's novels had some of the existential qualities of Sartre and Camus but differed in that Greene's characters always transcended the absurdity that the existentialists offered as a response to human life (Hynes, 75–78). See also Satnam Kaur, *Graham Greene: An Existentialist Investigation*, for parallels to existentialism.

14. Joseph Komonchak, *The Reception of Vatican II* (Washington, DC: Catholic University of America Press, 1987), 79.

15. Greene wrote on "The Assumption of Mary" for *LIFE Magazine*, 30 October 1950, referring to Mary, the mother of Jesus, as "the only figure of perfect human love" (51).

16. Though the news of Vatican II was a surprise to the ordinary lay Catholic,

many Scripture scholars, liturgists, systematic theologians, and Catholic intellectuals in both Europe and the United States had laid the groundwork during the 1940s and 1950s for what was to happen at the Council. For a humorous but accurate account of the effect of the Council on working-class British Catholics, see David Lodge's novel *How Far Can You Go?*, published in America under the title *Souls and Bodies* (New York: Penguin, 1980). The text follows a group of Catholic friends in London from their university days in the 1950s through the turbulent 1960s and 1970s. Each character reacts differently to the many changes, innovations, and experiments with liturgy and pastoral practice in the Church after the Council, with special focus on the upheavals surrounding the Church's position on artificial birth control. Concerning the liturgical changes ushered in by the Council, Evelyn Waugh spoke for many British converts of his generation when in 1962 he denounced liturgists as "modernists" who were trying to change the character of the Church. See *The Essays, Articles and Reviews of Evelyn Waugh*, edited by Donat Gallaher (Boston: Little, Brown, 1983), 606.

17. Roger Garaudy, *From Anathema to Dialogue: A Marxist Challenge to the Christian Churches* (New York: Herder & Herder, 1966), 31. In the introduction of Garaudy's book, Leslie Dewart lists an extensive bibliography from 1955 to 1966 of over 38 texts by mostly European writers who were attempting a dialogue between Marxism and Christianity.

18. Terrence Eagleton, *The New Left Church* (London: Sheed & Ward, 1966), vii, 16.

19. Greene was inclined to economic socialism unfettered by Marxist ideology and thought this the best recipe for economic success in Eastern Europe: "Now that the Stalinist period is over I've swung back to the way I used to feel when I was young. I can't imagine, for instance, how the East can realize itself except through Communism, or better, in some kind of accord between Communism and Christianity" (1966 interview in *Cassis*, 182).

20. Küng, *Theology for the Third Millennium* (New York: Anchor Doubleday, 1988), 132,143. See the collection of articles in Hans Küng and David Tracy, eds., *Paradigm Change in Theology: A Symposium for the Future* (New York: Crossroad, 1989), for a thorough investigation of the usefulness of Thomas Kuhn's theory of paradigm shifts in theology. Küng summarizes the consensus of the symposium (439–452).

21. Küng's use of the term "postmodern" is in the narrowest sense defined as an epistemological, paradigmatic moment that transcends enlightenment/modernist metanarratives and assumptions. In this way, there is the Hegelian echo of dialectical process positively incorporating into postmodernism the premodern and modern paradigms of religious faith.

22. See Küng's "Theology on the Way to a New Paradigm," in *Theology for the Third Millennium*, 182–203, for a thorough treatment of his argument. More broadly, Küng holds that a "Catholic" postmodern paradigm has four dimensions: biblical (the "meaning" of faith in the God of Jesus Christ), historical (one's subjective standpoint in relation to a common world history), ecumenical (from particularist to universalist), and political (a dissolving of theoretical and practical theological divisions).

23. Many historians and theologians list the aims, effects, and accomplishments

of the council. For two complimentary summaries, see John W. O'Malley, *Tradition and Transition: Historical Perspectives on Vatican II* (Wilmington, DE: Michael Glazier, 1989), and Christopher M. Bellito, *Renewing Christianity* (New York: Paulist Press, 2001).

24. O'Malley, 27–28.

25. Ibid., 108. O'Malley notes that the Fifth Lateran Council in 1512 opened with the proclamation that "men must be changed by religion, not religion by men" (107), a statement completely devoid of any historical consciousness on the part of church leaders. With the term *aggiornamento*, the church admitted to the historical development of Scripture, liturgy, canon law, and doctrinal formulation.

26. See John Noonan, "Development in Moral Doctrine," *Theological Studies*, 54.4 (1993), 662–677, for a discussion of the development of church teachings on usury, marriage, slavery, and religious freedom. Noonan cites Newman's influence, as well as other twentieth-century theologians.

27. Newman, Tract 73, "On the Introduction of Rationalistic Principles into Revealed Religion," in *The Essential Newman*, 100.

28. The chapter headings of the *Dogmatic Constitution on the Church* (*Lumen Gentium*), illustrate this attempt at compromise and inclusion: chapter one claims the Church as a mystery and sacrament, the second as the people of God, the third as hierarchy, and the fourth as laity. Each lays claim to central metaphors in which to imagine and understand the nature of the Catholic Church. A now classic if optimistic theological analysis of the diversity of images that came out of the Council is most fully articulated in Avery Dulles, *Models of the Church* (New York: Image Books, 1991).

29. Interview with Greene, in Couto, 206.

30. Citations of *Gaudium et Spes* will be noted in the text as *GS*, followed by the standardized sectional numeration of the document.

31. Graham Greene Papers, Boston College. A folder of correspondence between Greene and Mary Pritchett from the 1970s and early 1980s discusses recent books they had each read and their thoughts on the state of the Catholic Church, especially in light of *Humane Vitae*. Greene mentions in various letters his reading of Teilhard's works, as well as Andrew Greeley's *The Making of the Popes*, Flannery O'Connor's *The Habit of Being*, and John Haughey's *The Conspiracy of God*.

32. Pierre Teilhard de Chardin, *Science and Christ* (New York: Harper & Row, 1968), 17, 167.

33. Teilhard de Chardin, *Christianity and Evolution* (New York: Harcourt Brace Jovanovich, 1971), 212.

34. Greene was well read in Teilhard's thought, and interestingly, Teilhard was well read in at least one of Greene's novels, *The Heart of the Matter* (1948). Teilhard entitled his own autobiographical text *The Heart of Matter* (New York: Harcourt Brace Jovanovich, 1978), quite conscious of Greene's novel. In a letter to a friend dated 1948, Teilhard writes: "Incidentally, the Graham Greene title (*The Heart of the Matter*) would be wonderful for me (although a quite different meaning) for an essay I am dreaming to write since some time" (77).

35. Rahner, "Anonymous Christians," *Theological Investigations*, vol. 6 (Baltimore:

Helicon Press, 1969), 390. See also "Atheism and Implicit Christianity," *Theological Investigations*, vol. 9 (New York: Herder & Herder, 1972), 145–164; and "Theological Considerations on Secularization and Atheism," *Theological Investigations*, vol. 11 (New York, Herder & Herder, 1974), 166–184.

36. Council Documents, *GS* 22, 57; *Lumen Gentium* 8, 16; *Ad Gentes*, 7.

37. See Owen Chadwick, *The Secularization of the European Mind in the 19th Century* (Cambridge: Cambridge University Press, 1975), for a historical perspective that argues this point. Chadwick suggests that early Marxism developed as an "attribution of the secular to a Christian inheritance" (67).

38. Edward Schillebeeckx, *God the Future of Man* (New York: Sheed & Ward, 1968), 5.

39. Schillebeeckx, in *Paradigm Change in Theology*, 316.

40. Schillebeeckx, *God the Future of Man*, 76.

41. Ibid., 64. The above summary is taken from Schillebeeckx's diagnosis of the "death of God" movement (53–90). See also his *God and Man* (New York: Sheed & Ward, 1969) where he directly treats the relationship of Catholicism to nonreligious humanism. For an example of the death of God movement in theology, see T. Altizer's *The Gospel of Christian Atheism*.

42. Ibid., 84.

43. Küng, *On Being a Christian*, 224.

44. Schillebeeckx defines his use of the term "ideology" as "a totality of images, representations, and symbols which a particular society creates in order to justify its identity . . . the reproduction and confirmation of one's own identity through 'founding symbols'" (*Paradigm Change in Theology*, 314).

45. Robert A. Burns, *Roman Catholicism after Vatican II* (Washington, DC: Georgetown University Press, 2001), 20. Rahner's lecture, "Two Types of Christology" was published in *Theological Investigations*, vol. 13 (New York: Seabury Press, 1975), 213–223.

46. Greene had both an early edition of *On Being a Christian* in his library, as well as an abridged version called *The Christian Challenge*, signed by Küng as a gift on his eighty-fifth birthday. The dedication reads: "My personal Spero, to Graham Greene who remains young in Spirit for his 85th birthday in admiration and gratitude" (Graham Greene Papers). Father Leopoldo Duran's memoir *Graham Greene: Friend and Brother* (London: HarperCollins, 1994), 110–113, notes Greene's great interest in both the theology and controversy surrounding Schillebeeckx and Küng.

47. Küng, *On Being a Christian*, 400.

48. See *On Being a Christian* for Küng's discussion on the Resurrection, 343–380; preexistence, 445–447; Incarnation, 437–444; and Trinity, 472–478.

49. Ibid., 599–602.

50. Edward Schillebeeckx, *Jesus: An Experiment in Christology* (New York: Seabury Press, 1979), 699.

51. Schillebeeckx's conclusions on the "transhistorical reality" of the Resurrection caused great controversy in both the Vatican and Catholic theological institutions. Greene probably became interested in Schillebeeckx when this controversy was aired

in *The Tablet*. For a full discussion, see Schillebeeckx's *Interim Report on the Books* Jesus and Christ (New York: Crossroad, 1981).

52. Ibid., 672–673.

53. Küng, *Theology for the Third Millennium*, 185.

54. Hans Küng, *The Church—Maintained in Truth: A Theological Meditation* (New York: Seabury Press, 1980), 12, 26.

55. Allain, *The Other Man*, 155.

56. Ibid., 158–159. In *Graham Greene, Friend and Brother*, Fr. Leopoldo Duran cites a letter from Greene dated 30 April 1984: "Now paradoxically in the affair of Father Hans Küng and Father Schillebeeckx I find myself grateful to those two priests for reawakening my belief—my belief in the empty tomb and the resurrection, the magic side of the Christian religion if you like. Perhaps that is the unconscious mission of Father S. when he writes of the resurrection as being a kind of symbolic statement of the spiritual impression which the apostles experienced after the crucifixion. I remember again in St. John's Gospel the run between Peter and John towards the tomb. Peter leading until he lost breath, and then the younger man arriving first and seeing the linen clothes but afraid to go in, and then Peter overtaking him. It's like *reportage*. I can be interested in the *reportage* of a mystery: I am completely uninterested—even bored—by a spiritual symbol equally 'unhistoric' in Küng's sense as *reportage*" (289–290).

57. Allain, 163. Greene had marked out in Küng's text the following analogy, which echoes his distinction between faith and belief that he made in the interview: "Faith is like love. If I love someone but have to explain suddenly why I love that person, I may stutter, make mistakes, exaggerate one thing and understate another, say something distorted or even false, stress what is unimportant and even forget what is important. But this is not necessarily detrimental to my love. Love is dependent on statements if it is to find expression. But love persists even through untrue statements" (Küng, *The Church—Maintained in Truth*, 45).

58. *Lumen Gentium*, 1, 9, 48; *Gaudium et Spes*, 45; *Sacrosanctum Concilium*, 2, 5, 26; *Ad Gentes*, 5.

59. Edward Schillebeeckx, *Christ the Sacrament of the Encounter with God* (New York: Sheed & Ward, 1963), 13.

60. Ibid., 15.

61. Ibid., 47–48.

62. Aquinas systematized a form of sacramental causality called "instrumental," in which the materiality of the sacrament (water and bread) and the words of the rite are instrumental (secondary) causes of God's grace, God being the primary efficient agent. The effect was to separate the sign of God's grace (the sacramental rite) from the cause (God's action). Karl Rahner attempted to reunite notions of sacraments as signs and sacraments as causes of grace by using a Heideggerian understanding of symbol as participation: a symbol not only bears witness to the reality it symbolizes but also makes the reality present See Karl Rahner's *The Church and the Sacraments* (New York: Herder & Herder, 1963), 36–37. Schillebeeckx, in more Thomistic termi-

nology, concurs: "Sacraments effect what they signify." For a concise summary of Schillebeeckx and Rahner's contribution to post–Vatican II sacramental theology, see Kenan Osborne, *Sacramental Theology: A General Introduction* (New York: Paulist Press, 1988), 49–68.

63. Schillebeeckx, *Christ the Sacrament of the Encounter with God*, 208.

64. The term "transubstantiation" was first used at the Fourth Lateran Council (1215) and reaffirmed at both the Council of Trent (1551) and by Pope Paul VI at Vatican II.

65. *Sacrosanctum Concilium*, 7. Yet, to safeguard the traditional faith in the real eucharistic presence as unique, Pope Paul VI issued his encyclical *Mysterium Fidei* (1965), in which he notes that "this eucharistic presence is called *the real presence* not to exclude the other kinds as though they were not real, but because it is real par excellence." (par. 39).

66. *Sacrosanctum Concilium*, 48.

67. See *Lumen Gentium*, 28, and *Presbyterorum Ordinis*, 3, 4, 5, 9.

68. Greene, *Yours Etc.*, 154.

69. Graham Greene Papers. Greene's correspondence is found in a folder entitled "Liturgy in English," containing his objections to the vernacular liturgy and some literary suggestions for the translation from Latin to English.

70. See Adam Schwartz, " 'I Thought the Church and I Wanted the Same Thing': Opposition to Twentieth-Century Liturgical Change in the Thought of Graham Greene, Christopher Dawson, and David Jones," *LOGOS: A Journal of Catholic Thought and Literature* 1.4 (1998), 36–65, for a litany of Greene's objections to the vernacular Mass. Schwartz argues that Greene's defense of the Latin Mass is evidence of an antimodernist strain in Greene's allegiance to his faith. Schwartz quotes part of the 1971 joint letter to Rome, which protested that the vernacular Mass surrenders to "the materialist and technocratic civilization that is increasingly threatening the life of the mind and spirit."

71. Allain, 161.

72. Greene, *Yours Etc.*, 250.

73. "Why I Am Still a Catholic," interview with John Cornwell, *The Tablet*, 25 September 1989; in Cassis, 458. With the death of the British Jesuit theologian C. C. Martindale in 1962, Greene had lost a priest-confessor and friend. Father Duran's friendship with Greene began in 1964 when he was finishing a doctoral thesis on the notion of priesthood in Greene's novels. It developed into an intimate and lifelong friendship, which resulted in Duran's idiosyncratic memoir of their many conversations and travels the last 25 years of Greene's life.

74. Besides his friendship with Fr. Duran, Greene corresponded with the peace activist Fr. Roy Bourgeois of the United States and Fr. Ernesto Cardenal of Nicaragua, the minister of education in the Sandinista government. Greene's correspondence with the British missionary priest John Medcalf led him to write the forward to Medcalf's *Letters from Nicaragua*, letters about his life as a parish priest under attack by U.S.-backed contras.

75. Allain, 159.

76. Hans Küng, *Does God Exist? An Answer for Today* (New York: Random House, 1978), 569–578.

77. Graham Greene Papers. The letters of Greene and Pritchett in the archive extend from 1979 to 1981, often discussing their impressions of Catholic issues of the time (including those raised by Hans Küng and Pope John Paul II) and questions about papal infallibility and artificial contraception.

78. Allain, 157.

79. Letter to Mary Pritchett, 3 March 1980, in the Graham Greene Papers.

80. Letter from Greene to Cardinal Arns, Archbishop of Sao Paulo, Brazil, in the Graham Greene Papers. Greene thanks Arns for "all that you have done for human rights and for liberation theologians."

CHAPTER 4

1. Quoted in Gustavo Gutierrez, *We Drink from Our Own Wells: The Spiritual Journey of a People* (Maryknoll, NY: Orbis Press, 1984), 117.

2. Ernesto Cardenal, *La democratización del la cultura* (Managua: Ministerio de la cultura, 1982), 21.

3. From 1971 until his death in 1991, Greene wrote six novels, two autobiographies, two biographies, a new collection of short stories, and a personal account of his friendship with General Omar Torrijos Herrera of Panama called *Getting to Know the General.* He wrote and saw produced his final play, *The Return of A. J. Raffles*, in 1975, and he gathered together previously published collections of his short stories, a second collection of articles, and a collection of his early film criticism. Of his six novels, I am not considering two in my investigation: *The Tenth Man* (1985), a forgotten film script from the 1950s reworked into a novella and published in 1985, and *The Captain and the Enemy* (1988), a slight picaresque story published right before Greene's death. Both of these works of fiction are in many ways derivative and are rarely, if ever, discussed, whereas the other late novels I am investigating have become part of the collected critical canon of his work.

4. *A Burnt-Out Case* is indeed a "Catholic" novel in that religious belief and unbelief are central. Querry is the "burnt-out case," like a leper deformed by disease. His renewal or salvation comes in part from reaching out to his leprous servant, Deo Gratias, as well as from his ability to help the monks and the atheist doctor at the medical clinic. He dies an absurd death at the hands of a fanatic Catholic named Ryker. The novel ends with the mission superior making a Pascalian claim on Querry's spiritual state. Certainly, Greene's Catholic imagination serves as the primary substrate for exploring belief. Yet even so, the classic formulae of his Catholic cycle of novels are missing. Moreover, Greene pessimistically interrogates religious belief to such an extent that he compels the reader to forgo any claim that faith (or the Divine, for that matter) might triumph in the life of his character. There is insufficient evidence in Querry's behavior to warrant it, and thus existential absurdity is as compelling a reading of the end and purpose of the story as is a religious reading of the text.

5. In *Ways of Escape*, 296, Greene muses, "If *A Burnt-Out Case* represented the depressive side of a manic-depressive writer, *Travels with My Aunt* eight years later surely represented the manic at its height—or depth . . . I can only suppose it came from making a difficult decision in my private life and leaving England to settle permanently in France in 1966. I burned a number of boats and in the light of the flames I began again to write a novel."

6. Duran, *Graham Greene*, 240.

7. Greene, *Ways of Escape*, 297

8. Graham Greene, *Travels with My Aunt* (New York: Penguin, [1969] 1977), 265.

9. General Conference of Latin American Bishops, *The Church in the Present-day Transformation of Latin America* (Washington, DC: USCC, 1970), introduction, 4.

10. Gustavo Gutierrez, "Liberation, Theology, and Proclamation," *Concilium* 96 (New York: Herder & Herder, 1974), 19.

11. Gustavo Gutierrez, *A Theology of Liberation* (New York: Orbis Press, 1988), 24, 103. Liberation theology in Central and South America began as a movement with Gutierrez's seminal work, *A Theology of Liberation*. Other scholars in this group of thinkers include Jon Sobrino, Leonardo Boff, Juan Luis Segundo, and Enrique Dussel. Liberation theology continues the trajectory of post–Vatican II Christology by focusing on the message and mission of Jesus of Nazareth.

12. For a christological consideration of liberation theology, see Jon Sobrino, *Jesus the Liberator, a Historical-Theological View* (New York: Orbis Press, 1993), 67–87, 254–264.

13. Gustavo Gutierrez, *The Truth Shall Make You Free: Confrontations* (New York: Orbis Press, 1990), 68.

14. Gutierrez, *Theology of Liberation*, 64.

15. Gutierrez, "Liberation, Theology and Proclamation," 33.

16. Gutierrez, *The Truth Shall Make You Free*, 61.

17. See Enrique Dussel, *A History of the Church in Latin America* Grand Rapids, (MI: William Eerdmans, 1981) 14, for a hermeneutical discussion of the term "praxis" in liberationist thought. Schillebeeckx, a theologian more familiar to Greene, often uses the word "praxis" to suggest the dialectical interaction of theory and concrete action in witnessing to Jesus' proclamation of the Kingdom. Schillebeeckx argues that following Jesus involves a "praxis of the reign of God," which is at once mystical and political.

18. It should be noted that over time Gutierrez quoted sociologists and political theorists less often in his later work and cited more Church and papal social encyclicals.

19. Greene, *Ways of Escape*, 78.

20. Greene, *Reflections*, 278.

21. Greene, *Getting to Know the General, the Story of an Involvement* (New York: Simon & Schuster, 1984), 225–226.

22. Greene interview in Couto, 213. Greene wrote many editorials on Nicaragua and takes aim at President Reagan in the *Times* (London): "Why does [he] persist in calling the Nicaraguan government a communist government? Wouldn't it be equally

true, or equally false, to call it a Roman Catholic government?" (20 March 1986); he takes on the pope once again in *The Tablet*: "The Pope when he speaks of religious persecution in Nicaragua seems to be lamentably ill-informed. I have just returned from that country and I can only speak of what I saw—big placards displayed on the roads marked 'Revolution Yes. But Christian.' . . . [On the feast of the Immaculate Conception] the crowds would shout 'Who has brought us happiness?' and the answering cry was 'Mary the Immaculate.' . . . This may be described as Mariolatry but hardly religious persecution" (4 January 1986). In Greene, *Yours Etc.*, 230, 232.

23. Greene shares the preoccupation with the theme of personal exile that pervades modernist and postmodernist and postcolonial literature. Likewise, Greene's fusion of Christian and Marxist ends finds company in much postcolonial literature of Latin America: Ernesto Cardenal (already mentioned), Gabriel García Márquez, Isabel Allende, and Mario Varga Llosa. For articles that explore this political-religious fusion, see Susan VanZantan Gallagher, *Postcolonial Literature and the Biblical Call for Justice* (Jackson: University Press of Mississippi, 1994).

24. See David Brindley, "Orthodoxy and Orthopraxis in the Novels of Graham Greene, *Theology* 86 (January 1983), 29–36.

25. Greene, *Yours Etc.*, 225.

26. Couto, 212.

27. The novel also succeeds as one of Greene's most "postmodern" literary works. Greene playfully explores the nature of paternity, especially textual paternity— the literary fictions that have exerted an influence on characters, as well as on readers. Elliot Mallamet notes that "the novel has both characteristics of self-reflexive and overtly parodic intertextuality . . . a story about absent fathers, discussions of Jorge Luis Borges, the reading, writing and reflection on detective fiction, a gloss on the stories of Stevenson, Chesterton, and Conan Doyle, characters from of old in new clothes—all speak to the themes of artistic influence and originality that are prevalent in Greene's later works" (114–115).

28. Greene, *The Honorary Consul* (London: Bodley Head, 1973), 62. Page numbers of further references are parenthetically noted in the text.

29. The text suggests that the "cord" that binds the child is correlative to a post–Vatican II understanding of the theology of original sin: less about the guilt and stain on the individual soul from Adam's first sin, and more about the social and biological givens of individuals living in a network of sinful human structures and relationships that hinder their flourishing.

30. Greene based León Rivas on a composite of two priests. In the Graham Greene Files at the University of Texas, Austin, a newspaper cutting from the *Irish Times* (6 April 1970) has this headline: "Rebel Priest's Work Praised by Novelist." It refers to Greene's visit to the Corrientes province in Argentina, where the archbishop had excommunicated a liberationist priest, Fr. Oscar Marturet. The parish sympathized with their priest, and the bishop had to call in the police and the army's infantry brigade to quell the unrest. The other priest that Rivas is based on is Fr. Camilo Torres, a university chaplain in Colombia who was removed from his post by the cardinal archbishop because of his socialist preaching. He joined the communist rebels

and became know as a guerilla-priest, dying with a gun in his hand. Many details of Torres's life are incorporated into Greene's portrait of Rivas. See Duran, *Graham Greene,* 73–74.

31. Gustavo Gutierrez, "Speaking about God," *Concilium* 171 (Edinburgh: T. & T. Clark, 1984), 28.

32. In an early confrontation in the novel, Plarr had reflected, "León was able to make even the Trinity seem plausible by a sort of higher mathematics" (119).

33. The quote comes from the first two drafts of the novel, found in the Graham Greene Files (File 15.1) at the University of Texas. Much was edited out in the third draft, including religious conversations between the characters and especially the pointedly Catholic justifications León makes for his actions. A primary excision refers to a conversation on the historical situation of Latin America, in which Plarr, León, and Aquino mention the pope (most references to Rome are taken out in the final version) and other political leaders, as well as a clearer reference to Fr. Camilo Torres, on whom Leon's character is based.

34. Greene was quite familiar with Teilhard de Chardin's evolutionary vision, as has already been observed. Greene's letters from the 1950s and 1960s to his Jesuit friend and spiritual director C. C. Martindale suggest Greene's further study of Teilhard's works. Teilhard and Martindale had been stranded together in Copenhagen during World War II. Greene's correspondence with Martindale is found in the Graham Greene Papers.

35. For all of León's theological speculation in a divine-human revolution, his personal hope is centered on giving his trust and commitment to a worthy and just father. In the last scenes León feels the betrayal of his final surrogate father, El Tigre, his rebel commander. Textually El Tigre is a more absolute and remote father figure than even León's own father or the hierarchical fatherhood of the church.

36. David Leigh, "The Structures of Graham Greene's *The Honorary Consul,*" *Renascence: Essays on Values and Literature* 38.1 (Autumn 1985), 23.

37. Gutierrez, *The Truth Shall Make You Free,* 103.

38. Gutierrez, "Speaking about God," 31.

39. Kim Philby had secretly worked as a spy for the Soviet Union during and after World War II. Greene had written 25,000 words before Philby's announced defection and consequent publication of his memoir, *My Secret War,* both a defense and account of his actions. In April 1978 Greene sent the final proofs of the novel to Philby, now exiled in Moscow, for comments and alterations. See West's *Quest for Graham Greene,* 233–257, for an interesting account of Greene and Philby's relationship.

40. The title of the first draft of the novel, "The Cold Fault," alludes more fully to the metaphorical implications of the cold war on human relationships. In a personal note in the Graham Greene Files at the University of Texas (Box 17), Greene discusses this title before it changed to *The Human Factor:* "Perhaps in love lies the cold fault of the title—a commitment to private life rather than loyalty to country or to one political system more than another."

41. Conor Cruise O'Brien's review is one of the most explicit readings of the

novel as a religious work: "This novel, which appears to be political, is in fact metaphysical. It is about good and evil, love and hate, the quest for God, the imitation of Christ." Greene's Castle, *The New York Review of Books*, 1 June 1978, 3–5.

42. Paul O'Prey, *A Reader's Guide to Graham Greene* (London: Thames & Hudson, 1988), 136.

43. Graham Greene, *The Human Factor* (New York: Simon & Schuster, 1978), 145. Page numbers of all further references are parenthetically cited in the text.

44. Greene's original disclaimer in his preface to the book, that "Operation Uncle Remus" was merely a product of his imagination, proved once again his astute and prescient reading of the political situation during the cold war. Soon after the novel appeared, E. Cervenka and Barbara Rodgers published *The Nuclear Axis: The Secret Collaboration between the West and South Africa* (London: Julian Friedman, 1978), which reports that stolen documents from the South African Embassy in West Germany detailed an operation that has a striking resemblance to Greene's fictional invention.

45. Erdinast-Vulcan, 102.

46. Greene's intertextual references are evident, for the love between Maurice and Sarah Castle suggests comparison to his other passionate but unhappy couple of the same name, Maurice Bendrix and Sarah Miles in *The End of the Affair*.

47. Castle's need to right the balance is a more serious strain of Charley Fortnum's humorous commentary on drinking "the right measure." Fortnum's incessant worry over the right measure and Castle's desire to right the balance recounts the claim of a Catholic theological aesthetic in which one's actions participate proportionately in the actions of Christ, the ultimate standard. Both characters in the end "measure up" to that standard.

48. Graham Greene, "The Last Pope," address given in 1948 at Les Grandes Conférences Catholiques in Brussels, translated by Philip Stratford in Greene's *Reflections*, 120.

49. Greene, *Reflections*, 124. In this same collection is Greene's provocative 1969 address upon being given the University of Hamburg's Shakespeare Award. This time he compares Shakespeare to one of his contemporaries, the English Jesuit poet and martyr Robert Southwell. He notes that Southwell's literary achievements are enacted at a great price. Referring to the virtue of disloyalty in quasi-religious terms in writers such as Dante, Villon, and Solzhenitsyn, Greene names Shakespeare a poet of the establishment, where "the only line I can recall of Shakespeare's which reflects critically on the Reformation is a metaphor in the Sonnets which could easily be explained away" (266). This lack of religious sensibility in Shakespeare, Greene ruefully suggests, shows "the deepest tragedy Shakespeare lived was his own: the blind eye exchanged for the coat of arms, the prudent tongue for the friendships at Court and the great house at Stratford" (270).

50. Erdinast-Vulcan, 100. Erdinast-Vulcan entitles her study of the novel "A Priest without a Church: *The Human Factor*," suggesting that Castle is ontologically described as a priest bereft of both a religious and a secular community.

51. Ibid., 106.

52. Leopoldo Duran, "The Human Factor within the Inhuman System," *The Clergy Review*, August 1980, 287.

CHAPTER 5

1. Greene spent much of the early 1980s embroiled in a battle to uncover the influence of organized crime on the justice system of Nice in southern France. After writing letters to the press he published *J'Accuse* (1982) in French and English, a pamphlet documenting the criminal collusion of the mafia and the French justice system. The exposé's vaunted title is taken from Émile Zola's famous defense of Dreyfus. Greene's involvement was made personal when the daughter of Yvonne Cloetta, his long-time mistress in Antibes, unknowingly married a man involved in the mafia. He had manipulated the courts in order to get custody of their child after their divorce. See Duran, 247–259, for an extensive play-by-play of Greene's involvement in the affair.

2. This same stylistic technique is found in his other two works of fiction of the 1980s as well: *The Tenth Man* (1985; first written in the 1940s as a Hollywood script), reads like a thrilling morality play, in which the themes of sin, redemption, and the sacrifice of self for the sake of love are subsumed in the drama; and *The Captain and the Enemy* (1988) is a dreamlike fairytale of misfits and adventurers who find their hope in the personal commitments to those they love. See Brian Thomas, *An Underground Fate: The Idiom of Romance in the Later Novels of Graham Greene*, for a detailed exploration of Greene's turn to romance. Thomas argues that it is in some part a return to Greene's earlier structures from his texts of the 1920s and 1930s. These two novellas indeed recall the "entertainments" of Greene's earlier works.

3. DeVitis, 144.

4. The terms "carnivalesque" and "dialogical" are Mikhail Bakhtin's nomenclature. He argues that the novel is a "double-voiced" literary form in which "speech acts" in a text allude to, echo, and respond to other preexisting discourses. As a result, there is something "unfinalizable" and open-ended in the possible forms of cooperation, opposition, and interaction among the diverse voices in a novel. Such has been my reading of Greene's religious discourse in his texts, especially the late works. Bakhtin traces the "carnivalesque" pattern in Western literature (in the tradition of the literary grotesque) as a form that uniquely embodies a dialogic imagination: by turning upside down the usual hierarchical structures of both the social world and the more classical literary genres, the reader glimpses through a momentary revolution (carnival) a more profoundly complex and embodied experience of humanity. See his books *The Dialogic Imagination: Four Essays by M. M. Bakhtin*, edited and translated by Michael Holquist (Austin: University of Texas Press, 1981), and *Rabelais and His World*, translated by Hélène Iswolsky (Bloomington: Indiana University Press, 1984), for a detailed discussion.

5. Gaston, 131.

6. Greene, *Doctor Fischer of Geneva, or the Bomb Party* (New York: Simon & Schuster, 1980), 141. The page numbers of all further citations are noted parenthetically in the text.

7. Gaston, 131.

8. DeVitis, 143.

9. Gaston, 132, 134.

10. David Lodge, "Moral Entertainment: *Doctor Fischer of Geneva or the Bomb Party,*" *The Tablet* (29 March 1980), 318.

11. Couto, 8; John Spurling, *Graham Greene* (London: Methuen, 1983), 54. Spurling claims that *Monsignor Quixote* is "a second coda" because he places *A Burnt-out Case* (1961) as the first coda of Greene's Catholic cycle.

12. Greene, *Monsignor Quixote* (Toronto: Lester & Orpen Dennys, 1982), 15. The page numbers of all further citations are noted parenthetically in the text.

13. Much of the details of Greene's relationship with Fr. Duran and his travels in Spain are found in Duran's memoir, *Graham Greene*. He states that on a drive in 1977 "Monsignor Quixote was born in the cemetery at Salamanca [at] Miguel de Unamuno's tomb" (212).

14. *The Tablet* 23/30 (December 1978), 1238–1241. The next two chapters also appeared in serialized form in *The Tablet* in 1980 and 1981, before the publication of the novel. Tom Burns, the editor of *The Tablet* and a personal friend of Greene, is mentioned in the dedication of the novel.

15. Cervantes' *Don Quixote de la Mancha* (1605) tells the story of an old country gentleman so moved by his reading of chivalric romance that he sets out to do "battle against the windmills." With his squire, Sancho Panza, and his horse, Rocinante, he has numerous comic adventures but is ultimately defeated by those who find him mad. Near the end of his life, he renounces his role as knight-errant.

16. Greene's hope that there might be a practical relationship between Catholicism and Marxism is evident in his decision to divide the Spanish and Latin American royalties of the novel equally between the two communities in which he was most engaged during this time, the Trappist monks of Spain and the revolutionary forces (FMLN) fighting the oppressive government of El Salvador in the 1980s.

17. See Jae Suck Choi, *Greene and Unamuno: Two Pilgrims to La Mancha* (New York: Peter Lang, 1990), for a thorough reading of Greene's works through the lens of Unamuno's philosophy. Choi succinctly notes their religious affinity in the following ways: "Both were torn between rationalism and the affective religious sense; both struggled between dogma and faith; and both believe that those who are in agonic struggle can be spiritually alive and attain true faith" (31). And they share another distinction: for a time, Greene's *The Power and the Glory* and Unamuno's books *The Tragic Sense of Life* and *The Agony of Christianity* were placed on the church's Index of Forbidden Books by the Vatican's Holy Office.

18. Miguel de Unamuno, *The Tragic Sense of Life in Men and Nations*, translated by Anthony Kerigan (Princeton, NJ: Princeton University Press, Bollingen Series 85.4, 1972), 226–227.

19. Greene, *Ways of Escape*, 266. Greene quotes four influential passages from

Unamuno in reference to his short story "A Visit to Morin" and his novel *A Burnt-out Case* (265–267). The importance of Unamuno on Greene is substantiated in Duran's memoir of his travels with the author.

20. Cates Baldridge, for instance, discusses the apocalyptic implications in the novel: "Greene's form of Christianity is very much his own construction. . . . [His] objection is to both Christianity and Marxism's official eschatologies, for both systems insist upon their own versions of a coming time 'without doubt or faith.' " (170–171). Baldridge argues that Greene's understanding of doubt is much like Matthew Arnold's: "The truth of the matter is that sometimes the pounding that Marx and Christ deliver to each other . . . leave standing only a figure resembling Matthew Arnold, much as our author might wish to deny it" (172). Baldridge's argument holds only if one understands Christian eschatology as a parallel to Marxism, the achievement of a rationalized perfection of human nature instead of a transformation (divinization) of the human. In my reading of the text, Christ doesn't get the pounding from Marx that Baldridge claims. Quixote's doubt is not based on the liberal strains of enlightenment categories but on a personal doubt of one's ability to see the mystery in the manner of things. Far from implying Arnold's agnosticism, Quixote echoes Pascal. In the end, Quixote's God is an objective reality, not an idea, both known and yet total mystery. It is in the struggle of holding to this paradox that his doubts arise.

21. John F. Desmond, "The Heart of (the) Matter: The Mystery of the Real in *Monsignor Quixote*," *Religion and Literature* 22.1 (Spring 1990), 72.

22. Peter G. Christensen, "The Art of Self-Preservation: Monsignor Quixote's Resistance to Don Quixote," *Essays in Graham Greene: An Annual Review*, vol. 3, edited by Peter Wolfe (St. Louis, MO: Lucas Hall Press, 1992), 34.

23. Heribert Jone's *Moral Theology* was reprinted several times during the 1940s and 1950s and was used in major Catholic seminaries until the time of the council. In a letter to David Low, Greene mentions his amusement at reading the book and his hope to use it in *Monsignor Quixote*. For Greene's correspondence with David Low, a London bookseller and bibliophile, see *Dear David, Dear Graham* (Oxford: Alembic Press, 1989).

24. The critic Adam Schwartz makes much of this liturgical clash, calling the monsignor's final mass in Latin a "talisman" against modernity, a "rebellion" against the church's new liturgical law, and a "defiance" against the imposition of the hierarchy's will. He concludes, rather narrowly, "Greene's sense of what constitutes a proper Catholic opposition to modernity and its implications for liturgy and practice is ultimately an illustration of his faith's conditional nature" (41). This reading seems reductionistic, for Quixote's reversion to the old rite certainly doesn't convey his attachment to Tridentine conservativism; rather, it is the poet in Quixote (and, I think, in Greene) and not the ideologue that still responds to the old Latin Mass.

25. The novelist Muriel Spark, a fellow convert and friend of Greene, plays with this same sentiment in her satirical novel *The Abbess of Crewe: A Morality Play* (New York: Viking, 1974). The novel relates the story of the new abbess of the Benedictine monastery of Crewe, who uses her position to control both the liturgy and the lifestyle of her monastery in order to impede any implementation of the spirit of Vatican

11. Her main adversary is a younger, activist nun who wishes to modernize the order's rule and worship.

26. Desmond, 67. John Desmond's analysis deserves considerable mention in informing my own theological reading of the novel. Much that follows concerning the relationship of Lynch and Teilhard de Chardin to Greene's text stems from his work.

27. Ibid., 66–67.

28. William Lynch, *Christ and Apollo: The Dimensions of the Literary Imagination.* 188.

29. Sancho had taken the monsignor to lodge at a brothel in Salamanca, and the balloon refers to a prophylactic. Quixote sees "a little square envelope" lying next to Sancho's bed and blows up the "sausage-shaped balloon" inside. Bewildered, Sancho inquires, "Have you never seen a contraceptive before? No, I suppose you haven't" (102).

30. John Desmond makes a strong case in comparing Greene's use of Francis de Sales' notion of the hopping of Adamant to iron with Teilhard's personal account of his own conversion to an evolutionary theory of union between matter and spirit. In *The Heart of Matter* Teilhard tells of his youthful fascination with "a piece of iron" that led him to think in terms of spirit incarnated in matter (68).

31. Desmond, 73.

32. Lynch, *Christ and Apollo* 66. Lynch is critical of Greene's religious imagination in two novels: *The Heart of the Matter* is "a subtle if unconscious demonstration of the Manichean way" (168), and *The End of the Affair* is a "Catholic novel that is more Catholic than Catholicism" (169). Lynch's assessment of Greene's imagination is hindered by his narrow critique of Kierkegaard, whom he thinks Greene most resembles.

33. Ibid., 13.

34. Peter Christensen, in "The Art of Self-Preservation," argues that the Monsignor's attempt to preserve his status as a human being in the midst of doubts about his sanity is correlated to his resistance to Don Quixote's demise in Cervantes' tale: "Near death the Don repents, but the Monsignor does not repent after his last Mass. The Monsignor knows that doubting is not always a prelude to giving in; sometimes it precedes a resolve to go on" (35).

35. In an interview Greene revealed that his friend Fr. Duran was the source for Quixote's affirmation that he touches God: "[Fr. Duran] is possessed by an absolute faith. When I asked him to describe it, he modestly replied, 'I do not believe in God, I touch Him." Allain, 147.

36. The classical, Tridentine word "transubstantiation" necessarily isolates the focus of the eucharistic presence on the material of bread and wine, the accidental sign that persists in the consecration, as opposed to that presence in the gathered assembly.

37. Graham Holderness, in " 'Knight-Errant of Faith'? *Monsignor Quixote* as Catholic Fiction," *Journal of Literature and Theology* 7.3 (September 1993), sees the word "compañero" as key to the mutual effect of Quixote and Sancho on one another: "[Compañero] is a term which synthesizes picaresque companionship (cp. The chival-

ric term *compañero de armas*), political solidarity ('comrade') and reciprocal human affection (friend)" (268). It also suggests a fourth effect—the call of discipleship.

38. Michael W. Higgins, "Greene's Priest: A Sort of Rebel," in Peter Wolfe, *Essays in Graham Greene*, vol. 3, edited by Peter Wolfe (St. Louis, MO: Lucas Hall Press), 23.

39. Holderness, 280.

EPILOGUE

1. According to my reading of Greene, he would probably have accepted the title "liberal," but such a term must be qualified. His love for the old Latin mass, his belief in the importance of celibate priesthood, his sacramental ontology, and his disdain for modernist claims all show that Greene's Catholicism is much more complex than such easy categorization would allow.

References

Abercrombie, Nigel. *The Origins of Jansenism*. Oxford: Clarendon Press, 1936.

Adamson, Judith. *Graham Greene, The Dangerous Edge: Where Art and Politics Meet*. London: Macmillan, 1990.

Allain, Marie-Françoise. *The Other Man: Conversations with Graham Greene*. New York: Simon & Schuster, 1983.

Allit, Patrick. *Catholic Converts: British and American Intellectuals Turn to Rome*. Ithaca, NY: Cornell University Press, 1997.

Allott, Kenneth, and Miriam Farris. *The Art of Graham Greene*. London: Hamish Hamilton, 1951.

Altizer, Thomas. *The Gospel of Christian Atheism*. Philadelphia: Westminster Press, 1966.

Atkins, John. *Graham Greene*. London: Calder & Boyars, [1957], 1966.

Bakhtin, M. M. *The Dialogic Imagination Four Essays by M. M. Bakhtin*. Edited and translated by Michael Holquist. Austin: University of Texas Press, 1981.

———. *Rabelais and His World*. Translated by Hélène Iswolsky. Bloomington: Indiana University Press, 1984.

Baldridge, Cates. *Graham Greene's Fictions: The Virtues of Extremity*. Columbia: University of Missouri Press, 2000.

Balthasar, Hans Urs von. *Bernanos: An Ecclesial Existence*. San Francisco: Ignatius Press, 1996.

———. *The Glory of the Lord: A Theological Aesthetics*, vols. 1–7. San Francisco: Ignatius Press, 1982–1988.

Bataille, Georges. *Theory of Religion*. Translated by Robert Hurley. New York: Zone, 1989.

Bednar, Gerald J. *Faith as Imagination*. Kansas City: Sheed and Ward, 1996.

Begley, Ann M. "Georges Bernanos' Love Affair with God." *Religion and Literature* 33.3 (2001), 37–52.

Béguin, Albert. *Léon Bloy: A Study in Impatience*. Translated by Edith Riley. New York: Sheed and Ward, 1947.

Bellito, Christopher M. *Renewing Christianity*. New York: Paulist Press, 2001.

Bennett, John C. *Christianity and Communism Today*. New York: Association Press, 1970.

Bernanos, Georges. *The Diary of a Country Priest*. Translated by Pamela Morris. New York: Carrol & Graf, [1936] 2001.

———. *The Star of Satan (Sous le Soleil de Satan)*. Translated by Pamela Morris. New York: Macmillan, [1926] 1940.

Bloom, Harold. *The Anxiety of Influence: A Theory of Poetry*. New York: Oxford University Press, 1973.

Bloom, Harold, ed. *Graham Greene: Modern Critical Views*. New York: Chelsea House, 1987.

Bloy, Léon. *Choix de Textes et Introduction. Par Albert Béguin*. Fribourg: Editions de la Librairie de l'Université, 1943.

Boardman, Gwen R. *Graham Greene: The Aesthetics of Exploration*. Gainesville: University of Florida Press, 1971.

Bosco, Mark. "Seeing the Glory: Graham Greene's *The Power and the Glory* through the Lens of Hans Urs von Balthasar's Theological Aesthetics." *Logos: A Journal of Catholic Thought and Culture* 4.1 (2001) 34–53.

Brindley, David. "Orthodoxy and Orthopraxis in the Novels of Graham Greene. *Theology* 86 (January 1983), 29–36.

Burgess, Anthony. *Urgent Copy: Literary Studies*. New York: W.W. Norton, 1968.

Burns, Robert A. *Roman Catholicism after Vatican II*. Washington, DC: Georgetown University Press, 2001.

Cardenal, Ernesto. *La democratización del la cultura*. Managua: Ministerio de la cultura, 1982.

Cargas, Harry, ed. *Graham Greene*. St. Louis, MO: Herder, 1969.

Cash, William. *The Third Woman: The Secret Passion that Inspired* The End of the Affair. London: Little, Brown, 2000.

Cassis, A. F. ed. *Graham Greene: Man of Paradox*. Chicago: Loyola University Press, 1994.

Cervanka, E., and Barbara Rodgers. *The Nuclear Axis: The Secret Collaboration between the West and South Africa*. London: Julian Friedman, 1978.

Cervantes, Miguel de. *Don Quixote de la Mancha*. Translated by J. M. Cohen. New York: Penguin, [1650] 1950.

Chadwick, Owen. *The Secularization of the European Mind in the 19th Century*. Cambridge: Cambridge University Press, 1975.

Choi, Jae Suck. *Greene and Unamuno: Two Pilgrims to La Mancha*. New York: Peter Lang, 1990.

Christensen, Peter G. "The Art of Self-Preservation: Monsignor Quixote's Resistance to Don Quixote." In *Essays in Graham Greene: An Annual Review III*, vol. 3. Edited by Peter Wolfe. St. Louis, MO: Lucas Hall Press, 1992, 25–42.

Couto, Maria. *Graham Greene: On the Frontier. Politics and Religion in the Novels*. New York: St. Martin's Press, 1988.

Cunningham, Adrian. *Slant Manifesto: Catholics and the Left*. Springfield, Ill.: Templegate, 1968.

D'Arcy, Martin C. *The Nature of Belief*. London: Sheed & Ward, 1931.

Desmond, John F. "The Heart of (the) Matter: The Mystery of the Real in *Monsignor Quixote*." *Religion and Literature* 22.1 (Spring 1990), 59–78.

Detweiler, Robert. *Breaking the Fall: Religious Readings of Contemporary Fiction*. San Francisco: Harper & Row, 1989.

Detweiler, Robert, and David Jasper, eds. *Religion and Literature: A Reader*. Louisville, KY: John Knox Press, 2000.

Devereux, James A. "Catholic Matters in the Correspondence of Evelyn Waugh and Graham Greene." *Journal of Modern Literature* 14 (1987), 111–126.

DeVitis, A. A. *Graham Greene*, rev. ed. Boston: Twayne Publishers, 1986.

Donaghy, Henry J. "Graham Greene's Virtue of Disloyalty." *Christianity and Literature* 32 (1983), 31–37.

Doyle, Dennis M. *The Church Emerging from Vatican II*. Mystic, Conn.: Twenty-third Publications, 1992.

Dubois, E. T. *Portrait of Leon Bloy*. New York: Sheed & Ward, 1951.

Dulles, Avery. *Models of the Church*. New York: Image Books, 1991.

Duran, Leopoldo. *Graham Greene: Friend and Brother*. London: HarperCollins, 1994.

———. "The Human Factor within the Inhuman System." *The Clergy Review*, August 1980), 279–287

Dussel, Enrique. *A History of the Church in Latin America*. Michigan: William Eerdmans, 1981.

Eagleton, Terry. *The Ideology of the Aesthetic*. Oxford: Basil Blackwell, 1990.

———. *The New Left Church*. London: Sheed & Ward, 1966.

———. "Reluctant Heroes: The Novels of Graham Greene." In Harold Bloom, ed., *Graham Greene: Modern Critical Views*. New York: Chelsea House, 1987, 97–118.

Eco, Umberto. *The Aesthetics of Thomas Aquinas*. Cambridge, MA: Harvard University Press, 1988.

Eliot, T. S. *Essays Ancient and Modern*. London: Faber, 1934.

Erdinast-Vulcan, Daphna. *Graham Greene's Childless Fathers*. New York: St. Martin's Press, 1988.

Evans, Robert O., ed. *Graham Greene: Some Critical Considerations*. Lexington: University of Kentucky Press, 1963.

Flannery, Austin, ed. *Documents of Vatican II*. New York: Costello Publishing, 1996.

Foucault, Michel. *The Archeology of Knowledge & the Discourse on Language*. Translated by A. M. Sheridan Smith. New York: Pantheon Books, 1971.

Fraser, Theodore P. *The Modern Catholic Novel in Europe*. New York: Macmillan, 1994.

Friedman, Melvin J. *The Vision Obscured: Perceptions of Some Twentieth-Century Catholic Novelists*. New York: Fordham Press, 1970.

Gallagher, Susan VanZantan, ed. *Postcolonial Literature and the Call for Justice*. Jackson: University Press of Mississippi, 1994.

Garaudy, Roger. *From Anathema to Dialogue: A Marxist Challenge to the Christian Churches*. New York: Herder and Herder, 1966.

Garcia-Rivera, Alejandro. *The Community of the Beautiful*. Collegeville, MN: Liturgical Press, 1999.

Gaston, Georg M. A. *The Pursuit of Salvation: A Critical Guide to the Novels of Graham Greene*. Troy, NY: Whitston Publishing, 1984.

General Conference of Latin American Bishops. *The Church in the Present-day Transformation of Latin America*. Washington DC: USCC, 1970.

Gerhart, Mary. "What Ever Happened to the Catholic Genre?" In *Morphologies of Faith: Essays in Religion and Culture in Honor of Nathan A. Scott, Jr.* Edited by Mary Gerhart and Arthur C. Yu. Atlanta, GA: Scholars Press, 1990.

Giles, Paul. *American Catholic Arts and Fictions: Culture, Ideology, Aesthetics*. Cambridge: Cambridge University Press, 1992.

Goizeuta, Roberto. *Cominemos con Jesus: Toward a Hispanic Latino Theology of Accompaniment*. New York: Orbis Press, 1995.

Gordon, Haim. *Fighting Evil: Unsung Heroes in the Novels of Graham Greene*. Westport, CT: Greewood Press, 1997.

Greeley, Andrew. *The Catholic Imagination*. Berkeley: University of California Press, 2000.

———. *Religion as Poetry*. Somerset, NJ: Transaction Publications, 1996.

Green, Garret. *Imagining God: Theology and the Religious Imagination*. San Francisco: Harper & Row, 1989.

Greene, Graham. Antibes, to Hans Küng, Tübingen, Germany, 29 October 1989. Letter in the hand of Graham Greene. Used with permission of Hans Küng.

———. "The Assumption of Mary." *LIFE Magazine*, 30 October 1950.

———. *Brighton Rock*. New York: Penguin, [1938] 1977.

———. *A Burnt-Out Case*. New York: Penguin, [1961] 1977.

———. *The Captain and the Enemy*. Toronto: Lester & Orpen Dennys, 1988.

———. *Collected Essays*. New York: Penguin, 1969.

———. *Collected Short Stories*. New York: Penguin, 1986.

———. *The Comedians*. New York: Penguin, [1966] 1976.

———. *Dear David, Dear Graham*. Oxford: Alembic Press, 1989.

———. *Dr. Fischer of Geneva, or the Bomb Party*. New York: Simon and Schuster, 1980.

———. *The End of the Affair*. New York: Penguin, [1951] 1975.

———. *Essais Catholiques*. Paris: Seuil, 1953.

———. *Getting to Know the General: The Story of an Involvement*. New York: Simon & Schuster, 1984.

———. The Graham Greene Files. Ransom Research Library, University of Texas, Austin.

———. The Graham Greene Papers. John J. Burns Library, Boston College, Boston.

———. *The Heart of the Matter*. New York: Penguin, [1948] 1978.

————. *The Honorary Consul*. London: Bodley Head, 1973.

————. *The Human Factor*. New York: Simon & Schuster, 1978.

————. *J'Accuse: the Dark Side of Nice*. London: Bodley Head, 1982.

————. *The Lawless Roads*. New York: Penguin, [1939] 1982.

————. *The Man Within*. London: Heineman, 1929.

————. *Monsignor Quixote*. Toronto: Lester & Orpen Dennys, 1982.

————. *Our Man in Havana*, New York: Penguin, [1958] 1986.

————. *The Power and the Glory*. New York: Penguin, [1940] 1991.

————. *The Quiet American*. New York: Penguin, Viking, [1955] 1990.

————. *Reflections*. Toronto: Lester & Orpen Dennys, 1990.

————. *A Sort of Life*. New York: Simon and Schuster, 1971.

————. "Table Talk with Graham Greene." Interview with Père Jouve and Marcel
     Moré. Translated by Nancy Hargrove. *Dieu Vivant* 16 (1949); 127–137.

————. *The Tenth Man*. New York: Simon & Schuster, 1985.

————. *Travels with My Aunt*. New York: Penguin, [1969] 1977.

————. *Ways of Escape*. New York: Simon & Schuster, 1980.

————. "Why I Am Still a Catholic: Graham Greene on God, Sex and Death." Inter-
     view with John Cornwall. *The Tablet* (23 September 1989): 1085–1089.

————. *Yours, Etc.: Letters to the Press, 1945–1989*. Edited by Christopher Hawtree.
     New York: Penguin, 1989.

Gregor, Ian. "The End of the Affair." In *The Moral and the Story*. London: Faber &
     Faber, 1962.

Griffiths, Richard. *The Reactionary Revolution: The Catholic Revival in French Literature,
     1870–1914*. New York: Frederick Ungar, 1965.

Gremillion, Joseph. *The Gospel of Peace and Justice: Catholic Social Teaching since Pope
     John*. New York: Orbis Press, 1976.

Gutierrez, Gustavo. "Liberation, Theology, and Proclamation." *Concilium* 96. New
     York: Herder & Herder, 1974.

————. "Speaking about God." *Concilium* 171. Edinburgh: T. & T. Clark, 1984.

————. *A Theology of Liberation*. New York: Orbis Press, [1973] 1988.

————. *The Truth Shall Make You Free: Confrontations*. New York: Orbis Press, 1990.

————. *We Drink from Our Own Wells: The Spiritual Journey of a People*. New York:
     Orbis Press, 1984.

Haber, Herbert R. "The End of the Catholic Cycle: The Writer versus the Saint." In
     Robert O. Evans, ed., *Graham Greene: Some Critical Considerations*. Lexington:
     University Press of Kentucky, 1963.

Hanson, Ellis. *Decadence and Catholicism*. Cambridge, MA: Harvard University Press,
     1997.

Henry, Patrick. "Cervantes, Unamuno, and Graham Greene's Monsignor Quixote."
     Comparative Literature Studies 22 (1986), 12–23.

Herbert, Will. *Four Existentialist Theologians: A Reader from the Works of Jacques Mari-
     tain, Nicolas Berdyaev, Martin Buber and Paul Tillich*. New York: Doubleday, 1958.

Higgins, Michael W. "Greene's Priest: A Sort of Rebel." In *Essays in Graham Greene*,
     vol. 3. Edited by Peter Wolfe. St. Louis, MO: Lucas Hall Press, 1992, 9–24.

Holderness, Graham. " 'Knight-Errant of Faith'? *Monsignor Quixote* as Catholic Fiction." *Journal of Literature and Theology* 7.3. (September 1993), 259–283.

Hynes, Samuel, ed. *Graham Greene: A Collection of Critical Essays.* Englewood Cliffs, NJ: Prentice-Hall, 1973.

Jarrett, Bede, O. J. *Mediaeval Socialism.* London: Burns, Oates & Washbourne, [1913], 1935.

———. *Social Theories of the Middle Ages 1200–1500.* London: Frank Cass, 1926.

Jones, Graham C. "Graham Greene and the Legend of Péguy." *Comparative Literature* 21 (1969), 138–145.

Kaur, Satnam. *Graham Greene: An Existentialist Investigation.* Amristar, India: Guru Nanek Dev University Press, 1988.

Kellogg, Gene. *The Vital Tradition: The Catholic Novel in a Period of Convergence.* Chicago: Loyola University Press, 1970.

Kelly, Richard. *Graham Greene.* New York: Frederick Ungar, 1984.

Ker, Ian. *The Catholic Revival in English Literature, 1845–1961.* South Bend, IN: University of Notre Dame Press, 2003.

———. *Newman on Being a Christian.* South Bend, IN: University of Notre Dame Press, 1990.

Kermode, Frank. "Mr. Greene's Eggs and Crosses." In Samuel Hynes, ed., *Graham Greene: A Collection of Critical Essays* Englewood Cliffs, NJ: Prentice-Hall, 1973.

Komonchak, Joseph. *The Reception of Vatican II.* Washington, DC: Catholic University of America Press, 1987.

Küng, Hans. *On Being a Christian.* New York: Doubleday, 1976.

———. *The Changing Church: Reflections on the Progress of the Second Vatican Council.* New York: Sheed & Ward, 1965.

———. *The Church—Maintained in Truth: A Theological Meditation.* New York: Seabury Press, 1980.

———. *Does God Exist? An Answer for Today.* New York: Random House, 1978.

———. *Theology for the Third Millennium.* New York: Anchor Doubleday, 1988.

Küng, Hans, and David Tracy, eds. *Paradigm Change in Theology: A Symposium for the Future.* New York: Crossroad, 1989.

Kunkel, Francis. *The Labyrinthine Ways of Graham Greene.* New York: Sheed & Ward, 1959.

———. "The Theme of Sin and Grace in Graham Greene." In Robert O. Evans, ed., *Graham Greene: Some Critical Considerations,* Lexington: University Press of Kentucky, 1963.

Kurismmootil, Jospeh. *Heaven and Hell on Earth: An Appreciation of Five Novels of Graham Greene.* Chicago: Loyola University Press, 1982.

Lash, Nicholas. *Easter in Ordinary: Reflections on Human Experience and the Knowledge of God.* South Bend, IN: Notre Dame University Press, 1988.

Leigh, David. "The Structures of Graham Greene's *The Honorary Consul.*" *Renascence* 38.1 (Autumn 1985): 13–25.

Lewis, R. W. B. *The Picaresque Saint: Representative Figures in Contemporary Fiction.* Philadelphia: Lippincott, 1959.

Lodge, David. *Graham Greene.* Columbia Essays on Modern Literature. New York: Columbia University Press, 1966.

———. Introduction to François Mauriac, *The Viper's Tangle.* Translated by Gerard Hopkins. New York: Carroll & Graf, 1987.

———. "The Lives of Graham Greene." *The Practice of Writing.* New York: Penguin, 1996.

———. "Moral Entertainment: *Doctor Fischer of Geneva or the Bomb Party.*" *The Tablet* 29 March 1980, 317–318.

———. *Souls and Bodies.* New York: Penguin, 1980.

Lynch, William. *Christ and Apollo: The Dimensions of the Literary Imagination.* New York: Sheed and Ward, 1960.

———. *Images of Faith: An Exploration of the Ironic Imagination.* South Bend, IN: University of Notre Dame Press, 1973.

Lyotard, Jean-François. *The Postmodern Condition: A Report on Knowledge.* Minneapolis: University of Minnesota Press, 1984.

Malamet, Elliot. *The World Remade: Graham Greene and the Art of Detection.* New York: Peter Lang, 1998.

Maritain, Jacques. *Art and Scholasticism.* London: Sheed & Ward, 1923.

Mauriac, François. *God and Mammon.* London: Sheed & Ward, 1936.

———. "Men I Hold Great." In *Graham Greene: A Collection of Critical Essays.* Samuel Hynes, ed. Englewood Cliffs, N.J.: Prentice-Hall, 1973.

———. *Woman of the Pharisees.* Translated by Gerard Hopkins. New York: H. Hall, [1941] 1946.

———. *Les Pages Immortelles de Pascal: Choises et Expliquées.* New York: Longmans, Green, 1941.

———. *Thérèse.* Translated by Gerard Hopkins. London: Eyre & Spottiswoode, [1927] 1947.

McEwan, Neil. *Graham Greene.* London: Macmillan, Publishers, 1988.

Medcalf, John. *Parish at War: Letters from Nicaragua.* Springfield, IL: Templegate, 1989.

Miller, J. Hillis. *The Disappearance of God: Five 19th Century Writers.* Cambridge, MA: Harvard University Press, 1976.

Miller, R. H. *Understanding Graham Greene.* Columbia: University of South Carolina Press, 1990.

Mora, José Ferrater. *Unamuno: A Philosophy of Tragedy.* Translated by Philip Silver. Berkeley: University of California Press, 1962.

Morreall, John. *Comedy, Tragedy, and Religion.* New York: State University of New York Press, 1999.

Muford, Peter. *Graham Greene.* London: Northcote House Publishers, 1996.

Murphy, Francesca Aran. *Christ the Form of Beauty.* Edinburgh: T. & T. Clark, 1995.

Myers, Jeffrey, ed. *Graham Greene, a Revaluation: New Essays.* London: Macmillan, 1990.

Neary, John. *Like and Unlike God: Religious Imaginations in Modern and Contemporary Fiction.* Atlanta, GA: Scholars Press, 1999.

Newman, John Henry. *Apologia Pro Vita Sua*. New York: Penguin, 1994.

———. *An Essay in Aid of a Grammar of Assent*. Oxford: Clarendon Press, 1985.

———. *An Essay on the Development of Christian Doctrine*. London: Longmans, Green and Co., 1927.

———. *The Essential Newman*. Edited by Vincent Ferrer Blehl. New York: Mentor-Omega Books, 1963.

———. *The Idea of a University*. London: Longmans, Green, 1951.

———. *Parochial and Plain Sermons*, 8 vols. San Francisco: Ignatius Press, 1987.

———. *The Via Media of the Anglican Church*. Oxford: Clarendon Press, 1990.

Noonan, John. "Development in Moral Doctrine." *Theological Studies*, 54.4 (1993): 678–697.

O'Brien, Conor Cruise. "Greene's Castle." *The New York Review of Books*, 1 June 1978, 3–5.

———. *Maria Cross: Imaginative Patterns in a Group of Catholic Writers*. London: Burnes & Oates, 1963.

O'Grady, Joan. *Early Christian Heresies*. New York: Barnes & Noble Books, 1994.

O'Malley, John W. *Tradition and Transition: Historical Perspectives on Vatican II*. Wilmington, DE: Michael Glazier Publishing, 1989.

O'Prey, Paul. *A Reader's Guide to Graham Greene*. London: Thames & Hudson, 1988.

Orwell, George. "The Sanctified Sinner." In Samuel Hynes, ed., *Graham Greene: A Collection of Critical Essays*. Englewood Cliffs, N.J.: Prentice Hall, 1973.

Osborne, Kenan. *Sacramental Theology: A General Introduction*. New York: Paulist Press, 1988.

Pearce, Joseph. *Literary Converts*. San Francisco: Ignatius Press, 2000.

Péguy, Charles. *Basic Verities: Prose and Poetry*. Translated by Ann Green and Julian Green. New York: Pantheon Books, 1943.

———. *Oeuvres de Prose, 1909–1914*. Paris: Gallimard, 1961.

Pendleton, Robert. *Graham Greene's Conradian Masterplot*. New York: St. Martin's Press, 1996.

Populorum Progresso, Encyclical Letter, Catholic Church. Pope Paul VI, 1967.

Prévost, Jean Laurent. *Le Roman Catholique a Cent Ans*. Paris: Fayard, 1958.

Pryce-Jones, David. *Graham Greene*. London: Oliver & Boyd, 1963.

Rama Rao, V. V. B. *Graham Greene's Comic Vision*. New Delhi, India: Reliance Publishing, 1996.

Rahner, Karl. "Anonymous Christians." *Theological Investigations*, vol. 6. Baltimore: Helicon Press, 1969, 390–398.

———. "Atheism and Implicit Christianity." *Theological Investigations*, vol. 9. New York: Herder & Herder, 1972, 145–164.

———. "Concerning the Relationship between Nature and Grace." *Theological Investigations*, vol. 1. Baltimore: Helicon Press, 1961, 297–316.

———. *The Church and the Sacraments*. New York: Herder & Herder, 1963.

———. "Theological Considerations on Secularization and Atheism." *Theological Investigations*, vol. 11. New York: Herder & Herder, 1974, 166–184.

————. "Two Types of Christology." *Theological Investigations*, vol. 13. New York: Seabury Press, 1975, 213–223.

Reinhardt, Kurt. *The Theological Novel of Modern Europe: An Analysis of Masterpieces by Eight Authors.* New York: Frederick Ungar, 1968.

Ricoeur, Paul. *Interpretation Theory: Discourse and the Surplus of Meaning.* Fort Worth: Texas Christian University Press, 1976.

Salvatore, Anne T. *Greene and Kierkegaard: The Discourse of Belief.* Tuscaloosa: University of Alabama Press, 1988.

Schanz, John. *The Sacraments of Life and Worship.* Milwaukee, WI: Bruce Publishing, 1966.

Schillebeeckx, Edward. *Christ the Sacrament of the Encounter with God.* New York: Sheed & Ward, 1963.

————. *God and Man.* London: Sheed & Ward, 1979.

————. *God the Future of Man.* New York: Sheed & Ward, 1969.

————. *Interim Report on the Books* Jesus *and* Christ. New York: Crossroad, 1981.

————. *Jesus: An Experiment in Christology.* New York: Seabury Press, 1979.

————. *The Praxis of Christian Experience: An Introduction to the Theology of Edward Schillebeeckx.* Edited by Robert J. Schreiter and Mary Catherine Hilkert. San Francisco: Harper & Row, 1989.

Schloesser, Stephen. "Really, Really Dark: Inventing the Catholic Novel." *Explore* 5.2 (Spring 2002), 9–17.

Schwartz, Adam. " 'I Thought the Church and I Wanted the Same Thing': Opposition to Twentieth-Century Liturgical Change in the Thought of Graham Greene, Christopher Dawson, and David Jones." *Logos: A Journal of Catholic Thought and Literature* 1.4 (1998), 36–65.

Sharma, S. K. *Graham Greene: The Search for Belief.* New Delhi: Harman Publishing, 1990.

Sharrock, Roger. *Saints, Sinners, and Comedians: The Novels of Graham Greene.* South Bend, IN: University of Notre Dame Press, 1984.

Sherry, Norman. *The Life of Graham Greene,* vols. 1 and 2. New York: Penguin, 1989, 1995.

Smith, Grahame. *The Achievement of Graham Greene.* Totowa NJ: Barnes & Noble Books, 1986.

Sobrino, Jon. *Jesus the Liberator, a Historical-Theological View.* New York: Orbis Press, 1993.

Sonnenfeld, Albert. *Crossroads: Essays on the Catholic Novelists.* York, SC: French Literature Publications, 1982.

Spark, Muriel. *The Abbess of Crewe: A Morality Play.* New York: Viking, 1974.

Spurling, John. *Graham Greene.* London: Methuen, 1983.

Stagaman, David J. *Authority in the Church.* Collegeville, MN: Liturgical Press, 1999.

Stratford, Phillip. *Faith and Fiction: Creative Process in Greene and Mauriac.* South Bend, IN: University of Notre Dame Press, 1964.

Teilhard de Chardin, Pierre. *Christianity and Evolution.* New York: Harcourt Brace Jovanovich, 1971.

———. *The Heart of Matter.* New York: Harcourt Brace Jovanovich, 1978.

———. *The Phenomenon of Man.* Translated by Bernard Wall. New York: Harper & Row [1959], 1965.

———. *Science and Christ.* New York: Harper & Row, 1968.

Thomas, Brian. *An Underground Fate: The Idiom of Romance in the Later Novels of Graham Greene.* Athens: University of Georgia Press, 1988.

Tillich, Paul. *On Art and Architecture.* Edited by John Dillenberger. New York: Crossroad, 1987.

———. *Systematic Theology,* vol. 3. Chicago: University of Chicago Press, 1963.

———. *Theology of Culture.* New York: Oxford University Press, 1959.

Tracy, David. *The Analogical Imagination: Christian Theology and the Culture of Pluralism.* New York: Crossroad, 1981.

———. *Plurality and Ambiguity: Hermeneutics, Religion, Hope.* Chicago: University of Chicago Press, 1987.

Unamuno, Miguel de. *Life of Don Quixote and Sancho according to Miguel de Cervantes Saavedra.* New York: Knopf, 1927.

———. *The Tragic Sense of Life in Men and Nations,* Translated by Anthony Kerigan. Princeton, NJ: Princeton University Press, Bollingen Series 85.4 1972.

Waugh, Evelyn. *The Diaries of Evelyn Waugh.* Edited by Michael Davies. Boston: Little, Brown, 1976.

———. *The Essays, Articles and Reviews of Evelyn Waugh.* Edited by Donat Gallagher. Boston: Little, Brown and Company, 1983.

———. "Felix Cupla?" *The Tablet,* 5 June 1948, 191.

West, W. J. *The Quest for Graham Greene.* New York: St. Martin's Press, 1997.

Whitehouse, J. C. *Vertical Man: The Human Being in the Catholic Novels of Graham Greene, Sigrid Undset, and Georges Bernanos.* London: Saint Austin Press, 1999.

Index

absence (philosophical concept), 7
Aggiornamento, 79
Alden Pyle (protagonist of *The Quiet American*), 73
Alfred Jones (character in *Doctor Fischer of Geneva*), 131–134, 136–138, 157
Allende, Salvador, 103
analogical philosophy, 12, 27–28
  in *The End of the Affair*, 60
  in *Monsignor Quixote*, 148
  and sacramentalism, 54
Anna-Luise (character in *Doctor Fischer of Geneva*), 131–134, 136–138
Anxiety of Influence, The (Bloom), 20
Apologia Pro Vita Sua (Newman), 25, 35–36
Aquinas, Thomas, Saint. *See* Roman Catholic doctrine; theology (Catholic)
Arnold, Matthew, 5–6
atheism, 66–67, 80
Auden, W. H., 6, 155

Baiser au Lépreux, Le (Mauriac), 44–45
Bakhtin, Mikhail, 117, 183n. 4

Balthasar, Hans Urs von, 42, 51, 60, 152, 158
Barth, Karl, 78
Belloc, Hilaire, 46
Bendrix (Maurice, character in *The End of the Affair*), 42, 58–61, 64–67
  adultery of, 19
  agnosticism of, 38, 68, 154
  as Christ figure, 63, 157
  rationalism of, 62
Bernanos, Georges, 7, 42
  influence on Greene, 9, 40, 156
  Journal d'un Curé de Campagne, 42–43
  Sous le Soleil de Satan, 42–43
Blake, William, 20
Bloom, Harold, 20
Bloy, Léon, 7, 42
  influence on Greene, 40–41, 156
  La Femme Pauvre, 40
  Le Désespéré, 40
Brideshead Revisited (Waugh), 8
Brighton Rock (Greene), 19, 32, 58
  as "Catholic Novel," 3, 9, 17–18
  dialectical philosophy in, 38
  reference to Péguy in, 41–42
Browning, Robert, 99
Burns, Robert A., 85